All Things Needed for Godliness

"Al Truesdale has offered a wonderful resource on the subject of holiness, in the framework of what is known as Wesleyanism's "catholic spirit"—an expression that encapsulates an openness to learn from others. The theology of holiness is first and foremost a biblical doctrine that found articulation at the beginning of the early church. Now, two thousand years later, the doctrine finds different and important nuances expressed by diverse theological traditions. Recognizing these differences is key to understanding our own interpretation. Rich insights can be gained about God's holiness and humanity's call to be holy when we are open to other perspectives. The breadth of this study is remarkable because it covers the traditions of Orthodoxy, Catholicism, and major branches of Protestantism. Its depth will offer the reader fresh understandings well worth the exploration. This is a gift to the church."

—Diane Leclerc
Professor of Historical Theology
Northwest Nazarene University
Nampa, Idaho

"This book is a powerful reminder that there is one—and only one—defining moment in the history of the human race: the resurrection of Jesus Christ."

—Terence P. Jeffrey
The Editor-in-Chief of CNSNews.com

"What does it mean to be created, fallen, redeemed, and made holy? This book gathers insights from a variety of Christian traditions: Orthodox life in the Paschal mystery, Catholic formation into the image of God, and diverse Protestant approaches to a life of faith and discipleship. Readers will enjoy the side-by-side nature of these voices as they enter into these important conversations about what it means to be sanctified by the triune God."

—Rev. Dr. Martin J. Lohrmann
Assistant Professor of Lutheran Confessions and Heritage
Wartburg Theological Seminary
Dubuque, Iowa

"This book does an extraordinary job of setting out a range of Christian perspectives, from Eastern Orthodox to Pentecostal, on the work of God to make the people of God holy. In this, editor Al Truesdale and the contributors have performed a genuine service for the church, not only by providing a set of lucid and approachable essays on a sorely neglected topic but also through assembling a volume of varied denominational voices setting out God's work of sanctification in diverse but harmonious ways."

—Jason A. Fout
Associate Professor of Anglican Theology, Bexley Seabury Seminary Federation,
Chicago, Illinois
Coeditor in Chief, Anglican Theological Review, Sewanee, Tennessee

"In Jesus the beauty of holiness is displayed both in black and white and in many colors. Yet Christians in the Western world seem to have become increasingly blind to it in both its manifestations. For them nothing is sacred any longer. Worst of all, they are unaware of what they have lost. So these essays, which cover the teaching on holiness in eight main Christian traditions, are a welcome contribution for the recovery at least some of its splendor, with some inkling of its full-colored spectrum, and commendation of it to a new generation that may yet be fascinated by it and drawn to its tangible incarnation in Jesus."

—John W. Kleinig
Emeritus Lecturer in the Australian Lutheran College
The University of Divinity in Adelaide, South Australia

"At the heart of *All Things Needed for Godliness* is the enterprise of *holy* living. Beyond Christ's call to "come and follow" are found denominations and human lives steeped in *holy* living, the kind of living harmonious with God's ways and will, and only then reflective of a given polity or faith tradition.

"Expressed through Christian faith traditions, *All Things Needed for Godliness* is an insightful conversation convened and edited by Al Truesdale. The conversation partners provide salient reflections upon their faith tradition and upon how each tradition has inspired members to live a life of holiness. Although each tradition is featured through its unique Christian expression, the unifying element is each tradition's response to God's call to be a *holy* people in worship and especially through one's diverse if not surprising relationships.

"For Christian people, holiness is the result and reflection of the God who calls people out of darkness and places them in a light that reveals a godly identity. That identity becomes both means and mission for rescuing and restoring creation. That identity is also a vivid reminder that 'God is never aloof' from creation. The mission of the church is never solitary; rather, the mission and witness of the church speak of the solidarity it holds with the God who saves and who saves miraculously through the hearts and prayers of people who reflect and manifest God's holiness."

—The Rev. Dr. Augustus E. Succop III, Pastor
Quail Hollow Presbyterian Church
Charlotte, North Carolina

All Things Needed for Godliness

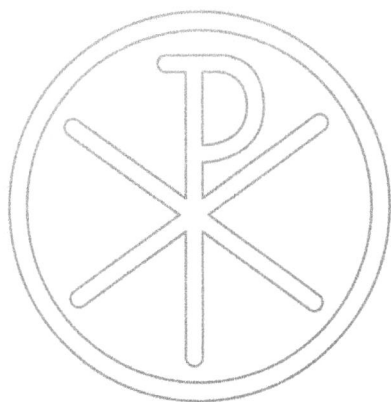

A Portrait of Holiness among Christian Traditions

Al Truesdale, Editor

f▸

THE FOUNDRY
PUBLISHING

Cover design: Arthur Cherry
Interior design: Sharon Page

Library of Congress Cataloging-in-Publication Data
A complete catalog record for this book is available from the Library of Congress.

The Internet addresses, email addresses, and phone numbers in this book are accurate at the time of publication. They are provided as a resource. The Foundry Publishing does not endorse them or vouch for their content or permanence.

"The gospels are consciously telling the story of how God's one-time action in Jesus the Messiah *ushered in a new world order* within which a new way of life was not only possible, but mandatory for Jesus' followers."
—N. T. Wright, *How God Became King*

"A holy life is not primarily the result of our efforts, of our actions, because it is God, the three times Holy (cf. Is. 6:3) who sanctifies us, it is the Holy Spirit's action that enlivens us from within, it is the very life of the Risen Christ that is communicated to us and that transforms us."
—*The Holiness*, Pope Benedict XVI, General Audience, Wednesday, April 13, 2011

"Although a difference in opinions or modes of worship may prevent an entire external union, yet need it prevent our union in affection? Though we cannot think alike, may we not love alike? May we not be of one heart, though we are not of one opinion? Without all doubt, we may. Herein all the children of God may unite, notwithstanding these smaller differences. . . . they may forward one another in love and in good works."
—John Wesley, "Catholic Spirit," Sermon 39, para. 4

Contents

Contributors

Kent Brower, PhD
Senior Research Fellow and Senior Lecturer in Biblical Studies
Nazarene Theological College
Manchester, United Kingdom

Don H. Compier, PhD
Episcopal Priest
Canon Theologian of the Episcopal Diocese of Kansas
Dean of the Bishop Kemper School for Ministry
Topeka, Kansas

T. Scott Daniels, PhD
Senior Minister, Nampa College Church of the Nazarene
Pastoral Scholar in Residence, Northwest Nazarene University
Nampa, Idaho

Robert M. Jack, DMin
Former Senior Pastor, Pleasant Hill Presbyterian Church
Charlotte, North Carolina

Glen W. Menzies, PhD
Former Dean of the Institute for Biblical and Theological Studies
Former Professor of New Testament and Early Christianity
North Central University
Minneapolis, Minnesota

Craig L. Nessan, ThD
Professor of Contextual Theology and Ethics
The William D. Streng Professor for the Education and Renewal of the Church
Wartburg Theological Seminary
Dubuque, Iowa

Jerry J. Pokorsky, MA
Pastor
Saint Catherine of Siena Catholic Church
Great Falls, Virginia

Harold Segura, PhD
Colombian Baptist Pastor and Theologian
Director of Faith and Development for Latin America, World Vision
Former Rector of the International Baptist Theological Seminary
Cali, Colombia

Al Truesdale, PhD
Emeritus Professor of Philosophy of Religion and Christian Ethics
Nazarene Theological Seminary
Kansas City, Missouri

Paul Wesche, PhD
Archpriest
Pastor, Saint Herman's Orthodox Church
Minneapolis, Minnesota

David Wheeler, ThD
Adjunct Professor of Theology, Palmer Theological Seminary, St. Davids, Pennsylvania
Former Senior Pastor, First Baptist Church, Portland, Oregon
Former Professor of Theology and Ethics, Central Baptist Theological Seminary,
    Shawnee, Kansas

Mi Ja Wi, PhD
Lecturer in Biblical Studies and Global Mission
Nazarene Theological College
Manchester, United Kingdom

Foreword

❖

From a young age I became familiar with the Wesleyan language of Christian holiness. This provided a vocabulary that conveyed specific values. I cherish this tradition; in it I practice my Christian faith.

As a seminary student my appreciation for my own tradition expanded. And so did my appreciation for how other Christian traditions understand Christian holiness. For example, I delighted in reading "The Universal Call to Holiness in the Church," issued by the Second Vatican Council (1962-65): "In the Church, everyone . . . is called to holiness, according to the saying of the Apostle: 'For this is the will of God, your sanctification.'" Holiness "is unceasingly manifested, and must be manifested, in the fruits of grace which the Spirit produces in the faithful."[1]

Readings from other sources highlighted the streams of Christianity that have, from time to time, come together, touched and influenced one another, and then branched off again, only to create a series of pathways that lead us to the holiness of God. This understanding has allowed me to cherish my own theological family while increasing my understanding of and appreciation for other parts of the church. Along the way, it becomes obvious that John Wesley drew upon many Christian sources that lead us to the holiness of God.

The beauty of God's holiness pervades the Old Testament, just as the call to Christian holiness pervades the New Testament. These themes are universally foundational for the church of God. From the beginning, Jesus's disciples have been called to, and empowered for, lives of Christian holiness, rooted in the holiness of God. In the preface to *Against Heresies*, Irenaeus (ca. AD 139–ca. AD 202) affirmed the essence of Christian holiness: "The Word of God, our Lord Jesus Christ, who did, through His transcendent love, become what we are, that He might bring us to be even what He is Himself."[2] More than a century later, Athanasius (ca. AD 296–373), in *On the Incarnation of the Word*, reaffirmed Irenaeus's conviction: "[Christ], indeed, assumed humanity that we might become God."[3] Both affirmations derive in large part from the declaration in 2 Peter 1:4: "Thus he has given us, through these things, his precious and very great promises, so that through them you may escape from the corruption that is in the world because of lust, *and may become participants of the divine nature*" (NRSV, emphasis added).

God's plan for his church, through Christ, is to cleanse Christians from sin and establish them in holiness. This transformation happens through formation in godliness by the Holy Spirit. This promise has characterized the church through the centuries, regardless of the church's diversity.

In a beautiful mosaic, the contributors to *All Things Needed for Godliness: A Portrait of Holiness among Christian Traditions* have expressed the church's diverse and complementary ways of envisioning and living out the "precious and very great promises" declared by the apostle Peter. They have explained what it means today to *"become participants of the divine nature,"* what it means to be formed by the Holy Spirit given at Pentecost.

The book invites us to listen to varied Christian voices, to discover the uniting thread, and to live out in the church and the world, God's "precious and very great promises." As we learn how to become more like God in the image of Christ, we will also learn how to be faithful participants in the mission of God.

Carla Sunberg, PhD
General Superintendent
Church of the Nazarene
June 2019

Introduction

❖

Worship the LORD in the splendor of his holiness.
—Psalm 96:9

❖

In richly varied ways, this theme is repeated from Genesis to Revelation. Worshipping the living God is humankind's most joyous, defining, consuming, and fulfilling activity.

All creation—the theater of God's glory—should participate:

> Praise the LORD from the earth,
>> you great sea creatures and all ocean depths,
> lightning and hail, snow and clouds,
>> stormy winds that do his bidding,
> you mountains and all hills,
>> fruit trees and all cedars,
> wild animals and all cattle,
>> small creatures and flying birds. (Ps. 148:7-10)

God's presence transforms nature; he alone makes dry ground fertile and the desert bloom with flowers (Isa. 35:1-3; 41:17-20).

For ancient Israel, worship was comprehensive; it was to be *enacted* in all of life. "I am the LORD your God; consecrate yourselves therefore, and be holy, for I am holy" (Lev. 11:4, RSV; see 19:2). The Torah (Law)[1] instructed Israel in how to glorify God by embodying his righteousness, mercy, and steadfast love. Worship, observes Walter Brueggemann, was meant to be a glad, unrestrained expression of awe, amazement, and gratitude.[2] Far from being just a slice of time reserved for festive days, worship, as Abraham Joshua Heschel explains, was to be "the grammar of living."[3]

At the beginning of Jesus's mission, the Tempter tried to convince him to turn away from the cross. Jesus responded, "It is written, 'You shall worship the Lord your God, and him only shall you serve'" (Luke 4:8, RSV). In unflinching obedience to his heavenly Father, Jesus the Messiah fulfilled what Israel had failed to do. By submitting to idolatry and thereby becoming culpably embroiled in the problem (Isa. 65:2-5; Jer. 2:5-9), Israel betrayed its mission as the bearer of redemption. Through Jesus's obedience, even to death on the cross (Phil. 2:8), our Lord opened for all people—Jews and Gentiles alike—a way to fulfill God's call for holy worship and holy living (2 Cor. 5:18, 21). He fulfilled the promise made to Abraham (Gal. 3:14) and became God's faithful "light to the nations" (Isa. 42:6; 49:6, RSV; see Luke 2:32; John 1:4-5, 9; 8:12).

Ransomed by "the precious blood of Christ,"[4] the apostle Peter says, members of Christ's body are called *to* and empowered *for* holiness in all their conduct (1 Pet. 1:13-16). This promise is made to ordinary members of Christ's church, not to privileged religious and social elites. In the Gospels Jesus indiscriminately promises the riches of God's kingdom to all who "hunger and thirst for righteousness" (Matt. 5:6, RSV). The cross of Christ, says Fleming Rutledge, radically undercuts "who is in and who is out."[5] Miraculously, Jesus can transform everyday people into a "royal priesthood" whose vocation is to "declare the praises of [God] who called [them] out of darkness into his wonderful light" (1 Pet. 2:9). Jesus's disciples, says N. T. Wright, are equipped by the Holy Spirit to "[reflect] God's glory into the world and the praises of creation back to God."[6] This is the vocation of Christian holiness, or righteousness.

In diverse ways, throughout the church's history, the call to Christian holiness has been viewed as normative for discipleship. Each faith or doctrinal tradition contributes distinctive shades of meaning; they are gifts employed "for one another" (1 Pet. 4:10, RSV).[7] However, even the whole is only an anticipation of its perfection when God's kingdom is complete.

This book offers a portrait of Christian holiness as it has been proclaimed and practiced in the various creedal or faith traditions, beginning with the Orthodox Church (chap. 3) and concluding with Pentecostalism (chap. 10).

Due to lack of space, some theological traditions are not represented. These include the Friends (Quakers) and the Anabaptists (the Radical Reformation).

The goal is fivefold: to promote worship of the living God, to affirm unity in the sanctified body of Christ, to bear witness to the transforming power of the risen Lord, to encourage conformity to his will, and thereby to serve the mission of God.

Being Human
A Holy Vocation

❖

Al Truesdale, PhD

Al Truesdale is emeritus professor of philosophy of religion and
Christian ethics, Nazarene Theological Seminary, Kansas City, Missouri.
He is the editor of the five-volume Book of Saints series (Foundry
Publishing). He is an ordained minister in the Church of the Nazarene.

❖

By the time O. E. Parker was twenty-eight, tattoos[1] covered most of his body—except his back. "I ain't got any tattoo on my back," he bragged to his homely wife, who was an expert at "sniffing up sin."

The only reason Parker worked was to pay for more tattoos. At age fourteen, he began by having an eagle, which was perched on a cannon, tattooed on the back of one hand. He advanced to tigers, panthers, and cobras and then to Elizabeth II and Prince Philip covering his stomach—but never a tattoo on his back.

Parker vigorously avoided religion. He was confident he could make himself beautiful without God, certainly without the assistance of any "straight gospel preacher." So far as Parker was concerned, there wasn't "anything in particular" to be saved from.

Everywhere Parker went during five years in the navy, he picked up more tattoos. For a month or so, each new tattoo would satisfy him. When the satisfaction wore off, he would be seized by unrest. He hoped that finally his accumulating tattoos would yield a symmetrical and colorful pattern of beauty to replace his emptiness. Instead, his tattoos became haphazard and chaotic. To correct the mess, Parker would return to the tattoo parlor. However, as empty spaces decreased, his listlessness and yearning intensified. Despair raged inside him. It was as if the panther and the lion, the serpents, the eagles and the hawks were warring inside.

While baling hay and thinking about a fitting tattoo for his back, a large tree in the middle of the field seemed to reach out to grab Parker.[2] His tractor collided upside down against the tree and broke out in fire. Landing on his back, his shoes aflame and his eyes cavernous, Parker cried out, "GOD ABOVE!" Scrambling backward, he fled shaken and barefoot (Exod. 3:4-6) to his truck. He drove straight to town—directly to the tattoo parlor.

"What are you interested in?"

"God!" Parker answered.

"Father, Son, or Spirit?" the artist questioned.

"Just God! Just so it's God!"

Parker searched the art books. Suddenly the all-demanding eyes of Christ seized him. He began to tremble. His throat became too dry to speak. He sensed he was being changed to a new life by a subtle power. Hours later, staring in a mirror at the completed tattoo, Parker was commandeered by the all-demanding eyes of Jesus.[3]

When Parker arrived home, the door was locked. "Let me in," he yelled.

"Who's there?" a sharp voice asked.

"Me," Parker said, "O. E."

He waited a moment.

"Me," he repeated impatiently, "O. E."

Still no sound.

Parker tried again. "O. E.," he said, beating the door. "O. E. Parker. You know me."

Silence. Then the voice said slowly, "I don't know no O. E."

"It's me, old O. E. I'm back."

Suddenly, a brilliant array of light burst over the skyline. Parker stumbled back against the door as if pinned by a lance.

In a tone of finality, the voice asked again, "Who's there?"

Parker bent down and whispered, "Obadiah [servant of God] Elihue [he is my God himself]!" "All at once he felt . . . light pouring through him, turning his spider web soul into a perfect [pattern] of colors, a garden of trees and birds and beasts."[4]

Parker as Parable

Flannery O'Connor, famous Southern author of "Parker's Back," was a perceptive revealer of humankind's misdirected hunger for God, as well as the disfiguring results of our failures. She was also an unfailing herald of God's transforming and characteristically astonishing grace. In her stories, O'Connor ingeniously provokes disdain for her crude characters until readers realize she is describing them in their unredeemed wretchedness. She coaxes readers to see that only through God's grace can their ruin be reversed and their lives changed into the harmony God intends.

True to the New Testament, O'Connor knew, left to ourselves, we are hopelessly "dead in trespasses and sins" (Eph. 2:1, KJV). Transformation requires crucifixion of the old self (Rom. 6:5-7; Gal. 6:14), resurrection (Eph. 2:6; Col. 3:1), new birth (John 3:3), and new creation (2 Cor. 5:17; Gal. 6:15).[5]

Parabolically, through O. E. Parker, O'Connor pictures humankind's desperate efforts to achieve peace and fulfillment by avoiding God. Her diverse characters confirm Augustine's timeless truth: "Man desires to praise thee, for he is a part of thy creation. . . . Thou hast made us for thyself and restless is our heart until it comes to rest in thee."[6]

Subtly, O'Connor's title leads us to question, Does Parker's back *belong* to him? Parker certainly makes this claim. Or do the words mean Parker comes "back to God"? Back to worship of God alone, back to restorative fellowship with him? Parker owns his name: "Obadiah [servant of the Lord] Elihue [he is my God himself]."

Parker was "back"! He surrendered his fragmented, idolatrous life to Jesus Christ. Parker was *back*, like King David:

> Have mercy on me, O God,
>> according to your unfailing love;
>> according to your great compassion
>> blot out my transgressions.
> Wash away all my iniquity
>> and cleanse me from my sin. (Ps. 51:1-2)

Parker was *back*, like the prodigal son (Luke 15:11-32); *back*, like Mary Magdalene (8:2; Matt. 28:1); *back*, like the apostle Peter conversing with Jesus by the Sea of Galilee (John 21:15-19); and *back*, like the apostle Paul on the road to Damascus (Acts 9:1-9).

21

Vocation Assigned

Genesis says that only humans were created by God "in his own *image*" and "after" his own *"likeness"* (Gen. 1:26-27, KJV, emphasis added; 5:1; 9:6).[7] Scholars have extensively discussed this unique claim. Some say it refers to some property of human nature that *resembles* God in some way. Others focus on *function* (what people do instead of what they are). Humans uniquely represent God in his activity of ruling the world. Still others understand "image" and "likeness" *relationally*. Humans are truly themselves only when they are in a right relationship with God and with other humans.[8] Abraham Joshua Heschel, the great Jewish interpreter of the prophets, explains that humans are meant to "imitate" God by "walking in His ways" (*miṣwôt*, "precepts," "how God is"). By living in "the likeness of God," Israel was to become "a kingdom of priests, a holy people" (Exod. 19:6).[9]

The explanations are complementary. They affirm God created us as his *expression* or *transcription* in creaturely form to be fulfilled through trusting and loving obedience (Gen. 2:15-17). We are to be "worshipping stewards within God's heaven-and-earth reality."[10] This is our "priestly vocation"; it consists of "summing up the praises of creation before the Creator" and "reflecting God's wisdom and justice into the world."[11]

Vocation Squandered

The staggering story in Genesis, and throughout the Bible, is that humankind rejected God's intention. As illustrated by O. E. Parker, when humans choose to construct an independent and contrary narrative, the end is death, not life, as the cunning deceiver promised (Gen. 3:1-5). The deceiver used the serpent (part of God's creation) as a wedge for separating humankind from God. His *purpose* was to impose chaos upon God's good and orderly creation. His *strategy* was to convince Adam and Eve to deny God's truthfulness and trustworthiness. He promised Eve, "If you disobey God, you will not die. Rather, God is withholding life from you" (vv. 1-5, paraphrased).[12]

Genesis 2 describes three trees in the garden of Eden. The first is "pleasing to the eye and good for food" (v. 9). Adam and Eve could freely eat its fruit (vv. 9, 16). Second is the "tree of life" (v. 9). The third is the "tree of the knowledge of good and evil" (v. 9). Adam and Eve were forbidden to eat of that tree (vv. 15-17). Knowing the difference between good and evil should be highly beneficial. Why the prohibition?

C. John Collins explains that by God giving free access to the first tree (v. 16), Adam and Eve had everything they needed. By acting obediently and living out of God's resources, they would arrive at a proper knowledge of good and evil. They would gain permanent access to the "tree of life" (v. 9; cf. Rev. 2:7). Instead, first Eve and then Adam flagrantly disobeyed God by eating of the "tree of the knowledge of good and evil" (Gen. 2:17). The tree symbolizes the option of trying to be fully human in defiance of God's will, by rejecting trustful obedience.[13]

Compliantly enticed by "the delusion of false emancipation,"[14] humankind's history of sin, the "mystery of iniquity," began (2 Thess. 2:7, KJV; Rom. 5:12). Arrested by God's questions, Adam and Eve fabricated excuses for personal benefit, regardless of the harm to their prior delight in God and harmony with each other.[15] Old Testament scholar John H. Walton says the Israelite reader would have understood the result of the serpent's work as "evil taking root among humanity."[16]

Genesis 4 portrays humankind's continued decline into sin and the results of disobedience as they spread through Adam's offspring. Adam and Eve's disobedience and idolatry led directly to the preflood judgment against the accumulated wickedness of the human race (6:5).

The apostle Paul confirms the judgment: "Although they claimed to be wise, they became fools" (Rom. 1:22). Often called the "great exchange," created to be God's wise agents, humans squandered their calling. They "exchanged" the "glory" of God for the glory of the world and commenced worshipping the creation instead of their "Creator" (vv. 23, 25; see vv. 18-32). Paul uses terms such as "ungodliness," "futility," "decay," and "enemies of God" to describe the results (see vv. 18-32; 5:10). Spiritual death (Eph. 2:1-3; Col. 2:13) and alienation from God (Col. 1:21) are consequences into which disobedience and idolatry spiral (3:5-6).

The indictment is universal. Paul told the Galatians that "Scripture" decisively levels the judgment against everyone (Gal. 3:22; cf. Rom. 3:9-19). Jesus taught his disciples that when the Holy Spirit comes, "He will convince the world concerning sin and righteousness" (John 16:8, RSV).

All of us, said Augustine and Martin Luther, are by nature "curved in upon ourselves."[17] An infinite array of twisted forms, idolatrous self-love, and disobedience is humankind's fundamental problem. John Wesley also emphasized our tendency to be idolatrous by loving the creature more than the Creator. Whether we are curved upon ourselves or curved toward others, God has been replaced. We are all "tattooed Parkers" (8:34; 1 John 1:8-10).

Abraham Joshua Heschel observed, "One of the great achievements of the prophets was the repudiation of nature as an object of adoration. . . . [For] Judaism, the adoration of nature is as absurd as the alienation from nature is unnecessary."[18] The prophet Isaiah lampoons the absurdity of idolatry. A carpenter cuts down a tree and burns half to warm himself and to cook a meal. He carves the other half into a "god." The foolish man does not consider that the halves could easily have been reversed (Isa. 44:9-17; cf. Deut. 4:19).[19]

By habitual worship of the creation, we—like O. E. Parker and Isaiah's carpenter—have grotesquely disfigured ourselves and all we touch. Our manifold "tattoos" are composed of parts of the heavens and earth, race and gender, religion and human sexuality, political and military power, intellect and natural passions. Our catalog of possible "tattoos" seems inexhaustible.[20] Like Parker, the more the "tattoos" increase, the greater our dissatisfaction and unrest become.

Vocation Regained

Tucked into the Genesis account of Adam and Eve's expulsion from the garden lies a divine promise. To the deceiver God says, "I will put enmity between you and the woman, and between your offspring and hers" (Gen. 3:15).[21] Although scholars disagree on the statement's meaning, clearly Satan will not have the final word. God the Creator is also God the Covenant Maker who redeems (Jer. 31:31-34).

New Testament scholar N. T. Wright connects the covenant God makes with Abraham (Gen. 12:1-3; 17:1-8) to the expulsion from Eden. God "called Abraham and his family to undo the sin of Adam, even though Abraham and his family became part of the problem as well as bearers of the solution."[22] From the expulsion from Eden to the cross of Christ, where "creation and covenant come together";[23] from the old creation to inauguration of the new; and from the exodus from Egyptian slavery to the new freedom for which Christ sets us free (Gal. 5:1), God has consistently shown himself to be the covenant-keeping Redeemer. His steadfast love[24] never fails (Isa. 54:8; Jer. 31:3; Lam. 3:22).[25]

If humankind's sorry condition is to be reversed and transformed, if the holy covenant is to be restored, if the universal yearning for redeemed life and peace with God is to be satiated, it must have two features: First, redemption will depend on divine initiative and grace alone, not on what defiled humans can generate. God must take upon himself the task of rescuing sinners "dead in trespasses and sins" (Eph. 2:1, KJV). Second, redemption must be directed *toward* and successful *in* removing the polluting and disfiguring effects of human sinfulness (Heb. 10:19-25; 1 Pet. 1:3-9).

Aware of this, N. T. Wright surveys humankind's lost estate, its rebellion, its bondage to idols and demonic powers, and its consequent estrangement from God. Nothing less than a mighty and successful divine revolution, Wright correctly insists, could reverse humankind's course toward destruction.[26] Only a revolution could restore humans to divine fellowship and to loving and obedient worship.

Just such a revolution began on a Friday afternoon, in AD 33. God, in love, "*set forth* [his Son] to be a propitiation through faith in his blood, to declare his righteousness for the remission of sins that are past, through the forbearance of God" (Rom. 3:25, KJV, emphasis added). In his sovereign love, manifest on the cross, the holy God drew evil into one place. God Incarnate, taking the full force of sin upon himself, "lay bare his holy arm in the sight of all the nations" (Isa. 52:10), and met us there as Redeemer. He became the place of meeting (Gk., *hilastērion*; "propitiation" [Rom. 3:25, NASB]; "mercy seat" [Heb. 9:5, NASB]), the place of reconciliation, between himself and sinful humankind. He replaced faithlessness and idolatry with covenantal fidelity and holy worship.[27]

In Christ Jesus, the Father brought heaven and earth together, thereby restoring our lost estate and preparing us to walk before him "in holiness and righteousness" (Luke 1:75). In his atonement, Christ removed all that could obstruct a meeting between God and sinful humankind.[28] Now, by Christ's life *in* us, unending transformation is possible. "If, while we were God's enemies, we were reconciled to him through the death of his Son, how much more, having been reconciled, shall we be saved through his life" (Rom. 5:10).[29]

Jesus's bodily resurrection "was the first visible sign that the revolution was already under way."[30] By raising Jesus from the dead, the eternally faithful God had inaugurated his new creation within the present world.[31] By the power of the Holy Spirit, God invites people of all nations to become new creatures and, *as sanctified vessels*, joyous participants in his project of new creation.

Vocation as Mission

Beginning in Genesis, the Bible anticipates a renewed human vocation within God's renewed creation. The book of Revelation calls that vocation a holy, sanctified priesthood. Glory "to him who loves us and has freed us from our sins by his blood, and has made us to be a kingdom and priests to serve his God and Father—to him be glory and power for ever and ever! Amen" (1:5-6; cf. 5:9-10; 1 Pet. 2:4-5). Through the revolution begun on the cross, confirmed in Jesus's resurrection and glorification, and empowered at Pentecost, the holy vocation has been renewed.[32]

The call to, and provision for, Christian holiness is liberally broadcast across the New Testament (Luke 1:74-75; Rom. 6:22; 2 Cor. 7:1; Eph. 4:24). Restoration of worship and loving obedience, transformation in the image of Christ (Rom. 8:29; 2 Cor. 3:18; Col. 3:9-10), and "participation in the cruciform character of God"[33] celebrate our Lord's victory and the riches he has won for us (Eph. 1:15-23). Christian holiness involves, by grace through obedient faith, coming to know "in all wisdom and insight the mystery of [God's] will, according to his purpose which he set forth in Christ as a plan for the fullness of time, to unite all things in him, things in heaven and things on earth" (1:9-10, RSV). "What we are promised in the gospel is the kingdom of God coming 'on earth as in heaven.'"[34]

The enabling Spirit of God equips Jesus's disciples to join the celebration of his victory. He empowers Christians to say yes to the power of Jesus's resurrection in every dimension of life, yes to new creation and yes to a new mode of existence. In the cross and resurrection, *"a new way of being human has been launched."*[35] It "starts with forgiveness (God's forgiveness of those who turn from their now defeated idols) and continues with forgiveness (the forgiveness offered by Jesus's followers in his name and by his Spirit to all who have wronged them). . . . Forgiveness is . . . the power of the revolution."[36]

As Wright explains, the vocation of Christian holiness means not only the restoration of worship but also mission. *"Christian mission means implementing the victory that Jesus won on the cross."*[37] It is the life and work of "reconciled reconcilers." Buried and raised with Christ, equipped by the Holy Spirit, Christians are to announce that *"a new reality has come to birth. Its name is 'forgiveness.'"*[38] Christian discipleship is meaningless—defeating and pointless—until fueled by a "chain-breaking, idol smashing, sin-abandoning power called 'forgiveness,' called 'utter gracious love,' called *Jesus.*"[39] Because of the Jesus revolution, new creation is the true reality.

"The early Christian message is not well summarized by saying Jesus died so that we can go to heaven. That . . . shrinks and distorts what the Bible actually teaches."[40] It ignores Jesus's claim to have inaugurated the long-awaited kingdom of God on earth. And it ignores our true Christian vocation as "image 'bearers'" of Jesus Christ, reflecting God's glory into the world.[41] If Jesus's death really did launch a revolution; if Satan, the Great Jailer, has been overpowered and his house plundered (Matt. 12:29; John 12:31; Col. 2:15); if sin's prison doors have been unlocked, someone needs to announce to the world that the enslaving powers and idols have lost their power (Eph. 2:1-10; Col. 2:13-15). In "cross-resurrection-Spirit kind of power," someone must "announce the amnesty to 'sinners' far and wide."[42]

Vocation as Journey

In the words of Eugene Peterson, Christian holiness proceeds from our "whole being staggered by a vision of God."[43] If we settle for less, God becomes monotonously predictable—a *means* to secondary *ends*—and we remain imprisoned in sinful self-interest.[44] The psalmist placed things in order:

> Ascribe to the LORD the glory due his name;
> worship the LORD in the splendor of his holiness. (Ps. 29:2)

> Come, let us bow down in worship,
> let us kneel before the LORD our Maker;
> for he is our God
> and we are the people of his pasture,
> the flock under his care. (95:6-7)

Joyfully, Jesus's disciples can become bustling construction sites for his "workmanship" (Eph. 2:10, KJV; Col. 3:5-17).[45] There are no elites among the redeemed. The provisions of Christ's atonement are indiscriminate in his church. They are intended for all his sisters and brothers. Peter addressed all of them as "sanctified by the Spirit for obedience to Jesus Christ" (1 Pet. 1:2, RSV). His counsel: "As obedient children, do not be conformed to the passions of your former ignorance, but as he who called you is holy, be holy yourselves in all your conduct; since it is written, 'You shall be holy, for I am holy'" (1 Pet. 1:14-16, RSV).[46]

In that spirit, Martin Luther said that those who by faith receive the word of the gospel become "the most free lords of all, subject to none." At the same time, they become "the most dutiful servants of all."[47] When by grace we reside completely in Christ, the true Lord of all things possesses and secures us. Nothing of significance in all creation can be added or subtracted. In Christ, we are "lord of all."

The entire creation again becomes what the Creator intended—the rich and magnificent arena in which we, God's vice-regents can "declare his glory among the nations, his marvelous deeds among all peoples" (1 Chron. 16:24). In the words of Catholic scholar R. J. Snell, "The grace of the Incarnation does not destroy human nature but perfects it, completes it, elevates it. . . . We have been purchased and saved *from something* and *for something*."[48] God's *revolution* begun in Christ guarantees that "his divine power has granted to us all things that pertain to life and godliness, through the knowledge of him who called us to his own glory and excellence" (2 Pet. 1:3, RSV).

As happened for Obadiah Elihue Parker, the Redeemer can turn our "spider web souls into a perfect [pattern] of colors, a garden of trees and birds and beasts."[49] "But we all, with unveiled face, beholding as in a *mirror* the glory of the Lord, are being transformed into the same image from glory to glory, just as from the Lord, the Spirit" (2 Cor. 3:18, NASB).

2

"On Earth as It Is in Heaven"
The Vocation of Holiness in Scripture

❖

Kent Brower, PhD and Mi Ja Wi, PhD

Kent Brower is senior research fellow and senior lecturer in biblical studies, Nazarene Theological College, Manchester, England. He is a layperson in the Church of the Nazarene.

Mi Ja Wi is lecturer in biblical studies and global mission, Nazarene Theological College, Manchester, England. She is copastor of Ye Dam Church of the Nazarene, Manchester.

❖

The vocation of holiness runs like a golden thread through the Scriptures. While vocational language only becomes explicit in Exodus 19:5-6 and Leviticus 19:2, and reread in 1 Peter 2:5, 9-10, this scarcely does justice to the theme.

Holiness in Scripture is both vocation and identity. God's people are holy only in relationship to the Holy One. This holy calling is not a static and self-possessed identity. It does not mean being independently holy as if holiness were a thing. Rather, holiness in Scripture is always derived—people, places, and things are only holy in relation to the Holy One. For people it is a life-giving relationship with the holy God that enables people to reflect God's holiness to and in the world. *Living* as God's holy people can never be divorced from *being* God's holy people.

Scripture describes the vocation of holiness primarily through its narrative. This grand narrative, stretching from creation to consummation, shapes the social and personal identity of the people of God. It undergirds the life of late Second Temple Judaism (about 530 BCE to 70 CE) and is central to the Christian story.

The existence of Scripture itself illuminates the vocation of holiness. Because Scripture is a living and authoritative text for believers, it speaks the word of God afresh in new contexts. The text is reread and reauthored in light of God's ongoing self-disclosure culminating in Christ. This occurs within Scripture itself, in the Old Testament but especially in the New Testament, with its "figural reading."[1]

Readers themselves exist in a dialogical relationship with the text. They bring their contexts and diverse cultures to the text. Moreover, readers of the text become a text to be read by others (James 1:22-25). The call to be God's holy people is also the vocation of faithful readers, who engage with and are engaged by the story—the story of the living God who is at work through the Holy Spirit in the midst of his created order and through his called kingdom of priests and a holy nation. Readers themselves become a text—part of the vocation to *be holy as I am holy!*

This chapter examines the way the narrative of God's calling to the vocation of holiness is set out and then reread at different points. It starts with creation, the call of Abraham, the exodus, and life leading up to the exile. The first rereading occurs during the exile. Next, the chapter looks at the New Testament rereading of the story in two parts: (1) following the Holy One of God and (2) living as God's holy people. It will become clear that the *new story* is the retold *old story* in a new setting; the text's story is retold.

Creation and Vocation

"Holiness is the quintessential nature of Yahweh as God."[2]

The biblical narrative begins with the story of a holy God—creating, forming, and shaping a holy people with a mission to embody his holiness in their way of life. The creation account reveals a holy God and does so particularly in his relation to creation.

The word "holy" occurs only once in Genesis. God blesses the seventh day and makes it "holy" (2:3). But as theologian Philip Jenson notes,

"Holiness has to be understood in relation to the actions and purposes of the holy God."[3] Thus the divine words "create," "bless," and "create life." Creation responds to them. It is structured and shaped by them. Most of all, God's actions fill the creation with "blessing and life," which are an integral part of God's holiness.[4] Creation is good (1:4, 10, 12, 18, 21, 25).

The goodness of creation reaches its zenith in Genesis 1:27-28. God creates humankind, male and female, in his image, blesses them, and gives them a mission. God forms human community in his likeness and breathes the breath of life into them. They are given their vocation, with power and authority to serve God's creation. As image bearers of the Creator, humans are "morally accountable for [their] actions" and are to represent God.[5] In a nutshell, humans are created to be holy in relationship with God, with one another, and with the whole creation. Creation is indeed "very good" (v. 31) in harmonious relationships.

The disobedience of humankind, however, engenders chaos that leads to curse and death instead of blessing and life. Relationships between God and humankind, human and human, and human and creation are marred (Gen. 3). No longer is God's holy presence a blessing, but it becomes a threat.[6] No longer does human community cherish living together, but it descends to injustice and violence. No longer is the relationship between God's creation and human community symbiotic, but it becomes parasitic and exploitative. Death as separation from the source of life enters the scene (chap. 3; see Rom. 5:12). The more humankind multiplies and grows, the more human violence and wickedness seem to increase. This is recounted in the flood and the Tower of Babel stories (Gen. 6, 11). Not only is "every inclination of . . . the human heart" evil, but also the earth is "full of violence" (6:5, 11).

Nevertheless, the narrative of a holy God continues. The thread of a righteous relationship with Noah leads to covenant renewal with the earth. God unceasingly reaches out, relating to and restoring human community to his mission. He calls and sets apart agents of blessing and life for the rest of his creation.

Holy God, Holy People

The holy God not only creates but also calls. God calls Abram, Moses, and Israel. Yet the "particularity" of the call narratives always serves the "universality" of God's interest for the whole creation.[7] In Gen. 12:1-3, God calls Abram to be a blessing to all people and to be blameless in his relationship with God (17:1). God's promise of blessing and life in Abram's call has been remembered and shared by many, including those who have become descendants of Abram by faith.

Abram is called to trust God, who speaks and blesses him. In turn, Abram obeys and follows the call (12:4) and believes him (15:6). He is called to "walk before [God Almighty] faithfully and be blameless" (17:1). Here "be blameless" is connected to "walk before [God]." The command to be blameless, or to be perfect, can only be possible when an ongoing and intimate relationship with God is maintained.[8] Walking in the presence of God makes "be blameless" possible.[9]

Walking as a way of life is elaborated in Genesis 18:19, where the focus is on doing what is right and just. Abraham (name changed from Abram; see 17:5) is chosen "that he may charge his children and his household after him to keep the way of the Lord by doing righteousness and justice" (NRSV). Abraham's call and blessing entails walking in the way of the Lord, manifesting who God is. What causes God to "go down" to Sodom and Gomorrah is not only their grave sin but also the cry for help (18:21, NRSV) from those who suffer from violence and injustice. He hears this cry and comes to act against the oppressors.[10] Doing what is right and just becomes concrete as a response to the outcry of the oppressed and against the injustice and violence of the oppressors. The story further reveals the character of God in Abraham's plea for Sodom (vv. 23-32). Abraham sees a God who is willing to extend mercy instead of destroying even those who are unrighteous and unjust.[11] The story repeatedly points to God's mercy and patience even after the destruction of Sodom and Gomorrah (19:16, 21, 29). Abraham learns the way of the Lord is merciful and just. This is what he is to teach his children and household.

The word "holy" occurs the second time when God calls Moses (Exod. 3:5). Here "holy" is linked to God's self-revelation of his name and character. In Jo Well's words, "From Exodus 3, holiness is tied up with the knowledge of God as Yahweh."[12] In many aspects, Moses's call resonates with Abraham's in Genesis 18. It is set in the context of the "outcry" of the Israelites who suffer from slavery, oppression, violence, and even genocide (Exod. 2:23-25). God responds to these outcries. He not only hears but also sees the peoples' distress. He knows their sufferings and comes to deliver them. Here God's holiness is revealed, and the self-disclosure of "the divine name acquires content."[13]

The ground where Moses stands is holy because of God's presence (3:5). But "far from the austerity and severity that one might have expected with some conceptions of holiness," God's holy presence is characterized by his concern for the outcry of the people under oppression and by delivering them from their oppressors (2:23-25; 3:7-10).[14] Moses is called to participate in the divine acts of deliverance. Later, God's holiness is praised because of this deliverance and redemption (15:11, 13). The very character of God "as holy, as compassionate, as deliverer" is disclosed in the account of the call of Moses.[15]

The call narratives culminate when God creates and calls Israel to be "[his] treasured possession," "a kingdom of priests and a holy nation" (Exod. 19:5-6). The word "holy" is finally tied to a people called holy. Here holiness is indeed an *identity* given to Israel. They are called to live out this holy identity as their *vocation* "both in relation to [God] and also in relation to other nations."[16] Similar to the call of Abraham in Gen. 12:1-3, Israel is called to be a blessing to all the peoples and the whole earth through her priestly role (Exod. 19:5). Priests are "set apart" for their particular vocation (v. 6). It is not simply the cultic "nature of the priestly function" but their mediatory role between God and other nations, and the whole creation that draws our attention.[17] Moreover, the call happens in conjunction with what God has done for them and against their oppressors (v. 4). Israel's relationship to God is defined as *his* treasured possession, as a priestly kingdom, and as a holy nation. While all peoples and the whole earth belong to God, this call distinguishes Israel from others because of their particular way of relating to this holy God. Thus holiness is required. C. H. Wright's observation on holiness in this context is illuminating:

> Being holy did not mean that the Israelites were to be a specially religious nation. A fundamental part of the meaning of the word is "different or distinctive." Something or someone is holy when set apart for a distinct purpose and kept separate for that purpose. For Israel, it meant being different by reflecting the very different God that YHWH revealed himself to be, compared with other gods. Israel was to be as different from other nations as YHWH was different from other gods.[18]

Israel's holiness, understood as its distinction from the surrounding nations, needed to be embodied in its daily life (Lev. 18:2-3). Israelites were to live out their holy identity by acting justly and rightly in relation to others and to the whole creation.[19] The Torah details how life should be lived in response to who God is and what God has done. In particular, Leviticus 19 makes holiness concrete as embodied in all areas of life. It begins with the imperative: "Be holy because I, the LORD your God, am holy" (v. 2). The command to be holy is founded upon Israel's special relation to a holy God (v. 2; 20:26).

A call to imitate God's holiness in Leviticus 19 combines ritual and ethical aspects of holiness. Anthropologist Mary Douglas explains, "Holiness requires in ritual contexts correspondence to what God's people must do for each other in secular contexts."[20] Hence, beginning with a command to honor parents, to keep Sabbaths, and to avoid turning to idols (vv. 3-4), Leviticus 19 expounds holiness in the context of harvest, neighborly relations, and business and judicial dealings (vv. 9-18, 34-35).

In all these, however, the main concern centers on the protection of the weak members of the community: the landless (the poor and immigrants) when it comes to harvest (vv. 9-10); the disabled (v. 14); and hired laborers, whose lives hang on their daily wages when it comes to neighborly relations (v. 13). Israel's holiness has to be characterized by its just and right dealings with those who are particularly vulnerable in the community. A call to be holy (v. 2) centers on justice that is always expressed in particular relationships and contexts.[21] Moreover, the vocation of holiness is articulated in positive and inclusive terms. It combines justice with mercy and extends to loving neighbors and immigrants alike (vv. 18, 34). In fact, the Bible speaks more of loving foreigners than of loving those like us. Hence Leviticus 19 provides "the finest commentary on the call of Israel to be [a] 'kingdom of priests and a holy nation'" (Exod. 19:6).[22]

Thus far, God's holiness is revealed and stated in who he is and what he has done. As Creator, his divine acts of creation bring blessing and life. As a merciful God, he attends to the cries for help and looks compassionately upon the oppressed. As a mighty savior, he delivers the oppressed and executes righteousness and justice. Based on how God reveals himself as holy, the call to live likewise is expressed in Deut. 10:12-19:

> And now, Israel, what does the LORD your God ask of you but to fear the LORD your God, to walk in obedience to him, to love him. . . .
>
> To the LORD your God belong the heavens . . . , the earth and everything in it. Yet the LORD set his affection on your ancestors and loved them, and he chose you, their descendants, above all the nations. . . . For the LORD your God is God of gods . . . , who shows

no partiality and accepts no bribes. He defends the cause of the fatherless and the widow, and loves the foreigner residing among you, giving them food and clothing. And you are to love those who are foreigners, for you yourselves were foreigners in Egypt.

Living in the Land: Kings and Prophets

With the presence and guidance of a holy God, Israel arrives at the promised land, which is also a land of strangers and enemies. God's call to walk in his ways and to choose life and blessing faces real challenges as Israel encounters other nations. Israel is chosen "as the instrument through which [God] would . . . bring blessing to the whole world."[23] Then how does the Bible, particularly in the story of violence and conquest in Joshua, describe Israel's vocation of holiness?

This is perhaps the most problematic, if not distressing and embarrassing, question to address in the vocation of holiness. Careful readers pay close attention to ancient contexts. Scripture was written in a time when "the massacre of populations was commonplace."[24] That fact, however, cannot eliminate the problem. Interpretation of ancient texts also faces the challenge of whether they are to be read literally or metaphorically.

Perhaps a more telling question is this: Can we apply these texts as divine mandates to practice similar violence? By no means. They need to be heard as strong warnings against sinful acts, but not to be taken literally. Similarly, texts of violence demand of Israel a total commitment and allegiance to God in the places where other gods are in play. Israel's particular identity as God's chosen people requires undivided loyalty but, at the same time, needs to be embodied in their relations with others. While this does not solve many of the problems regarding texts of violence, we need to hear stories of mercy in the midst of war and violence. The book of Joshua introduces Rahab, a prostitute in Jericho, as "Israel's first contact with 'the enemy.'"[25] The Israelites not only spare Rahab and her family, who put their faith in the God of Israel, but also embrace them as their own (2:6). The Gibeonites, unlike other peoples in Canaan, make a similar profession of faith. To save themselves they make a covenant with Israel, even though by trickery (chaps. 9–10). Thus, joining God's people is always a possibility regardless of ethnic or religious backgrounds. Living in the promised land, Israelites are repeatedly reminded that they are to show mercy and justice to foreigners living among them; they, too, were once foreigners in Egypt. In fact, Israelites are "permanently" foreigners residing in God's land, for it belongs to him (Lev. 25:23).[26]

Beginning with the reign of David, Israel establishes a hereditary monarchy. Kings were to represent God, who reigns with justice and mercy. He defends the cause of the poor—the fatherless, widows, and foreigners (Ps. 72). The Davidic kingship reminds us of God's *particular* covenant with Israel (2 Sam. 7; 1 Chron. 17), anticipating its *universal* reign by which "all nations will be blessed" (Ps. 72:17). At the dedication of the temple in Jerusalem, the prayer of Solomon once again includes foreigners who come and pray to God. It includes all people of the earth who come to know God (1 Kings 8:41-43, 59-61). Kings must embody God's reign for this *particular* covenant, with its *universal* effect, to succeed.

Thus the vocation of holiness for rulers is twofold: (1) to lead their people to follow God unreservedly and (2) to rule them with justice—that is, to rule "not by power but by their concern for the powerless; not by wealth but by how they treat the poor."[27] A king's responsibility is to build a just society. Failure to do this is judged by the prophets. Because Israel fails to live out her identity and vocation to be holy, it eventually leads her into exile.

The book of Isaiah begins with God's condemnation of Judah and Jerusalem for their inequity (1:2-4). Their worship is detestable before God because of injustice and their oppression of the vulnerable (vv. 12-17, 21-23). Ritual purity is inseparable from social justice. Israel, called to walk in the way of the Lord—the way of justice and righteousness—has become like Sodom and Gomorrah (vv. 9-10). Israel, called to bring life and blessing, has become "a channel for oppression and injustice."[28] Isaiah proclaims, "[God] looked for justice, but saw bloodshed; / for righteousness, but heard cries of distress" (5:7). In this context, Isaiah champions God's holiness and reminds Israel of its vocation of holiness. "Holy, holy, holy" is Isaiah's vision of God (6:3). God's name is holy (57:15). God is the Holy One *of Israel*. Relational holiness is intrinsic to God's name and nature.[29]

God's exalted holiness is expressed as justice and righteousness. Isaiah 5:16 declares, "But the LORD of hosts is exalted by justice, and the Holy God shows himself holy by righteousness" (NRSV). Divine holiness is deeply concerned with the cries of the oppressed and victims of injustice (vv. 1-15). Encounter with divine holiness cleanses Isaiah and commissions him as a prophet to the people (chap. 6). Likewise, the Holy One of Israel demands Israel cleanse its impurities by embodying his holiness;

it must do what is just and right by God's standard. The vocation of holiness extends beyond Israel to all who obey God's word by maintaining justice and doing what is right (56:1-8). Indeed, the Holy One of Israel is the Creator, Redeemer, and Savior of all the nations. But in spite of Isaiah's hope for universal restoration and renewal, failure to follow the way of the Lord leads Israel into exile.

Was all hope lost? Not at all. Jeremiah promised a new covenant with Israel in which "I will put my law within them, and I will write it on their hearts; and I will be their God, and they shall be my people" (Jer. 31:33, NRSV). Ezekiel promised a "new heart" and a "new spirit" (Ezek. 36:26-27, NRSV). These texts are central to the hopes of the people of God in their later rereading of this narrative.

Rereading the Story: Part 1

Exile and Return

In Ezra and Nehemiah the identity and vocation of Israel as God's holy people are reshaped. The returned exiles restore the temple and the Torah to renew their covenant with God and to renew covenant communities. The exile strengthened their desire to be faithful to God and to enable God to return to dwelling in their midst.

But in the process, holiness as separation becomes dominant in their interpretation of "the function of the Temple and the Torah."[30] The returned exiles refuse help from the people of the land in rebuilding the temple (Ezra 4:3). They exclude those of foreign descent from worshiping in the temple (Neh. 13:3). The temple is no longer envisioned as a house of prayer of all nations, but an exclusive place of worship for ethnically pure Israel. The temple and the Torah secure their identity. A call to be holy is no longer for God in service to others, but separation from the people of the land. Identity becomes an exclusive possession. The returned exiles understand their identity as a holy seed (Ezra 9:2), which refers to genealogical purity. They establish an impenetrable boundary based on lineage.

Thus intermarriage is of particular concern in both Ezra and Nehemiah. Intermarriage is now understood as defilement and uncleanness that leads to unfaithfulness (Ezra 9-10; Neh. 13:28-30). The rereading of the Torah's prohibition against intermarriage with certain nations is expanded or intensified, if not misinterpreted. In the Torah, unjust and immoral ways of other nations are the main concern regarding the prohibition of intermarriage (Deut. 7:3-4; 23:2-6). But after the exile, the prohibition is interpreted as defilement of Israel's holiness. It is therefore used to establish boundaries. Keeping Israel's identity as a holy seed becomes its vocation. Israel maintains its genealogical purity by prohibiting intermarriage. They no longer cleanse themselves by promoting justice and righteousness: holiness becomes defined as protection against ethnic impurity. So separation becomes a watchword during the postexilic period.[31]

Rise of Holiness Movements

The return from exile has happened, but Israel is still overrun by Gentiles and has a sense of remaining in exile.[32] As hostility and resistance to Gentile power and influence intensify, the quest for holiness as separation increases.[33] It serves to maintain and preserve identity as God's chosen people, and it ensures "future security" as a nation.[34] With this understanding of holiness, purity and impurity become critical issues in the postexilic community. Hence, holiness movements emerge in various forms.

Two of them are instructive for our purposes. First, the Qumran community calls itself the "holy ones." To maintain their purity as the holy ones, separation from society becomes essential, including separation from other Jews. With their rigorous study of the Torah and radical (literal) interpretation of it, the community chooses to live a communal life in the wilderness along the Dead Sea. They describe themselves as the "house of holiness for Israel" and thus the true priesthood (see *Rule of the Community* from Qumran, 1QS VIII, 5). They exclusively apply "a kingdom of priests and a holy nation" (Exod. 19:6) to themselves. For the Qumran community, holiness as separation is both "means and end."[35]

Second, unlike the Qumran community, the Pharisees "democratize" their understanding of Israel as "a kingdom of priests and a holy nation" (v. 6). All Jews are called to be priests and are to keep purity regulations pertaining to the call to holiness. But the regulations are applied not so much to embody the priestly mediatorial role as to maintain purity laws in cultic settings. The Pharisees' strict observation of purity laws is intended for "separation within society."[36] Living in the land, which is impure due to the presence of Gentiles, the Pharisees meticulously develop ways Israel can maintain purity in daily life. John the Baptist appears in this context with his message of a baptism of repentance. He cries out for the renewal of God's people.

Rereading the Story: Part 2A

Following the Holy One of God

Longings for restoration are reflected in Luke's stories of the righteous people surrounding John's and Jesus's births. At the center of these hopes is hope for a prophet like Moses, or the Messiah,[37] who would herald renewal of the people of God under the son of David.

Into this scene comes John the Baptist. Full of the Spirit from his mother's womb, he prepares the way for the Coming One. John is the link between promises in the prophets and hopes for restoration that form part of the rereading of Israel's story with reference to the coming of Jesus of Nazareth. In words echoing Genesis 1, Luke pictures a new beginning through the Holy Spirit's overshadowing of Mary. Her baby is son of Adam and Son of God. Matthew's genealogy recapitulates the line of Abraham that culminates in Jesus. He is the obedient Son called out of Egypt who is also Immanuel, "God with us" (1:23). For Mark, Isaiah's "new thing" (Isa. 43:19) is happening in Jesus. It is signaled by the voice from heaven and the rending of heavens when the Spirit descends like a dove upon the beloved Son (Mark 1:9-10). He is the true representative of the people of God. Jesus announces the arrival of the kingdom of God in fulfillment of God's promises (vv. 14-15).

This disclosure of Jesus's identity is vital for understanding the renewal of God's holy people. Gospel readers know that he is Messiah Jesus, Son of God.[38] Immediately after the call of four disciples, Jesus's identity is revealed by an unclean spirit—Jesus is the Holy One of God.[39] Only the centurion gives human voice to this confession (Matt. 27:54; Mark 15:39; Luke 23:47), and he speaks more than he knows.[40]

While the Gospels are ancient biography,[41] a significant theme has to do with discipleship. Jesus first calls four disciples. Exorcisms and healings follow; they demonstrate God's opposition to evil and show compassion for the hurting. Jesus is reconstituting the holy people of God for their holy vocation: the announcement and inauguration of the kingdom. The culmination of the kingdom's beginning occurs in Mark 3:13-15. In a scene echoing Exodus 24, Jesus goes to the mountain and calls and names twelve apostles. They are the vanguard of the renewed and regathered people of God. The Twelve are given authority over the powers of evil, are commissioned to proclaim the kingdom of God, and, most importantly, are to be present with Jesus.[42]

The Twelve, although confined to one or two tribes of Israel, represent the twelve tribes (see Luke 22:28-30). For Jesus, ethnicity no longer matters. In Mark 3:31-35, Jesus's blood relations urge him to leave the throngs. Jesus's response is significant: "Who are my mother and my brothers?" (v. 33, NRSV). He answers his own question: "Whoever does the will of God" (v. 35, NRSV). Jesus establishes a new social reality. His redefinition of "family" is both revolutionary and provocative. In Second Temple Judaism, genealogy lay at the heart of identity. This new definition of family changes all that. Jesus is "gathering around himself a disparate group. . . . And he transforms them into his holy community—the restored kingdom of priests and the holy nation. . . . Their core characteristic is doing God's will."[43] The new covenant community is determined by proximity to the Holy One of God and to engaging in his mission.

The meal settings confirm Jesus's new community orientation. He eats with tax collectors and sinners.[44] But the Pharisees question why he crosses purity boundaries. In response, in Luke 15 Jesus invites them to join him in celebrating the arrival of the kingdom. They are "the righteous" and he is offering them a welcome, as the parable of the lost son makes clear. Even the wealthy are invited to join. But their participation depends on their willingness to embrace the poor.[45]

Jesus calls his followers to be perfect as their heavenly Father is perfect. That vocation seems impossible if read out of context. But the statement echoes Lev. 19:2. It is recast by Luke to focus upon mercy shown even to enemies. According to Matthew and Luke, this is a radical return to the original mission of God. It reiterates God's call to Abraham to "walk before Yahweh and be perfect" (Gen. 17:1, author's translation). This call included righteousness and justice as the way Abraham was to be a blessing to the nations.

Redefining Purity and Reenvisaging the Holiness Vocation

Purity in Second Temple Judaism was a complex system designed to allow God to dwell in the midst of his people. Holiness was centered in the temple. Extending from the holy of holies, there were circles of holiness that required diverse levels of purity.[46]

Jesus challenges that system at its heart. The presence of God in the midst of his people is relocated to center in Jesus.[47] The Spirit of God dwells in Jesus, the Holy One of God. In turn, in the power of the Spirit, he embodies and enacts God's rescue mission. In the Gospel of John, the Word, who is God, becomes flesh and dwells among us. His body is now the temple of God—the dwelling of God among his people (1:14).

The relocation of holiness in Christ also "represented an extension and intensification of holiness. . . . The people, the land, the Temple and the Torah could be understood no longer as sufficient testimony to God's presence in holiness."[48] This meant redefining the purity system. In the old purity system impurity could be controlled by keeping pure people or things from contact with the impure. In that system, when purity was compromised, the contagion was dealt with through remedies found in the Torah (Law).

Jesus challenges the contagion of impurity. He cleanses lepers, heals on the Sabbath, exorcises unclean spirits, and declares all food clean. Andy Johnson observes that "this dislocation of holiness [from being about] . . . separation from impurity and its relocation in the Spirit-inhabited, boundary-crossing Son of God is nothing less than a shakeup of cosmic proportion."[49] Jesus's actions display "the very character of God, and thus . . . the nature of holiness."[50] Holiness is no longer defined by separation but by nearness to the Holy One. Purity still matters, but it comes from within. It reflects the compassion, mercy, and love at the heart of God, and it issues in community-affirming action.

The call to a holy vocation that comes from Jesus is not for the distant future. It is for today. All people are called to follow Jesus in the mission of God.[51] The vocation of holiness is both corporate and personal; it is a call to follow Jesus, the one who embodies the vocation of Abraham and Israel. It resets the relationships between God and his creatures and between people and the creation.

Rereading the Story: Part 2B

Living as People of the Spirit

The vocation of holiness is lived in the power of the Spirit. The New Testament writers share the conviction that the age to come has dawned. Jesus comes in the fullness of time. The narrative of Jesus's life, death, resurrection, and ascension is the example for believers to follow in working out their salvation.[52] In Acts, the Twelve are reconstituted, signaling the embodiment of the purposes of God fulfilled in this new people. The

Twelve are the vanguard of God's "new thing" (Isa. 43:19) that embraces the mission of the holy God to the nations. But the Twelve are to wait in Jerusalem until they receive the promise of the Father, the outpouring of the Spirit.

The central markers of the "last days" (Isa. 2:2; Mic. 4:1) are the resurrection of Christ and the outpouring of the Spirit. Jesus's resurrection is the first fruits of God's ultimate purposes. The purification of God's people, with a new heart of flesh and a new spirit within them, signals the arrival of the new day. Through Ezekiel, God says, "I will sanctify my great name . . . when through you I display my holiness before their eyes" (Ezek. 36:23, NRSV; see also vv. 24-27). God's holiness will be displayed "through Israel's restored life together."[53]

Peter explains Pentecost as Joel's promised outpouring of the Spirit on all flesh, personally and corporately. He doesn't know it yet, but that is *all* flesh, not just all Jewish flesh. And it includes daughters as well as sons, old as well as young. In short, this is Isaiah's "new thing" now coming to rest in the Spirit poured-out-on-all-flesh, the (re)new(ed) holy people of God, whose vocation is to be the agent of God's mission. The renewed people of God are empowered to bear witness to Christ, with signs of the new age confirming its arrival.

In their communal life, the holiness of God is displayed: no one is in need. Hospitality is a defining characteristic of God's holy people, who have been invited into the generous hospitality of the triune God. Hospitality is part of the biblical vocation of holiness.[54] Without hospitality in word and deed, God's hospitable holiness is not displayed. Hospitality as holiness welcomes the stranger, embraces the alien, and hosts the dispossessed, the refugee, and the immigrant at the table. Disabled people are welcomed and included in the community of faith.[55] Inclusion of the marginalized and vulnerable into the hospitality of God's people is at the heart of reflecting God's character.

The renewed people of God are also a prayerful and reflective community; they devote themselves to loving God and neighbor (cf. Acts 2:42). Implicit in holy vocation is the necessity of prayer, worship, and adoration. Breaking bread together may have soon acquired sacramental overtones. They are as important as acts of justice and mercy. The book of Acts emphasizes this by pointing to the apostles' teaching and prayers.

The mission of proclaiming God's good news is in continuity with that of God's people in Scripture. Now this good news is centered in Jesus. Like the purity map, the missional direction is reconfigured. Instead of people streaming into Jerusalem, the message goes out from Jerusalem. Samaritans and Gentiles are now brought into the people of God, whose only characteristic is the "heart purified by faith."[56] They, too, are to be transformed into the image of God while on the journey as God's Spirit people proclaiming the good news of Jesus.

For Peter and the Jerusalem apostles, grasping the far-reaching implications of the new day was neither quick nor easy.[57] The welcome of an excluded eunuch (see Deut. 23:1) is promised in Isaiah 56:1-5. The agenda-setting Cornelius story (Acts 10:1–11:18) shows how the Jerusalem apostles, despite the pressure to maintain boundaries, came to accept the Gentiles as Gentiles. Peter did not get there easily, but the lessons are clear: the purification of the Gentiles is an inward matter. Hearts are purified by faith.

The gospel was also problematic for the civil powers. Those engaged in God's holy mission are accused of turning the world upside down. In one episode that Robert Wall calls "the demythologization of magic,"[58] the gospel is perceived as a threat to the Artemis cult in Ephesus and to "the city's culture, its way of life, both economic and social."[59] This accusation is, of course, true. In the proclamation of the gospel "there is danger . . . that this trade of ours may come into disrepute" (Acts 19:27, NRSV). The statement is telling. Worship of Artemis is used to exploit people. Idolatry is shown to be an empty shell. But, more subtly, it challenges the exploitative systems of the world organized in opposition to the holy God.

These stories are mold breaking. The last days were to require a bold rereading of Scripture. The excluded, both Jews and Gentiles, are welcomed into the holy people of God, solely on the basis of the Spirit's work in their lives. The remapping of the purity universe continues: God creates the holy people of God by purifying their hearts by the work of the Spirit. This happens without reference to any of the usual scriptural criteria of what purity might look like and as interpreted by the "holiness people" of Jesus's day. The vocation of holiness embodies the themes of justice and mercy that come from the heart of God as reread for the new day.

Become Who You Are in Christ through the Spirit

Although this vocational calling is intensely personal, it is never individualistic or isolationist. To be "in Christ" is to be incorporated into

43

the body of Christ. Just as God called Israel as a people, so those who are in Christ, the true Israelite, are part of the people of God together. As Colossians 3:3 states, "Your life is now hidden with Christ in God." The language is chosen carefully: the life in Christ is one life, together, in which you (plural) are hidden.

Followers of Jesus are "holy ones," "the saints." They are reconciled to God through the death of Christ, are brought into a right relationship with the holy God, and have received the ministry of reconciliation. Their calling is due entirely to the faithfulness of Jesus, through whom God demonstrates his covenant faithfulness and love.[60] God's love in the community reflects the love between Father, Son, and Spirit, and so "binds everything together in perfect harmony" (v. 14, NRSV).

Those who are in Christ are a new creation; they display the image of the Creator. The identity markers of God's holy people describe Christlikeness: "compassion, kindness, humility, meekness, and patience" (v. 12, NRSV). In that light, the saints reflect the direction of God's good purposes in their life together. "There is no longer Greek and Jew, circumcised and uncircumcised . . . ; but Christ is all and in all" (v. 11, NRSV; see vv. 10-15). Marred relationships are restored. Traditional boundaries are challenged, divisions are abolished, and diversity is celebrated because God's love has been poured out through the Holy Spirit. Divine justice is expressed in this community where the old hierarchies of race, gender, and status are replaced by the patterns of the new community in Christ.

Paul is particularly clear on identity and its implications in Romans 6. Christians have been baptized into Christ's death; those in Christ are, through Christ, dead to sin's reign and have been raised to newness of life. They are no longer slaves of sin, but slaves of righteousness. God's people have been made holy by the Holy Spirit, who has sanctified them entirely through their participation in Christ.

This new identity is summed up in one phrase: *in Christ*. This is participation language. It is more than simply the imitation of Christ, although being Christlike depends upon imitation. Through God's incorporation of believers into Christ's body, the people of God live lives of missional holiness in service to God and others. So, if this is who you are, "count yourselves dead to sin but alive to God in Christ Jesus" (v. 11). The imperative of Paul's language is based on the statement of identity—become who you are—and live into that identity in the power of the Spirit.

The Vocation of Missional Holiness

The vocation of holiness will be lived out in a hostile environment. Jesus reminds his followers they are hated because, like him, they do not owe allegiance to the world. He prays for their protection from the evil one, not for deliverance. He gives his peace and commissions and empowers his disciples for the mission: "As the Father has sent me, I am sending you. . . . Receive the Holy Spirit" (John 20:21-22).

The vocation of holiness is a cruciform life.[61] Paul endures suffering himself, and as children of God, believers are "joint heirs with Christ—if, in fact, [they] suffer with him" (Rom. 8:17, NRSV). He reminds his readers in Philippi, where Roman citizenship was prized, that "our citizenship is in heaven" (Phil. 3:20, NRSV). Deliverance comes from God, not Caesar. So Christians are to "live as worthy citizens of the gospel" (1:27).[62]

The vocation of holiness is, therefore, costly because it actually challenges structures and the patterns of the world. It participates in the ongoing redemptive work of the Messiah. The vocation is "a real participation in this Triune God's mission . . . [through] faithfulness to God and cruciform loving actions for others."[63] Paul describes his own work as participating in "completing what is lacking in Christ's afflictions" (Col. 1:24, NRSV). Together, believers are called to be "colonies of cruciformity."[64]

Paul is not alone in this view. The writer to the Hebrews rereads Israel's story as promise and example. His readers endure suffering as they "pursue peace with everyone, and the holiness without which no one will see the Lord" (12:14, NRSV). They join Jesus "outside the camp and bear the abuse he endured" (13:13, NRSV). The journey implies impermanence: "For here we have no lasting city, but we are looking for the city that is to come" (v. 14, NRSV). They must press on, following Jesus, *the pioneer and perfecter.* The holiness vocation is not, however, seen as separation (see "Exile and Return" above). Rather separation is "displaced by *holiness as solidarity,* the solidarity of the great high priest in sharing human nature as flesh and blood and, above all, in accepting the defilement of death."[65] This solidarity is worked out in the people of God.[66] Obedience is possible by establishment of the promised new covenant relationship through Christ.[67]

First Peter rereads Israel's foundational holiness texts in light of Jesus's example. Tellingly, readers are called "elect aliens" (1:1, author's translation). This is not a geographical or political statement but is rather a theological description of people called to be holy as God is holy (1:16).[68] It is a consequence of the new relationship to God and participation in God's people. The "elect aliens" are marginalized because of their belief. But 1 Peter transforms their diaspora (disperse) existence into a "legitimating category of respectability."[69] They should now celebrate their new kinship; they are participating in the people of God. In fact, 2 Peter states that they are "participants of the divine nature" (1:4, NRSV); they share in God's holiness by being transformed into the image of Christ.

Life is difficult, but Christians are not to flee: "This was not at root a call for retreat from the world, but a vocation to identify with God's own character."[70] So the advice in 1 Peter 2:12–3:17 is about staying alive. Shively Smith shows that what looks like the sanctification of sinful hierarchical structures is "a private prescription, supplying multicultural and vulnerable Christian populations with a strategy for functioning and surviving in hostile environments."[71] Suffering is endured but not sought. Indeed, suffering for its own sake is merely suffering (see 2:19-20) rather than a witness to Christ in the hostile context of social injustice. As a kingdom of priests and a holy nation, the saints' vocation is to "proclaim the mighty acts of him who called you out of darkness into his marvelous light" (v. 9, NRSV).

The "saints," however, are not flawless. Failings affect vocation and require repentance and transformation. When Paul addresses the Corinthians as "the holy ones in Corinth," eyebrows are often raised.[72] One Corinthian dispute involves the Lord's Table: the behavior of the powerful toward others shows contempt for the church (1 Cor. 11:22). In the Corinthian congregation the poor are invisible, even despised. By failing to discern the body of Christ in which all the people of God participate, the Corinthian elite are bringing the cultural standards of the fast-fading social structure into the body of Christ.

For Paul, the Lord's Table is missional because it proclaims the Lord's death. But because of divisions, this is not happening. This is not Paul's only concern. The exercise of charismata is also dividing the people. The declaration that Jesus is Lord is possible only in the power of the Spirit. The Spirit brings unity, not division.

This same emphasis surfaces in Romans. The controversy over days, food, and drink was anything but trivial. It threatened community life. Without harmony, the Roman Christians were not able to bear witness to the God of peace (see 15:5-7). The focus is relentlessly on mission. Unity enables the display of God's holiness before the world. Divisiveness does exactly the opposite. It evidences the chaos of broken relationships characteristic of the world apart from Christ. When conflicts, no matter how important, become paramount, they eclipse the mission of God.

"Holy God among [His] Holy People in a Holy Place"

The culmination of the biblical story ends with the "holy God among [his] holy people in a holy place."[73] The holiness of God and the Lamb seated upon the throne are the starting points for the holiness vocation in Revelation (5:1-14). The picture of the holy people is reconfigured from "a single elect nation (e.g., Lev. 27:11-12; Ezek. 37:27), to a multicultural chorus of worshipers drawn from all the people of the world. . . . They are *hagioi* [holy] because they participate in the holiness of God" both in identity and in mission.[74]

Theirs is to be an active engagement. As Dean Flemming argues, the call to holiness is not to "retreat into a cocoon of pious irrelevance, but to *resist* Rome's dominant ideology through its prophetic witness (*martys*)."[75] Flemming sums up the vocation of God's holy people:

> [They are] to stop accommodating with the worldly powers. Instead, they are to incarnate the purity and wholeness of their glorious future in anticipation of it. Within the Roman world, local assemblies of believers are called to be outposts of another kingdom, another empire than that of Caesar and Satan—the empire of God and the Lamb. Their corporate life is to model real peace and justice, and the true human community that embraces the world's diverse peoples (e.g., Rev. 21:3), of which Caesar's empire could only make counterfeit boasts.[76] Their obedient witness offers a foretaste of the future, when the holy city comes down from heaven and the transforming presence of God fills the whole earth.[77]

The book of Revelation has much to say to contemporary believers at risk of missing their holy vocation by succumbing to the beguiling blandishments of current manifestations of empire, no matter how great they might claim to be, or glittering their facade.

Conclusion[78]

We have reread Scripture with Jesus's glasses in a way that uncovers the scriptural vocation of holiness. It is inextricably linked to the mission of God in Scripture. God calls and creates a holy people to participate in his rescue mission to his battered creation, bleeding from self-inflicted wounds that lead to death.

Three features have stood out. First, we are to be holy as God is holy, reflecting who God is: loving, just, merciful, hospitable, and missional. The vocation of holiness embodies these characteristics. This calling is for all of God's people today. Our lives are part of the answer to the prayer: "on earth as it is in heaven." This holy calling is ours through the power of the Spirit in Christ.

Second, the vocation of holiness is a missional calling that embraces and loves the other. When we see others as persons created in God's image for whom Christ died, we respond in love. The otherwise excluded are welcomed by God's holy people because God names and loves them.

Third, the purity that matters is the pure-in-heart (Matt. 5:8), motivational center of the person aligned with the will of God. This kind of purity is transformative in our communities of faith. It is God reflecting: faithful, generous, open, welcoming, redemptive, transformative, compassionate love.

In the last question from his interlocutors, Jesus and the scribe agree that the heart of the vocation of holiness is to love God with all your being and your neighbor as yourself. On these hang all the law and the prophets. Mark concludes the episode: "After that no one dared to ask him any question" (12:34, NRSV).

$$\left(\,3\,\right)$$

Out of Egypt
The Vocation of Holiness according to the Doctrine of the Orthodox Church

❖

Archpriest Paul Wesche

Fr. (Kenneth) Paul Wesche is rector of St. Herman's Orthodox Church, Minneapolis, Minnesota, an assignment he has held since 1992. In 1986 he completed a PhD in Greek patristics, Fordham University, Bronx, New York, under the direction of Fr. John Meyendorff, a leading theologian of the Orthodox Church of America. He and his wife, Nancy, are parents of five children.

❖

To readers of this anthology, the Orthodox Church may be the least known of the traditions represented. They may have heard of the Russian Orthodox Church or of the Greek Orthodox Church (*My Big Fat Greek Wedding*). There are yet others—Romanian, Serbian, Bulgarian, and Antiochian, to name a few—and, since 1970, an Orthodox Church in America.[1] These are not different churches, but different jurisdictions within the one Orthodox Church. Their doctrine, sacraments, and worship are the same. Their differences go no deeper than ethnic identity or cultural heritage. For example, the one is Greek and the other is Russian. The Orthodox Church in America is American. But all are the one Orthodox Church.

"The modern Orthodox Church is—from the viewpoint of history—the Church of Byzantium."[2] But "orthodox" does not mean "eastern" or "Byzantine." It means "true worship and doctrine," or "worship in Spirit and in truth." Orthodox worship and doctrine, not Eastern culture, make the Orthodox Church Orthodox.

Beneath her Byzantine coat of many ethnic colors, the Orthodox Church, in the Spirit of her theology, worship, and sacraments, is the body of Christ. Here, she is not one denomination among others, "not *a* Church but *the* Church." The "Orthodox Church is a living embodiment of an uninterrupted tradition, in thought and devotion. . . . She stands not for a certain 'particular' tradition, but for the Tradition of the ages, for the Tradition of the undivided Church."[3]

"Vocation" or "calling," from the Latin *vocatio*, could be a synonym for the Greek word for "church" (*ekklēsia*): "those called out of." This reveals the church—the body of Christ, the Word of God, who called the world into being—as the incarnate presence in the world of the Lord's command to "stand forth" as a new creation (see Ps. 33:9; 2 Cor. 5:17). This vocation or call of the church enters the world through the prophet Hosea: "Out of Egypt have I called my son" (Hos. 11:1, quoted in Matt. 2:15, KJV). It becomes flesh and dwells among us in the birth of Christ (Matt. 2:15; John 1:14). This call is the vocation of holiness according to the doctrine of the Orthodox Church. It is nothing less than the mystery of the church.

Entering the church, one enters this call of the Lord. It transfigures one's life into an exodus out of Egypt and into the promised land of the new creation in the death, resurrection, and glorification of our Lord God and Savior, Jesus Christ.

The Paschal Shape of Holiness

I am writing during the Afterfeast[4] of Pentecost. Pentecost is the Eighth Sunday of Pascha, Pascha being what Western Christians call Easter. Pascha is the Passover that initiated Israel's exodus to the promised land. The real Pascha, of course, is the Lord's Pascha, when he passed over from death to life in the mystery of his cross.

Like a shadow shaped by the person casting it, Israel's Pascha is the shadow shaped by the Lord's Pascha yet to come (1 Cor. 10:1-4; Heb. 10:1). Following the image of Israel's Pascha, then, I undertake to trace an outline of the Lord's Pascha, or the vocation of holiness according to the Orthodox Church.

The Liturgical Structure of Pascha

As indicated above, Pascha or Easter in Orthodoxy is a festal season of fifty days culminating on the Feast of Pentecost, the Eighth Sunday of Pascha (eight is a symbol of the Resurrection). This liturgical structure shows the Lord's victory over death and his ascension into heaven to be the prelude to another kind of self-emptying (cf. Phil 2:7)—Pentecost, when the Savior pours out his Holy Spirit on his disciples.

The goal of the Lord's Pentecostal self-emptying is set before us in the Gospel reading for the Seventh Sunday of Pascha, the Sunday between the Feasts of Ascension and Pentecost. The Lord prays to his Father, "That they may be one, as we are" (John 17:11, KJV, see also v. 22).

That is, the purpose of the Lord's death, resurrection, and ascension into heaven is to pour out his "spirit upon all flesh" (Joel 2:28-29, KJV) that we may become one with him and, in the power of his Holy Spirit, answer his call to come out of Egypt and begin our own Pascha. We follow him into the promised land of the new creation in the glory of his resurrection and ascension.

An Exodus of Ascent

The liturgical structure of Pascha shows holiness to be a paschal movement in the Holy Spirit. It is a journey, an exodus; and the exodus is an ascent in Christ's holy Pascha, to our inheritance—the promised land of the new creation, which is Christ himself. "For the inheritance and portion of Christians is God Himself. 'The Lord Himself,' it says, 'is the portion of mine inheritance and my cup.'"[5]

A paschal movement, this exodus of ascent is centered on the Lord's tomb. It is rooted in his death and burial, or in his Sabbath rest, which he sanctified (Gen. 2:3).

What about the Lord's cross? This is the weapon of victory by which he descended into hell and shattered its brass gates. He smashed the iron bars of death, as the psalmist foresaw, and delivered those held prisoner there (Ps. 107:9-16; Heb. 2:15). He did this just as he had once delivered Israel from her Egyptian bondage.

We therefore enter upon the vocation of holiness as we take up our cross according to the Lord's command to deny ourselves and follow him

(Mark 8:34-35). As Israel descended with him into the Red Sea (Exod. 14:13-31), we descend with him into the mystery of his death (Rom. 6:1-5) and into his Sabbath rest. There we are delivered from the devil, who held us in the power of death (Heb. 2:14). United with him in the likeness of his death, we are united with him in the likeness of his resurrection,[6] and we begin our exodus to heaven. The ascent of holiness therefore begins with a descent—namely, a descent into the sanctified waters of Holy Baptism (Rom. 6:1-5).

In Holy Baptism, we descend into the mystery of God "hidden throughout the ages" (Col. 1:26, NRSV; Eph. 3:1-13). He had already proclaimed the mystery to Adam and Eve in the garden: "From the earth you were taken; to the earth you shall return" (Gen. 3:19, author's translation).[7] In the terrible mystery of Christ's tomb, the curse opens onto a blessing. The curse is revealed as God's word revealing the way back to Eden and communion with God. In the font of Holy Baptism, we enter the mystery of Christ's tomb. We return to the earth from which we were taken. God refashions us and opens Eden to us again.[8] The vocation of holiness, in other words, is the return to Eden.

An Inner Exodus

The vocation of holiness, this exodus of ascent back to Eden, is obviously not a terrestrial journey. And Eden is not a geographical place. But neither is it a fable or myth. This is a mystery, a spiritual exodus, unseen. It is a theological mystery accomplished wholly within the mystery of the church through our union with Christ in Holy Baptism and Holy Eucharist (John 6:53, 58). To the world, this mystery is a riddle (1 Cor. 1:18). Let's spell out the riddle.

A Riddle

The Lord's descent into hell, his resurrection, and his ascension take place wholly on the *other side* of the grave. Yet the risen Lord appeared to his disciples on *this side*. But he was not a ghost. He came to the disciples in the same body that was crucified, dead, and buried (Luke 24:38-39). See how the *other side*, in the mystery of the risen Christ, is bodily present on *this side* of the grave. See how *this side*—in the mystery of the church, Christ's crucified and risen body (Eph. 1:23)—opens onto the *other side*.

The ascent of holiness, the ascent to heaven in Christ's resurrection and ascension, therefore, begins where this life ends: in the grave. Does this mean that holiness doesn't begin until we die physically? That can't be, for "in death there is no remembrance of thee" (Ps. 6:5, KJV). Yet Scripture clearly indicates that the vocation of holiness begins and ends in the grave, on the *other side* (Ezek. 37:12-14). "Grave" and "other side" must have a spiritual meaning. In fact they do, as we shall see in the pages that follow.

Let's continue to spell out the riddle. In the grave, on the other side—in Jesus's resurrection—the ascent of holiness begins and ends where the eyes of this world cannot see. Nor can the mind shaped by the knowledge of this world comprehend it (1 Cor. 1:18; 2 Cor. 4:4). Yet even as it transpires on the *other side*, it transpires in the world on *this side* because it transpires within us who live in this present world or age. If it transpires in the grave in us who are still on this side of the grave, does that not mean that it transpires in our death even as we are living? We've now stated the riddle. What does it all mean? The riddle has produced more riddles!

Setting our ear to the music of the lyre (Ps. 49:4), the liturgical worship of the church, let's solve the riddle.

The Sanctuary of the Heart

In the Septuagint we read, "The heart is deep beyond all things, and it is the man" (Jer. 17:9 [5 LXX], Brenton). The Greek rendering of Jeremiah sets forth the biblical understanding of the heart as our true self, our personal center. According to the Septuagint, God fashions man from a mound of earth (Gk., *choun*). This suggests an image of God molding our body into a temple around an inner chamber (Gen 2:7). The inner chamber is the heart, the sanctuary (Gk., *tameion*, Matt. 6:6) of our body, which is a temple of the Holy Spirit (1 Cor. 6:19).

In our heart we open onto the unfathomable depths of God.[9] Here we approach the beginning of our riddle's solution. Our heart is where we open onto the other side even while we live on this side.

The sanctuary of our heart was made for God to dwell in (John 15:4). A biblical image central to Orthodox doctrine is the heart as a bridal chamber (Song of Sol. 4:8-15; Isa. 61:10; Ezek. 16:1-14; Matt. 25:6). The heavenly Bridegroom would come to consummate his union with his bride, the human soul, in the bridal chamber of the heart—if she so desires (Rev 3:20).

If she so desires! This is what the test of the two trees in the garden of Eden (Gen. 2:15-17; 3:1-7) was and is meant to discover in each of us.

The Creation Unfinished

After "God blessed the seventh day [Saturday] and sanctified it, because in it He rested from His works," the Septuagint adds, "which God began to make" (Gen. 2:3, author's translation). The creation was not yet finished. We then read, "When no plant of the field was yet in the earth and no herb of the field had yet sprung up, for the Lord God had not yet caused it to rain on the earth, and there was no man to work the ground" (*ergazesthai gēn*, Gen. 2:5, LXX, author's translation). It seems clear that God is calling Adam to finish the work of creation. How is this supposed to happen?

What It's All about, Alfie!

"God is love," writes Saint John the Theologian (1 John 4:8, 16). Love is the primary principle of creation because the God who created it is love (vv. 7-12). The persons of the Father, Son, and Holy Spirit are each an eternal loving Beloved and a beloved Lover. Made in the image of God, mankind is created as persons, male and female, "beloveds" of God. Created as persons, they are called to love the God who first loved them.

Love is freely given and freely received. Self-determination or free will is therefore the essential property of our nature.[10] "Our soul was honored with free will and independent life," Saint Gregory Palamas (AD 1296–1359) explains, "since without this honor, it would have been pointless for man to be rational [i.e., to be like Christ]."[11]

Love does not seek its own way (1 Cor. 13:5; Rom. 15:1-2). In the beginning, then, the Lord stood outside the bridal chamber of the heart, waiting for Adam to receive him in love—as he does now (Rev. 3:20). The vocation of holiness now comes into view as the call to receive God into the bridal chamber of our heart that we may become one with him (1 John 4:19; Deut. 6:5; Mark 12:30-31) and finish God's creation in love.

Adam in the Garden

To complete the creation, then, God places Adam in the garden after he has fashioned him from the earth (Gen. 2:7-8). The true Eden is the mystery of the heart. Spiritually, God is leading Adam into the garden of his heart. He is led there, Scripture says, to work [*ergazesthai*] and guard it (1:26-31; 2:15).

Immediately follows a description of Eden's topography. According to early Syriac Christianity, the Tree of the Knowledge of Good and Evil is halfway up the mountain of Eden.[12] The Tree of Life, which is the "mystery of Christ" (Prov. 3:18; 1 Cor. 1:24), is at the mountain's summit.[13] To ascend beyond the Tree of Knowledge and attain the Tree of Life at Eden's summit, Adam needed to deny himself and obey the divine command not to eat of the Tree of the Knowledge of Good and Evil (Gen. 2:17).

Is this not the same commandment the incarnate Lord gives to his disciples today? "Whoever wants to be my disciple must deny themselves and take up their cross and follow me" (Mark 8:34). Obedience to this command is how we "love Him" who "first loved us" (1 John 4:19, NKJV) and who denied himself for our sake (cf. Phil. 2:5-6). This is how we answer God's call to become holy as he is holy; this is how we begin the exodus of holiness and ascend to the summit of Eden.

In the garden, then, we see the original biblical image of the vocation of holiness. It is the call of God to his son Adam (cf. Luke 3:38) to come out of Egypt and begin an exodus of ascent up God's holy mountain (Isa. 56:7). Attaining to the Tree of Life at Eden's summit, Adam would have become one with Christ in love. Creation would have been finished.

The purpose of God's commandment is to bring our free will to the surface so that we might master it. Saint John of Damascus (AD 676–749) compares the place before the Tree of the Knowledge of Good and Evil to a gym (Gk., *gymnasion*), a place where one's strength and resolve are tested. Adam was given what the Damascene calls a test (Gk., *apopeiran*) to prove (Gk., *dokimazō*) his heart.[14] Would Adam deny himself out of love for God or deny God out of love for himself?

Orthodox hymnography interprets Eve spiritually as the human soul.[15] When Adam turned the ear of his soul to accept the serpent's lie, he brought the serpent, not the Word of God, into his heart. Satan came into the bridal chamber of his soul. Instead of denying himself, Adam denied God. Instead of becoming one with God, he became one with the serpent.[16]

A Mortal Wound

"If a man does not first sin in his mind, he will never sin in action," writes Saint Maximos the Confessor (AD 580–662). Moreover, the power that draws us toward evil is our own negligence.[17] Negligent, Adam engaged in conversation with the serpent and received its lies into his mind. Its lies excited his desire precisely where, made in God's image, Adam was called to become like God, to be holy. He chose not to master his desire but allowed his desire to master him. He did in fact become like God, knowing good and evil,[18] but he did not become holy; he did not become one with God. Instead, Adam became self-righteous, a "little god" outside of God.[19] Rather than God, the serpent began to dwell in the bridal chamber of Adam's heart.[20]

The Greek word for devil is *diabolos*, a divider. Embracing the serpent's lie, Adam was separated from God. He became alienated from the primary principle of his nature—namely, his being created in God's image. Consequently, he was divided against himself. Saint Diadochos of Photiki (AD 400–486) taught that "the perceptive faculty natural to our soul is single, but it is split into two energies following upon Adam's disobedience."[21]

Hieromonk Damascene explains:

When man first . . . departed from the Way . . . , he corrupted his primal simplicity and became fragmented. . . . His will became divided. Now his "natural will," which remained inclined to follow the Way in all things, was set against his "free will," which had now taken on itself an inclination to depart from the Way. . . . He was essentially making himself into a little god. . . . Instead of regarding the Way, . . . he chose to regard what was easier and closer at hand: his own visible self. Instead of rising with God, he fell in love with himself.[22]

Can we not see this in ourselves? The source and fulfillment of the beauty and goodness we desire are in God.[23] Yet in fear of death (Heb. 2:14) we seek refuge, not in the beauty of God, but in pleasures entwined by death—"the lust of the flesh, the lust of the eyes, and the pride of life" (1 John 2:16). We give ourselves unwittingly to what we hate (Rom. 7:13-15)—namely, to death and all its fruits: anxiety, fear, hopelessness, and despair. In spiritual blindness, we are led by the "spoiler hidden in the depths who calls men [not to holiness and the exodus of ascent, but] to follow the path that leads to destruction."[24]

The serpent's lie subsequently divided Adam and Eve from each other (Gen. 3:8-13). Their sin alienated them from the ground from which they had been taken (v. 18). Now the toxin of the serpent's lie continues to work even in our physical death: our soul is divided from our body, and our body divides from itself, disintegrating into dust.

With his heart set against God and against itself, man died spiritually on the day of his transgression.[25] Death of the heart was "necessarily followed by the body's death."[26] The law of sin, death, became incarnate, embodied, in us (Rom. 7:22-23). In man's fall, the creation remained unfinished, subjected to "futility" (8:20, NRSV). Spiritually dead, man could no more make himself alive in the "true sense"[27] than a corpse can raise itself to life.

His heart opened onto the other side, but not onto the depths of God. He opened himself to the abyss of death. As portrayed by the psalmist, man's soul was brought down to the earth. He sat in the darkness as one forever dead. His spirit dried up within him. His heart was troubled (Ps. 142:3-5, LXX). Man's soul thirsted. It fainted for the living God. The earth of his body became a trackless, arid desert (63:1, LXX).

The Heart a Tomb

Saint Diadochos taught us to understand that "evil has no [independent] substance of its own, and no one is evil by nature; for, God did not make evil. When, by the desire of one's heart, one gives form to what has no substance, then the evil, which one's desire has created, begins to exist."[28] When Adam desired what did not belong to him, "covetousness began to exist and [he] died," so says Saint Paul (Rom. 7:7-10, author's translation).

Saint Maximos the Confessor identifies covetousness as self-love. Self-love, he says, is the origin and mother of evil. "When self-love is absent, not the slightest trace or form of evil can exist in any way at all."[29] Having believed Satan's lie, covetousness poisoned man's heart and became the root of our soul and body.[30]

The serpent's venom spread through our nature like a deadly toxin; it weakened, even paralyzed, our will (cf. Deut. 32:36, LXX) and left us for dead (Luke 10:30). Separated from God and expelled from Eden, the bridal chamber of our heart became a grave. "When you hear of sepulchers," writes Saint Macarius (ca. AD 300–391), "do not think only of visible ones. Your own heart is a sepulcher and a tomb. When the prince of wickedness and his angels burrow there, and make paths and thoroughfares there, on which the powers of Satan walk into your mind and thoughts, are you not a hell, a tomb, a sepulcher, a dead man towards God?"[31]

Saint Macarius has now solved our riddle. The true grave is not where we will be buried. Instead, it is our heart where we died in the "true sense," as Saint Maximos explains.[32] Our heart is the "grave" the vocation of holiness calls us to enter so that we may begin the exodus of ascent that ends on the other side, in the kingdom of heaven, the kingdom "within you" (Luke 17:21, KJV).

We must be healed of death, not from the outside, but from within. This is where the serpent's poison penetrated and divided us against God and against ourselves. The blood of bulls and goats cannot heal or cleanse our heart (Heb. 9:1-14). But neither can we be healed by coercion, for then we would be robots, not persons created in God's image. The vocation of holiness, then, is the Lord Jesus calling us, not coercing us, to follow him back to Eden in the depths of our heart. But first we must be delivered from bondage to the devil and be "brought out of Egypt by the Lord's outstretched arm" on the cross! (Deut. 26:8, author's paraphrase).

The Creation Completed

Only the Lord can heal the incurable wound of our heart, writes Saint Macarius. "For this reason, He came in His own Person; because none of the ancients, nor the Law itself, nor the prophets, were able to heal this wound. He alone by His coming healed that sore of the soul, that incurable sore."[33]

But the Lord could not come unless first he was received. When the all-holy Virgin in obedience submitted to the Lord's will (Luke 1:37-38), the temple of her body received God into the sanctuary of her heart, and the healing of creation began.

Paradise on Earth

Eve received the liar (John 8:44) into the bridal chamber of her heart. The all-holy Virgin received the Truth (John 14:6; Luke 1:46-55). Through Eve, sin entwined and mingled with the soul. It became "like a member of it" and "united with the bodily man."[34] But in the womb of the Blessed Virgin, the Resurrection and the Life (John 11:25) was entwined and mingled with her soul. It became a member of it and united with the bodily man (1:14; Heb. 2:14). Mary's womb became the palace of the King, more spacious than the heavens; her body became the Lord's throne (Ps. 44:6, LXX), the ark of holiness (131:8, LXX).

In Eve, all creation groaned as it fell into futility. In the Blessed Virgin, all creation rejoices, for in the sanctuary of her heart, it received the Creator of all. Mary became the all-holy Mother of God (Gk., *Theotokos*; Lat., *Mater Dei*; see Luke 1:43). The Son of God was born of her as the Son of Man, who "works the renewal of us who have grown old through the ancient transgression."[35]

In the all-holy Virgin, the Holy One of Israel (Isa. 43:3) now dwelt in the bridal chamber of man's soul. The Lord Jesus Christ dwelt in the holy of holies of the Living Temple—that is, in the heart of the Blessed Virgin. The Theotokos is the Living Temple,[36] whom the Old Testament temple prefigured (Ezek. 44:1-3).[37] In the Theotokos, creation was no longer rooted in death. It was now rooted in the Holy One of God, in Christ (Rev. 15:4), in him who is himself the Resurrection and the Life of God (John 11:25).

The word of the Psalmist was fulfilled; its meaning illumined: "The LORD is in His Holy Temple [the Theotokos]; the LORD, His throne [the Theotokos], is in heaven [in the mystery of Christ]" (Ps. 10:5, LXX, author's translation). In the joy and mystery of Christmas, the Blessed Virgin brings forth her Son and our God in the temple of his body (cf. John 1:14; 2:19-21), which he received from the Holy Virgin, his mother, the Living Temple.

Eden held the Tree of Life, the mystery of Christ. Our Lady held Christ in her womb. She is the mystery of Eden, and Eden is the mystery of the Temple of God. And so, the church hymns the holy Theotokos: "O sanctified Temple and Spiritual Paradise." "Rejoice, O Paradise who ever hast within thee the Tree of Life, O all-glorious Palace of the Word!"

Each feast of the Theotokos[38] is radiant with joy: "Today is the beginning of joy for all the world; today the winds blow that bring tidings of salvation!"[39] For in the all-holy Virgin, the Eden that was lost has again appeared on earth. "The Ancestors of our race rejoice in thee, O all-pure Virgin, receiving through thee the Eden [Christ] they lost through transgression."[40]

The church rejoices in the birth of the ever-Virgin Mary. Her nativity is the dawning of our salvation, for it means that the Lord's mother has come. And that means the incarnation of Christ the Savior is on the horizon. "Thy nativity, O Theotokos, has brought joy to the whole universe. From thee has shone forth the Sun of Righteousness, Christ our God. He has loosed us from the curse and bestowed on us a blessing. He has made death of no effect and bestowed on us eternal life."[41] The nativity of the Blessed Virgin, the new Eve, proclaims that the Tree of Life, the new Adam, is making ready to descend from Eden's summit, even to the depths of hell. It means that the true Light is beginning to shine on those who sit in the region and shadow of death (Isa. 9:2; cf. John 1:9; Matt. 4:16).

The Inner Exodus Begins

Descending into Jordan's depths, Christ at his baptism bears "the creation down into the stream, bringing it to a better and changeless Path that ascends to God."[42] When the Lord ascends from the Jordan, the heavens open (Matt. 3:13-17; Mark 1:9-11; Luke 3:21) because that's where he is going.

But Christ himself is the "better and changeless Path" (John 1:51). He is the Path of holiness that *descends* and *ascends* to God (14:6; Eph. 4:10). The Orthodox prayers for baptism identify the waters of the baptismal font with the waters of the Jordan. Christ's baptism in the Jordan, then, reveals where the exodus of ascent begins and where it ends. It begins in Christ in the waters of baptism and ends in the heavens that now are opened.

Orthodox baptismal prayers identify the baptismal font also as the tomb of Christ. The exodus of ascent on the "better and changeless Path," then, begins and ends in the tomb of Christ, or in the mystery of Holy Baptism, in which our heart is transfigured from a grave into a bridal chamber. Here is the full solution to our riddle. The grave, in which the vocation of holiness begins and ends, and in which we open onto the other side—the eternal life of the Holy Spirit—even as we are on this side, the earthly life of the body, is the mystery of Christ's tomb, the fountain of our resurrection.

The Gospels show that immediately after Jesus's baptism, the "better and changeless Path" was led by the Holy Spirit into the desert to be tempted by Satan (Matt. 4:1-11; Mark 1:12-13; Luke 4:1-13), just as Israel was led by the Holy Spirit through the desert to the border of the promised land. From there, the Path was led to Golgotha and descended into the tomb, just as Joshua (Jesus) descended into the Jordan at the entrance to the promised land. And just as Joshua passed through the Jordan and ascended to the promised land, so the Path led through the tomb and out onto the other side in the resurrection.

In this, the Lord has laid down the pattern (Exod. 25:9) of holiness. The exodus of ascent on the "better and changeless Path," Christ our God, leads into the desert of our soul (Ps. 63:1) and then into the tomb of our heart, where we were dead in our sins and trespasses (Eph. 2:1). There, in our hidden "inward parts" (Ps. 51:6, KJV), we are called to "work out [our] salvation with fear and trembling" (Phil. 2:12). This was the work given to Adam (Gen. 2:15). It is the work of denying ourselves and putting to death what is earthly in us (Col. 1:27)—namely, "the lust of the flesh, the lust of the eyes, and the pride of life" (1 John 2:16). This is the work of our repentance (Mark 1:14-15) in which we follow the Lord Jesus into our heart so that we may find our life (8:35) in his tomb and become one with him in the likeness of his death and resurrection.

The New Adam in the Garden

The Lord leads us into the garden of the heart, where Adam is fallen. In the "garden" (Luke 22:42) is where we find the new Adam praying to the Father: "Not my will, but thine, be done" (KJV).

Because we died through disobedience, we are not able to produce living fruit to God (cf. Rom. 7:4-5). "They have all gone astray, they are all alike corrupt; there is none that does good, no, not one" (Ps. 14:3, RSV; 53:3; Rom. 3:23). Even if we were obedient, we could no more make ourselves alive than could a corpse (Eph. 2:1), nor could we make ourselves holy any more than a corpse could make itself fragrant (Matt. 23:27; John 11:39). But what we cannot do, the Lord Jesus has done for us in his human will as man. In his obedience to the Father, even unto death on the cross (Phil. 2:8), he healed the "incurable sore" (1 Pet. 2:24) at its source, in man's heart (Heb. 10:22). He healed the conflicted, paralyzed human will (Deut. 32:36, LXX; Mark 2:4-12).

Golgotha was the "place of the skull" (Mark 15:22) or the place of death. Even today the faithful in Jerusalem say this is the very spot where Adam fell. This is absolutely true,[43] for the spot where Adam fell is not a geographical place; it is our heart.

As God, the Lord Jesus Christ is the only Lover of mankind (Ps. 103:11-13). As man, love for God was his food and drink (John 4:34). In the "gym" of the heart, the Lord, as the new Adam, was tested. He denied himself out of love for his Father and for the world (3:16). He was obedient unto death on the cross (Phil. 2:8); and he passed the test. When on the cross the divine Word by whom all things were made cried out "It is finished" (John 19:30), it was the creation he finished.

On the cross, the new Adam finished the work of creation Adam was meant to do. "The world is established; it shall never be moved," says the psalmist (Ps. 93:1, ESV). The world of God's creation, his holy church, shall never be moved. The powers of death shall not prevail against it (Matt. 16:18), for it has been established on the Rock of Golgotha in the person of the Rock himself (1 Cor. 10:4), the God-Man.

Christ is the embodiment, the incarnation, of God's love for man, and of man's love for God. He is the "Alpha and the Omega, the First and the Last" (Rev. 22:13). As God, he created the world; as man, he finished it. And we magnify with inexpressible love his most-holy mother; for "she gave birth to the Source of our salvation and eternal life."[44]

Uniting ourselves to her Son and God, Christ our Lord and Savior, in the garden of our heart, we are healed of our spiritual death and raised to life with him. Made one with him in the likeness of his life-creating death, we are finished, made holy as a "new creation" (2 Cor. 5:17). Even though we die, yet shall we live with him (John 11:25) in the joy and glory of his resurrection and ascension (16:22, 24; 17:13).

The Tomb of Christ

We are told in the Gospels that the Lord was buried in a new tomb where no one had been laid (Matt. 27:60; Luke 23:53; John 19:41). This is a theological veil that, once lifted, reveals a new kind of death that no one had died before.

Death is the result of disobedience, the final result of sin. "Sin, when it is finished, bringeth forth death" (James 1:15, KJV). The Lord's death, however, was the result of his obedience. Life not death is the end of obedience (Ezek. 20:13, 21). Death therefore could not hold the Lord Jesus (Acts 2:24) because he was "obedient unto death" (Phil. 2:8, KJV). By his obedience to death on the cross, he shattered the iron bars of our disobedience (Ps. 107:10-16); he destroyed death (Heb. 2:15).

By his death, the Lord answered the cry of David: "Create in me a clean heart, O God; put a new and right spirit within me" (Ps. 51:10, NRSV). He fulfilled his promise to the prophets: "A new heart I will give you, and a new spirit I will put within you; and I will take out of your flesh the heart of stone and give you a heart of flesh" (Ezek. 36:26, RSV).

A stony heart is a dead heart. A new heart of flesh is a living heart. To be given a new heart of flesh is to be raised from death and restored to life, to holiness. On Holy Saturday, Orthodox faithful read from Ezekiel: "I will . . . raise you from your graves, O my people. . . . I will put my Spirit within you, and you shall live, and I will place you in your own land" (37:12-14, ESV). "Your own land" is not a geographical place. It is our true inheritance—Christ (44:28).

Conclusion: The Robe of Light

In Holy Baptism, we unite the grave of our heart to the new tomb of Christ. We are clothed with the Robe of Light. This is Christ's sanctified humanity in which he was crucified, risen, and glorified. Baptized into his death (Rom. 6:3-14), we are united to his obedience. His new kind of death is now the principle of our life (2 Cor. 4:10-11).

In the baptismal font, we were united to Christ in the likeness of his Sabbath Rest, which he sanctified (Gen. 2:3).[45] In our baptism, we were therefore sanctified, made whole and holy, a "new creation" (2 Cor. 5:17). In the mystery of our heart, we ascend in joy with the Bridegroom (Ps. 19:5) on the exodus of ascent to the Tree of Life at Eden's summit. We ascend *in* holiness; we ascend *to* holiness (2 Cor. 3:18), for we ascend to the Tree of Life in the Holy Spirit. We ascend *in* Christ; we ascend *to* Christ, who is the Tree of Life.

We ascend by descending in obedience, in self-denial. The ascetic disciplines of the church such as prayer, fasting, and deeds of mercy[46] are called "the flower of abstinence" that grows for all the world "from the tree of the Cross."[47] They are the cross given to us by which we descend in order to ascend. Through them, we unite ourselves with Christ, not just in theory or imagination, but concretely.

Taking up the church's ascetic disciplines as our cross to follow Jesus, the life-creating power of his cross becomes embodied in us. His new kind of death and life become active in us. Through the church's ascetic disciplines, the cross of Christ shapes our inner man in the likeness of Christ (2 Cor. 3:18). Our heart is enlarged (6:11) in love for God. We are led into the deepest mystery of the heart described by Saint Paul: "It is no longer I who live, but Christ who lives in me" (Gal. 2:20, ESV).

Nursed in the healing salve of the heavenly Spirit working in us through the church's ascetic disciplines and her liturgical and sacramental worship, we are daily transformed by the renewing of our mind (Rom. 12:2). Becoming one with the Lord Jesus Christ, we are restored to our original beauty. The Savior counts us worthy to be citizens of heaven,[48] finished and perfected as a "new creation" (2 Cor. 5:17) in the grace of our Lord Jesus Christ, in the love of God the Father, and the communion of the Holy Spirit. Amen!

For Further Reading

George, Archimandrite (abbot of the Holy Monastery of St. Gregorios on Mount Athos). *Theosis: The True Purpose in Human Life*. Mount Athos, GR: Holy Monastery of St. Gregorios, 2006.

Schmemann, Alexander. *For the Life of the World: Sacraments and Orthodoxy*. 2nd ed. 1973. Reprint, Crestwood, NY: St. Vladimir's Seminary Press, 2002.

Sophrony, Archimandrite. *The Monk of Mount Athos: Staretz Silouan, 1886–1938*. Crestwood, NY: St. Vladimir's Seminary Press, 1973.

4

The Catholic Quest for Holiness

❖

Rev. Jerry J. Pokorsky

Fr. Jerry Pokorsky is a Roman Catholic priest for the Diocese of Arlington (ordained 1990) and is the pastor of Saint Catherine of Siena Church in Great Falls, Virginia. He holds a master of divinity and a master's degree in moral theology. He cofounded CREDO and Adoremus, both of which are committed to authentic liturgical renewal.

❖

Catholics believe the church was founded by Jesus Christ on the rock Peter, the first of the apostles (Matt. 16:18). The day of his ascension into heaven, Jesus commissioned the apostles to continue his saving work by baptizing all nations in the name of the Blessed Trinity (28:19).

The church, with distinct apostolic roots, developed a hierarchical shape that includes clergy and laity. The mission of the Catholic Church is, quite simply, the sanctification of the faithful (holiness) and the salvation of souls. For Catholics, holiness cannot be reduced to an abstraction; holiness is in the person of Jesus of Nazareth, the incarnate Word of God, and the Blessed ever-Virgin Mary, the new Eve.

I offer this chapter in the hope that it will provide a concise introduction to how Catholics understand Christian holiness.

The Glory of the Resurrection

The desire for holiness is a response to the hope and possibility that life does not end with death. We sense the tug of eternity. But what will our experience of eternity be? Will we encounter eternal bliss, or is there a possibility of eternal horror?

The Christian vision of eternity rests entirely on the foundation of the resurrection of Jesus Christ from the dead (1 Cor. 15:3-34). The desire to participate in the holiness of God depends upon our accepting, by God's grace and without any equivocation, the fundamental dogma of our faith: the bodily resurrection of Jesus (vv. 13-14).[1]

As a recorded historical event, the resurrection cannot be proved by scientific inquiry. It can only be accepted by faith based on the testimony of biblical witnesses and the martyrs of the early church.

When, with goodwill, the resurrection is tentatively accepted as plausible, it becomes reasonable through consideration of the entire narrative of God's encounter with humanity, repeatedly presented through the Sacred Liturgy and during the liturgical year.

Abraham's test of faith foreshadows the crucifixion. The promised land of the Israelites is replaced by the new and heavenly Jerusalem (Rev. 21:2). With the prospect of eternal life, all history has changed course and become intelligible. The tortured philosophical questions of Ecclesiastes are resolved; all is not vanity (1:2).

Because of Jesus's resurrection, all is also coherent. The resurrection allows us to recalibrate and assemble the entirety of God's revelation within the framework of the Apostles' Creed. The Word of God has returned to the Father and now beckons us to follow him. God sends forth his Spirit and renews the face of the earth (Ps. 104:30) in the sacraments. Even human suffering takes on a new and redemptive meaning in Christ, all because of the empty tomb.

God's triumph does not require humanity's obliteration or subordination. With his resurrection as reported by the four Evangelists, and as witnessed by the martyrs of the early church, Jesus, the Word made flesh, definitively accomplishes what God intends: our liberation from sin and death.

God's revelation as recorded in the Bible is the comprehensive history of the power of God's Word. And his encounter with humanity not only reconciles us to God but in Christ also gives our life new meaning.[2] We are forever reconciled by the promise of the life to come.

With every passing day, consciously or unconsciously, by the Holy Spirit we enter the history of the living Word of God as presented by the church. Jesus in his humanity directs attention to God as the source of goodness.[3] Christian holiness is free participation in the goodness of God in history.[4]

The Integrity of the History of Revelation

As we proceed in pursuit of true holiness, we need confidence in the reliability and coherence of revelation. It is common to refer to God's self-revelation as the history of salvation, and so it is. Revelation fundamentally reveals to human beings the essentials of their origin, duty, and destiny. Revelation is—or should be—the reference point for every historical narrative. All human progress and decline can be measured against God's self-disclosure. Fully accepting revelation is essential to our quest for holiness.

Jesus Christ, the second person of the Blessed Trinity, the Word made flesh, the Messiah, our Lord and Savior, is the center of human history. Revelation prior to Christ is anticipatory and imperfect.[5] The works of the Mosaic law (such as circumcision, the sign and price of being identified with the "chosen people") have been fulfilled and forever replaced by the single sacrifice of Christ. Discipleship entails interiorizing the spiritual and moral goods to which the law pointed and which Christ provides.

Jewish worship in the synagogue and the temple sacrifices has been fulfilled and replaced by the single sacrifice of Christ. But Jewish worship provides the foundations for celebrating the Mass: reading Scripture in the synagogue (Luke 4:17-21) gives way to the liturgy of the Word, and the temple sacrifices give way to the sacrificial liturgy of the Eucharist—re-presenting and mystically participating in the eternal sacrifice of Christ.

Christianity is "new" because Christ sums up in his person and perfectly completes all that God revealed of old. "Think not that I have come to abolish the law and the prophets; I have come not to abolish them but to fulfill them" (Matt. 5:17-18, RSV). That all things are fulfilled and renewed in Christ includes this demanding and very encouraging truth.

The fundamental truths of the faith, as handed down through the ages in the church's custody, never contradict one another. Hence, radical change in doctrine is not part of the Catholic lexicon. And if attempted, regardless of the source, the unholy effort violates the true deposit of the faith received from the apostles.

Revelation is consistent, intelligible, and reliable.

History and the Three Ages of the Spiritual Life

Persuaded of the reliability of revelation, the believer's next step is to enter, apply, and live the truths that God has revealed.

The spiritual classic *The Three Ages of the Interior Life* provides a road map for our struggle and quest as we enter communion with Christ.[6]

The *first age* is the "Purgative Way." Through prayer we identify our violations of the Ten Commandments—sins against God and neighbor— and repent of them. The *second age* is the "Illuminative Way." We contemplate God's self-revelation and apply the truths of faith to our lives. The *third age* is the "Unitive Way," the pinnacle of holiness when we enter mystical communion with God.

But the Three Ages are not only stages of personal prayer but also descriptions of distinct communal and historical dimensions of the faith. Old Testament history is a chronicle of God's fidelity to his people, their worship of the one God, and their repeated lapses into idolatry and wickedness. The preaching of John the Baptist sums up the "Purgative Way" of the Old Testament in a single sentence: "Repent, for the kingdom of heaven is at hand" (Matt. 3:2, RSV).

In the "fulness of the time," Jesus Christ, the second person of the Blessed Trinity, is born into the world (Gal. 4:4, KJV). He is God's Word made flesh (John 1:14) and the "image of the invisible God, the firstborn of all creation" (Col. 1:15, RSV). For he is "the way, and the truth, and the life" and "no one comes to the Father" except through him (John 14:6, RSV). The person and teachings of Christ represent the "Illuminative Way" in our return to God. The Beatitudes (Matt. 5:1-11), the self-portrait of Jesus, offer a vision of the pinnacle of true holiness.

Jesus wants us to be holy, to be in communion with him. "The only-begotten Son of God, wanting to make us sharers in his divinity, assumed our nature, so that he, made man, might make men gods."[7] Holiness is our destiny ordained by God.

On the day of Pentecost—upon the descent of the Holy Spirit—the church is born (Acts 2:1-4). Through the Holy Spirit, Mary and the disciples are definitively incorporated into the mystical body of Christ. This mysterious communion is truly the "Unitive Way," the age of the Holy Spirit. Through the church and her sacraments, we intimately encounter the risen Lord and deepen our communion with him.

The church herself is the sacrament of Christ and the instrument of this holy union. We encounter Jesus and his holiness through the church.

The Absolute Holiness of God

Our encounter with Jesus is an encounter with God, the author of holiness. His holiness provides the context—the "idea" of the holy—for our participation.

The first mystery of our faith is the Blessed Trinity, definitively revealed with the descent of the Holy Spirit at Pentecost. God is three distinct persons in one Godhead. The absolute simplicity and unity of the Three-in-One God is a mystery beyond human comprehension. But as we shall see, Trinitarian life is foundational for understanding ourselves.

God is revealed in the Old Testament as the one God and Creator. He intervenes in history after the fall of Adam and Eve to direct the chosen people along their pilgrim way. Jesus is the Word of the Father; he accomplishes his Father's will by rescuing and redeeming sinful humankind. On Pentecost, the Holy Spirit is definitively revealed as the bond of divine love by his descent upon Mary and the disciples.

There is an infinitely perfect union of love within the Blessed Trinity; there is absolute unity, but there are mysteriously three distinct persons, a pronounced distinction of persons disclosed through the perfection of divine love: the Father loves the Son, and the Son loves the Father, with infinite perfection in union with the Holy Spirit.

These final revelations of triune life are conclusive and carry an iron-clad logic. God is all-powerful, all-knowing, and ever-present and does not depend upon his creation for anything.[8] We can add nothing to the perfection of God's life and love.

Nevertheless, God reveals himself to us in the mysterious selfless generosity of his love. Even though there is absolute perfection of love within the Blessed Trinity, God shares his love. Saint Philip Neri (1515-95) states this succinctly: "God has no need of men."[9] Still, God creates. For reasons unknown, but highly speculated upon, he shares his love. He does this in covenantal communion with us, created in God's image.

All holiness is a participation in the life of the Blessed Trinity.

Created in the Image and Likeness of God

In view of the absolute and perfect holiness of God, dare we aspire to participate in his holiness?

In the Sacrament of Confirmation, Catholics encounter and receive the Spirit of Pentecost. From the vantage point of Pentecost, we can revisit the account of creation in the book of Genesis with new insights.

In Genesis we read, "God created man in his own image, in the image of God he created him; male and female he created them" (1:27, RSV). With the divine imprint of the Blessed Trinity on the heart of every human being, we can begin to explain otherwise inexplicable inclinations and behavior. The divine imprint defines and directs our nature. Every human being has an inestimable God-given dignity from the moment of conception. By nature, we are hardwired to be inclined to participate in the communion of his love and similarly to selflessly share his love in the world. This is the basis of the church's teaching on natural moral law— communion and creation.

These two elements—communion and creation—are identifiable in the Genesis account of creation. Love delights in the beloved (2:23). In their communion, Adam and Eve represent the nuptial characteristic of holiness. And the Lord sends them forth to be his cocreators: "Be fruitful and multiply, and fill the earth and subdue it" (1:28, RSV).

By God's plan and command, male and female become the ministers of new life in God's service. A newly conceived baby is therefore not the property of the parents; a newborn is a gift of God's generous love. Mother and father participate in his love and have the privilege and indispensable duty to be loving stewards of God's gift. Marriage is a covenant of generous love between one man and one woman, with Trinitarian love as its foundation and with Christ and his church as the model (Eph. 5:21-33). God is the giver and master of life. As we participate in Trinitarian love, we become ministers and stewards of God's gift. Our faith in the Blessed Trinity explains every impulse of human generosity.

The faith that we are created in the image of the triune God gives us the confidence to seek and participate in the holiness of Trinitarian selfless—and, in time, sacrificial—generosity.

Original Sin and the Mystery of Suffering

Seeking God's holiness is replete with many tests and obstacles, including human weakness and suffering.

Eternal life in Christ is boundless.[10] God will give us eternal life only if we love him—that is, if, by grace, we freely choose him. The test reveals the dignity of our personal freedom. The test of the authenticity of our love carries the most serious of consequences. We ourselves choose our destiny: heaven or hell.

Our first parents, Adam and Eve, failed the test of love. They succumbed to the "you will be like God" (Gen. 3:5, RSV) temptation of the Serpent, the fallen angel who rebelled against God before history began. It is a temptation that continues throughout history. Scripture also reveals the mysterious and dreadful temporal consequences of Adam and Eve's disobedience: suffering and death (cf. vv. 16-19). But God is not the author: "God did not make death, and he does not delight in the death of the living" (Wis. 1:13, RSV).

Mysteriously we participate in the original sin of our first parents and its consequences. Original sin has gravely wounded our nature but has not obliterated God's image. The full restoration of our humanity in holiness requires a lifetime of cooperation with God's healing grace.

Like our first parents, we, too, are called by God to "Seek good, and not evil, that you may live" (Amos 5:14, RSV). Created in God's image, we participate in God's goodness. But sin violates and distorts our humanity, consequently alienating us from God. Our evil choices bring suffering on ourselves and others, distorting God's image in us. When we sin, personal holiness is diminished and we become liable to God's just punishments; God often uses suffering as a grace to restore the scales of justice and bring us to conversion.

History is replete with accounts of the innocent suffering at the hands of wicked people. But some suffering—for example, the decline of health in old age—is also mysteriously linked to a world disrupted by the effects of original sin (Rom. 8:18-25). It is holy and good to continue the work of Jesus in comforting those who are afflicted, healing them with the miracle of modern medicine, and assisting those in pain. It is the hard work of compassion, suffering with those who suffer (12:15; Gal. 5:22-23).

Suffering can be a true test of faith. Hence, with life-threatening illnesses and serious declines in health, the church's Sacrament of the Anointing of the Sick is the outward sign of the compassionate presence of Christ in the midst of suffering. Extreme Unction—Anointing of the Sick—provides the graces of spiritual healing and the strength to remain faithful and, if God so wills, includes physical healing.

The book of Job suggests God may even permit that we endure, with his grace, immense suffering as we struggle to hold fast to his law. Suffering with Jesus in generous love is necessary for discipleship. "If any man would come after me, let him deny himself and take up his cross daily and follow me" (Luke 9:23, RSV). Suffering with Jesus is holiness (Matt. 16:24-26). Such is the great witness of the martyrs who would not be budged in their fidelity to Jesus. There is even great holiness in bearing with the faults of others (Eph. 4:1-7).

With God's grace, suffering need not be an obstacle to holiness; rather, suffering in Christ is a means of holiness.

Holiness and the Voice of Conscience

Confidence in the ability to know the difference between good and evil is crucial to the quest for holiness. Hence God endows every person with a conscience. But a conscience can easily be suppressed. For a time, King David lived happily after his adultery and murder, until the prophet Nathan ignited his conscience with his famous indictment: "Thou art the man" (2 Sam. 12:7, KJV).

Conscience is to be obeyed as the voice of God. A good conscience is refined and informed by revelation as received through the church. Conscience directs us to choose the good and disturbs us when we plot or commit evil. Conscience makes us aware of our sinful inclinations. Conscience is sensitive to the temptations of the devil and the world. Conscience distinguishes between mortal sin that expels the life of God (sanctifying grace) in the soul and venial sin, which is not deadly but can severely distort the purity of virtue (1 John 5:17).

The more we respond to the directives of conscience by making good choices, the more we become virtuous. When we repeatedly neglect the voice of conscience, we become vicious—that is, vice filled. Viciousness comes in many forms and is not restricted to acts of violence. One can be filled with vice and still be considered a very nice person!

When we reject the sting of conscience, when we bury it with self-justification of our sins, we win only for a time. By winning through the defeat of conscience, we lose. Nobody can escape the "four last things": death, judgment, heaven, and hell.

A good conscience needs revelation for its continuous formation. In seeking holiness, we always need to be attentive to forming our consciences according to the authentic teachings of the church.

Restoration in Christ

Violations of conscience offend God and need God's forgiveness. It is impossible to forgive ourselves on our own authority. But Catholic teaching does not abandon us in despair. The church reveals Christ and his mercy as our divine remedy.

The incarnation at the "fullness of time" (Gal. 4:1-4, NRSV) provides the definitive revelation of our redemption and salvation. "Behold, an angel of the Lord appeared to him in a dream, saying, 'Joseph, son of David, do not fear to take Mary your wife, for that which is conceived in her is of the Holy Spirit; she will bear a son, and you shall call his name Jesus, for he will save his people from their sins'" (Matt. 1:19-21, RSV).

The parable of the prodigal son (Luke 15:11-32) is a poignant depiction of the saving mission of Jesus. The wayward son, suffering because of his sins, comes to his senses. He makes his way back to the father and humbly acknowledges—though imperfectly—that he has sinned against heaven and his father. The merciful father welcomes him with open arms, and a celebration begins. A loving father rejoices at the return of his son who expresses true, if imperfect, repentance, no matter how serious the sin.

But the suffering and death of Jesus on the cross further reveals the true horror of our sins. Our sins not only ruin our lives—as the parable demonstrates—but also, in a mysterious way, wound the body of Jesus, along with his mystical body, the church. With every act of pride, unjust anger, lust, gluttony, sloth, envy, avarice, and selfishness—great or small—Christ is tormented and crucified in innocence. When we gaze upon the cross, this great mystery becomes evident and should fill us with true dread for our sins.

The triumphant return of Jesus after his glorious resurrection is loving and merciful. He exhibits no desire for vengeance despite the humiliation of the cross. His first recorded word at the tomb is, simply, "Mary" (John 20:16, RSV). This is a beautiful reminder that Jesus knows us by name. He appears to two disciples on the road to Emmaus and patiently explains how the Messiah needed to suffer and die to fulfill Scripture (Luke 24:13-35). He appears to the frightened apostles in the upper room and confers peace upon them. He reveals the wounds in his glorified body (vv. 36-48). There will be no acts of retribution, no humiliations before Jesus's ascension.

But there is no time for complacency. The work Jesus requires of his apostles is urgent. He breathes on his first priests the gift of the Holy Spirit and beckons them to forgive sins in his name. "Receive the Holy Spirit. If you forgive the sins of any, they are forgiven; if you retain the sins of any, they are retained" (John 20:22-23, RSV). Holiness comes through the forgiveness of sins that Jesus readily offers to a contrite spirit. Christ forgives and saves if we turn to him in trust. And the forgiveness of sins prepares us to reignite our resolve to be transformed by Christ.

The Ministry of the Hierarchy

God's plan for our salvation includes shepherds. So he calls bishops and priests to direct us in our quest for holiness.

In the Old Testament God sends the prophets to do his bidding. They prophesy in obedience to God's will and carry out other assignments. But after the incarnation, there is a significant shift in how God chooses and retains his representatives for their apostolic work. Jesus relies on his human instruments to continue his sacred ministry. Peter, the first of the apostles, is the model of the church's hierarchy and chief shepherd. After Peter witnesses to the divinity of Christ, Jesus names him first among the apostles. "You are Peter, and on this rock I will build my church, and the powers of death shall not prevail against it" (Matt. 16:18, RSV). Christ chooses Peter to safeguard the faith through the office of the papacy. And he is given "keys of the kingdom of heaven," with the power to loose and bind (v. 19, RSV).

But Peter is a deeply flawed recipient of the honor. He continues to need fortification by the grace of Christ in the exercise of his office. Only Christ can restore him to his favor after Peter's threefold denial (Luke 22:54-62). Hence, the authority of Peter and the apostles depends not upon personal piety or even orthodoxy. It rests with Jesus, and the church's valid conferral of holy orders and the "chair" of Christ.

Peter's authority is conspicuously religious, maintaining the distinction made by Jesus: "Render therefore to Caesar the things that are Caesar's, and to God the things that are God's" (Matt. 22:21, RSV). Peter and the hierarchy govern the church. The role of the laity is to sanctify the world according to their state of life, married or single.

The church's celebration of the "chair of Peter" accentuates the infallible authority of Peter's office as founded on Christ. But the demands of the ecclesial office are fulfilled by faithfully carrying out the duties of priest, prophet, and king according to the mind of Christ and his church.

Despite the personal failures of popes, bishops, and priests—or perhaps foreseeing those failures—Jesus promises the gates of hell will never prevail against the church, the holy and spotless bride of Christ (Matt. 16:18). This truth is not a question of faith alone. Significantly, as history unfolds, the role of human logic becomes part of the guarantee. The promise made by Christ is supported by the intellectually rigorous principle of noncontradiction. There can be no substantial contradictions in the sources of revelation. Scriptures, sacred tradition, and the magisterium (teaching authority of the church) must always remain in agreement.

The Mystical Body of Christ

After the resurrection, there occurs the touching scene of Mary Magdalene's encounter with the Lord. After realizing he is not the gardener, but the risen Lord, Mary clings to her beloved Jesus. But Jesus gently and mysteriously refuses Mary's tender expression of affection (John 20:17).[11] This prompts us to ponder our relationship with Jesus and his church. As important as human affections are in our relationships, Jesus wants us to have a thoroughly new kind of relationship with him as head of his mystical body.

The love that Christ asks of us goes beyond personal relationships and affections (Matt. 10:37-39; Mark 8:34-38). Jesus explains: "If you love me, you will keep my commandments" (John 14:15, RSV). And the resolve to keep Jesus's commandments requires faith in him and hope of eternal glory. Faith is essential to our hope for final salvation and a true relationship with Jesus.[12]

Without the ascension of the Lord and the resurrected Lord now living among us, faith in him would be unfulfilled. Without faith grounded in the resurrection and the ascension, our union with Christ would be limited to human features, no matter how beautiful and sentimental. And we might easily compete with each other for Jesus's attention and affection, just as James and John lobbied the Lord for most-favored-disciple (Matt. 20:21-22).

Faith, on the other hand, is universal and directs us to eternity. It is trust in things unseen (2 Cor. 4:18).[13] Faith brings us to the baptismal font to be born anew of water and the Spirit (John 3:4-5), blotting out sin, instilling grace, branding us as Christians, and incorporating us into the mystical body of Christ.

Our union with Christ is one of love, but a love that is directed by faith rather than by transient human affection (Heb. 11:1-3; 12:1-2). After the ascension, we cling to Christ in love, faithfully obedient to him as head of his mystical body. As members of his mystical body, our dialog with Christ is not primarily one of pious affection, as attractive as that can be (John 20:17). Instead, it is a consuming inner dialog in union with Jesus by faith, keeping his commandments and trusting that his heavenly graces will mysteriously but certainly guide us on our pilgrim way.[14] This explains why Christian holiness may not exclude a disturbing spiritual desolation that impels a disciple to remain faithful to Christ without losing hope and confidence (2 Cor. 4:6-9, 16-18).

The light of faith also helps us apply Christian teaching to the details of our life's decisions. The laity in particular has the right and privilege to apply the principles of the gospel with grace-inspired prudential judgments in their communities and the world regarding questions of politics, economics, medicine, war, and the environment.

By God's grace and in faith, human sentiment and affection find true meaning and fulfillment. As members of Christ's mystical body, we represent to others his face and the bonds of his love. Here we find "divine affection" for others: "A new commandment I give to you, that you love one another; even as I have loved you, that you also love one another" (John 13:34, RSV).

Living the sacrificial love of Jesus in union with his mystical body, the church, transforms us in his holiness (Gal. 2:20).[15]

"Do This in Remembrance of Me"

The love and virtue originating from God is sustained by the grace of the Eucharist. At the Last Supper, Jesus celebrates the new and everlasting Covenant, the first Mass. It anticipates not only the horror of Good Friday but also the glory of Easter Sunday. He commands his first priests, "Do this in remembrance of me" (Luke 22:19, RSV), thus guaranteeing that redemption and sanctification continue throughout history.

In the Sacred Liturgy, the priest and laity communicate a spirit of thanksgiving to God through vocal and mental prayers. Prayers of adoration, contrition, thanksgiving, and supplication celebrate the right relationship between God and humanity established by Christ. Human beings are God's handiwork and are accountable to the Creator as they live and when they die.

After years of Mass attendance, we begin to recognize our humble station and dependence upon God alone; and in doing so we recognize that we are not insignificant. "For God so loved the world that he gave his only Son, that whoever believes in him should not perish but have eternal life" (John 3:16, RSV). Above all we pray for a Holy Communion with Christ's most sacred body, blood, soul, and divinity.

The repetition of the liturgical ritual and the recurring cycle of liturgical seasons inspire us to be led ever deeper into the sacred mysteries with holy inquisitiveness, intellectual effort, and contemplative prayer. In the context of the Sacred Liturgy, we boldly repeat the most sublime prayers as we receive the words of Jesus himself, and make the Lord's prayer our own, "Our Father."

The liturgy of the Mass also repeatedly calls to our attention the mighty words and deeds of Christ. Each year, as the Easter season unfolds, the church uses literary flashbacks when presenting the Gospels. The flashback passages encourage us to revisit—within the liturgical cycle—the early ministry of Christ in the light of his resurrection.[16]

There is great meaning and consolation in the pursuit of holiness when mystically entering the entire course of human history during the celebration of Mass. In this celebration, we are in union with the entire church; this fact gives us courage to endure every evil in every age. With eyes of faith informed by reason, we recognize the Mass as a piece of heaven on earth, directing us to our eternal home. Eucharist means "thanksgiving." Praising God for his great glory and vowing to do his will is indeed the highest possible expression of a holy, sanctified spirit of thanksgiving.[17]

The Mass: Gateway to History and Holiness

The Mass re-presents the cross and resurrection and the entire history of salvation. Hence we can expect the liturgy to display the classic Three Ages of the Interior Life noted earlier: (1) the Old Testament Purgative Way; (2) illumination by the teachings of Christ; and (3) ultimate union with him through the church.

The "Purgative Way" is present in the Penitential Rite. Here we place ourselves in God's presence, express sorrow, and repent of our sins: "through my fault, through my fault, through my most grievous fault."[18]

Next we move directly to the "Illuminative Way," found in the readings of the liturgy of the Word. Here God reveals himself through Scriptures. The homilist, with the help of the Holy Spirit, has the responsibility to explain the Word of God and apply it authentically in our lives. We ponder God's revelation in faith and hope.

Finally, the liturgy of the Eucharist discloses the "Unitive Way." We stand at the foot of the cross during the consecration of the bread and wine into the body, blood, soul, and divinity of Christ. We conclude our encounter with the resurrected Christ in Holy Communion, the real presence of Jesus. In the Eucharist we are in loving communion with Jesus and his entire church throughout history. This includes the church militant on earth, the church suffering in purgatory, and the church triumphant in heaven.

The Three Ages encompass all of human history. And the Sacred Liturgy encloses the Three Ages for our sanctification, in communion with one another. The Catholic quest for holiness, therefore, includes a love for Scriptures and the sacraments. This entails a true love for the history of salvation re-presented at Mass.

Mary, Model of Holiness

A sincere quest for holiness seeks perfection (Heb. 6:1; Gk., *teleiotēs*, "completeness"), and perfection includes complete acceptance and responsiveness to God's will, a seemingly impossible task. Hence, we look to Mary as a model for guidance and help.

The angel Gabriel appears to Mary and tells her, "The child to be born will be called holy, the Son of God" (Luke 1:35, RSV). Mary accepts the conferral with humility: "Behold, I am the handmaid of the Lord; let it be to me according to your word" (v. 38, RSV). God chose Mary to be the Mother of God, but only along with her faithful assent.

The holiness of Mary teaches us to question God with reverence, with faith seeking understanding: "How shall this be, since I have no husband?" (v. 34, RSV). But Mary's exalted role is never a cause for sinful pride or presumption. At the wedding feast in Cana, Mary instructs the wine stewards (and us): "Do whatever he tells you" (John 2:5, RSV). Mary always defers to the Father's will as known through her Son.

Mary is the model of few words, with a faith wrapped in silence (Luke 2:19). At the foot of the cross, Mary experiences the fulfillment of Simeon's prophecy; a sword of sorrow pierces her heart (v. 35; John 19:25-

27). Mary's faith is pure and unique. Because in her heart she ponders the words of the angel Gabriel, only Mary could be certain that the horror of the crucifixion would not be the last word.

Mary has no ecclesial office to exercise. She is a member of the laity. She is, simply and sublimely, the Mother of God in history—the mother of Jesus, true God and true man. Yet Mary's feast days are numerous, dignifying every liturgical season. Her immaculate conception reminds us of how the church—from the cross and at Pentecost—is conceived in grace and holiness. And her glorious assumption, body and soul, into heaven directs our attention to the resurrection of the dead, our glorified bodies with the risen Christ, and the destiny of the church, purified of all evil and glorified in the new and heavenly Jerusalem (Rev. 21:1-8).

Mary is forever without sin; she is true, beautiful, and good. Hence, Mary is truly the model of the flawless and saving magisterial teachings of the church, handed down throughout history under the guardianship of flawed bishops and priests.

Holiness Is Living the Life of Christ

In the midst of sin and suffering, Jesus commands us to be holy: "You, therefore, must be perfect, as your heavenly Father is perfect" (Matt. 5:48, RSV). We soldier on with his boundless grace (John 1:16) in a lifelong pursuit of holiness and virtue, in Christ, "the hope of glory" (Col. 1:27, RSV).

But if holiness is possible in this life, why is there so much conflict and turmoil? Why do we fall short? There seem to be plenty of reasons to walk away from the quest, especially in times of weariness and discouragement. But during lonely spiritual battles—temptation, spiritual desolation, suffering, and even the terrors of persecution—revelation reminds us, through the sacraments, that we participate in the same spiritual struggles and faith-filled strength of our forefathers (Heb. 12:1-2). We share the same history. And in union with them as members of the mystical body of Christ, we seek their guidance and intercessory prayers for fidelity and courage.

And if we remain in his grace and still fall short in perfection, the Catholic faith provides an unexpected consolation. We have the confidence that the Lord's finishing school of purgatory[19] will purify us of all evil and definitively prepare us for the end of history and his beatitude (Rev. 21:1-5).

Conclusion

Personal holiness in this life is often confused with the absence of all turmoil, error, and failure. But realism informed by Catholic faith does not confuse true holiness with the illusory effects of narcotic drugs. Our individual return to God is a reasonable and holistic spiritual journey, along with the entire people of God in history. The path of our return in God's loving providence includes the light of revelation, the graces of fervent prayer, the Sacred Liturgy, and the sacraments. And we must fervently claim the promise of Revelation as our own: "He who testifies to these things says, 'Surely I am coming soon.' Amen. Come, Lord Jesus!" (22:20, RSV).

(5)

The Relation of Justification and Sanctification in the Lutheran Tradition

❖

Craig L. Nessan, ThD

Craig L. Nessan is academic dean, professor of contextual theology and ethics, and the William D. Streng Professor for the Education and Renewal of the Church, Wartburg Theological Seminary, Dubuque, Iowa. He belongs to the Evangelical Lutheran Church in America.

❖

The Lutheran tradition began with the efforts of Martin Luther (1483–1546) to address theological questions and introduce renewal into the late medieval Roman Catholic Church. A key moment was the posting of ninety-five theses for debate on October 31, 1517, a date that has come to mark the beginning of the Protestant Reformation. When Luther's proposals for reform were not accepted, this led to the formation of Lutheran churches, initially in Germany and Scandinavia, from which the Lutheran movement has spread throughout the world.

When interpreting differences among Christian traditions, one distinguishing factor involves where in the New Testament each tradition grounds its decisive biblical warrants. While each denomination bases its teaching on New Testament foundations, theological consequences derive from where each tradition locates its emphasis, its "canon within the canon."[1] In this book, certain Christian traditions orient themselves more explicitly to particular biblical texts—for example, texts that deal with Christian holiness. The chapters on the Wesleyan and Pentecostal traditions illustrate this. While all Christian traditions deal with holiness, several place the center of gravity for theology and practice on other topics in the New Testament. This is true for the Lutheran tradition, which concentrates on the New Testament witness to justification by grace alone through faith alone in Christ alone, especially as witnessed by the apostle Paul.

The American Holiness Movement, which emerged from the theology of John and Charles Wesley and spread through the nineteenth-century Second Great Awakening, emphasizes personal regeneration and sanctified living through the work of the Holy Spirit. Reformation theology discusses these themes in relation to the work of the Holy Spirit as confessed in the third article of the Apostles' Creed ("I believe in the Holy Spirit . . ."), especially as aspects of the Holy Spirit's work of sanctification. Martin Luther operated with a robust understanding of the active involvement of the Holy Spirit in the life of the church, particularly as mediated through Word and sacraments.[2]

Through the Word of God—Jesus Christ, Scripture, and proclamation as the Word's three central expressions—and through the sacraments of Holy Baptism and the Lord's Supper as means of grace, the Holy Spirit mediates the gifts of Jesus Christ. Luther writes in the Small Catechism (1529):

> I believe that by my own understanding or strength I cannot believe in Jesus Christ my Lord or come to him, but instead the Holy Spirit has called me through the gospel, enlightened me with his gifts, made me holy and kept me in the true faith, just as he calls, gathers, enlightens, and makes holy the whole Christian church on earth and keeps it with Jesus Christ in the one common, true faith. Daily in this Christian church the Holy Spirit abundantly forgives all sins—mine and those of all believers. On the Last Day the Holy Spirit will raise me and all the dead and will give me and all believers in Christ eternal life. This is most certainly true.[3]

The Holy Spirit works through the gospel to bestow spiritual gifts on the whole church. The Lutheran tradition centers on the gospel of Jesus Christ. While the Holy Spirit can and does work in other ways, the Lutheran focus is on those means of grace—Word and sacraments—where

Christ has promised to reveal himself. Through these particular means of grace, Christ bestows all promised gifts: forgiveness of sin, deliverance from death and the power of the devil, and eternal life.[4]

Sanctification and the Righteousness of Christ

The Lutheran tradition inseparably joins the work of the Holy Spirit with the work of Jesus Christ. Because of the theological issues that gave rise to the Reformation, the central concern was justification by grace alone through faith alone in Christ alone, not sanctification or Christian holiness. The insistence on "alone" (Lat., *sola*) highlights what was at stake: whether good works performed by people prior to justification are necessary for salvation. Many of the pious practices of the late medieval period had obscured the gospel of Jesus Christ as the exclusive basis for salvation. Such pious works included earning merit before God by performing private masses, making pilgrimages, reverencing relics, and purchasing indulgences. Luther judged acts of piety, performed to earn salvation, as "works righteousness." Instead, Luther insisted that salvation is based on the alien righteousness received by the work of Jesus Christ, not by any "righteousness" humans perform or achieve. Justification is based on the *passive righteousness* of faith. Passive righteousness is not earned by the believer but is received as a gift by trusting in Jesus Christ alone. Regarding personal holiness, the primary focus in the Lutheran tradition is on the holiness of Jesus Christ ascribed to the believer by faith in Christ's justifying work.

According to the Augsburg Confession (1530), one of the central confessional writings in the Book of Concord,[5] justification was the central article of faith under contention during the Reformation:

> Likewise, they teach that human beings cannot be justified before God by their own powers, merits, or works. But they are justified as a gift on account of Christ's sake through faith when we believe that Christ has suffered for us and that for his sake our sin is forgiven and righteousness and eternal life are given to us. For God will regard and reckon this faith as righteousness in his sight, as St. Paul says in Romans 3[:21-26] and 4[:5].[6]

This conviction is reaffirmed in the Smalcald Articles (1537), another important Lutheran confessional document: "Nothing in this article can be conceded or given up, even if heaven and earth or whatever is transitory passed away."[7] Lutheran theology centers on the doctrine of justification as that article by which the church stands or falls according to Scripture, the Lutheran Confessions, and Lutheran doctrine. Lutheran tradition holds that justification by grace through faith in Jesus Christ remains the central article of teaching for every generation.[8]

The Lutheran Achilles' Heel

The laser focus on justification during the Reformation created a theological dilemma for subsequent Lutheran efforts to explain Christian discipleship. Understanding the relationship between justification and sanctification became and remains a challenge. The dilemma is illustrated by Lutheran theologian Gerhard Forde: "Sanctification, if it is to be spoken of as something other than justification, is perhaps best defined as the art of getting used to the unconditional justification wrought by the grace of God for Jesus' sake."[9] Forde's statement reduces sanctification to an extension in time of what it means to live by justification alone.

The most pointed and enduring critique of Lutheran theology's failure to spell out the implications of justification for Christian life came from Lutheran theologian Dietrich Bonhoeffer (1906-45). In *Discipleship*, Bonhoeffer contrasts "cheap grace" with "costly grace." He organized his theology around the Christological center of justification. "Cheap grace," Bonhoeffer charged, is the Lutheran Achilles' heel.

Amid the catastrophe of Nazi Germany, Bonhoeffer severely judged the general failure of Lutherans to generate a life of discipleship:

Like ravens we have gathered around the carcass of cheap grace. From it we have imbibed the poison which has killed the following of Jesus among us. The doctrine of pure grace experienced an unprecedented deification. The pure doctrine of grace became its own God, grace itself. Luther's teachings are quoted everywhere, but twisted from their truth into self-delusion. They say if only our church is in possession of a doctrine of justification, then it is surely a justified church! They say Luther's true legacy should be recognizable in making grace as cheap as possible. Being Lutheran should mean that discipleship is left to the legalists, Reformed, or the enthusiasts, all for the sake of grace. They say that the world is justified and Christians in discipleship are made out to be heretics. A people began Christian, became Lutheran, but at the cost of discipleship, at an all-too-cheap price. Cheap grace had won.[10]

Bonhoeffer's sharp critique serves as the point of departure for the rest of this chapter. We will examine six Lutheran efforts to resolve the "Lutheran dilemma."

Lutheran Theology on the Question of Sanctification: Six Approaches

Martin Luther's pivotal treatise *The Freedom of a Christian* (1520) provides a key for understanding the relationship between justification and Christian discipleship (sanctification). According to Luther, the gospel of Jesus Christ means freedom. Christian freedom has a twofold, complementary meaning:

A Christian is a perfectly free lord of all, subject to none.

A Christian is a perfectly dutiful servant of all, subject to all.[11]

The first claim refers to justification. A Christian is subject to no lord except Jesus Christ. Christ's lordship is exercised according to the content of justification by faith alone. Luther explains: "Faith alone is the saving and efficacious use of the Word of God."[12] The gifts of Jesus Christ become the gifts of the sinner-made-saint through a sweet exchange. "Christ is full of grace, life, and salvation. The soul is full of sins, death, and damnation. Now let faith come between them and sins, death, and damnation will be Christ's, while grace, life, and salvation will be the soul's."[13] By faith the sinner receives freedom *from* sin, death, and the devil.

The second claim refers to service to one's neighbors. Not only does the gospel of Jesus Christ set sinners free *from* sin's bondage, but it also sets the justified person free *for* service to others. Good works performed to demonstrate one's worthiness before God are excluded; they constitute worthless "works righteousness." But good works freely performed in service to others, in response to the gospel, are the proper expression of civic righteousness. While good works cannot justify the sinner before God, in free response to the gospel the proper and necessary performance of good works is always in service to the neighbor's needs. "Here faith is truly active through love [Gal. 5:6], that is, it finds expression in works of the freest service, cheerfully and lovingly done, with which [one] willingly serves another without hope of reward."[14]

This explanation of the relationship between faith and works appears in Luther's sermon "Two Kinds of Righteousness" (1518; Phil. 2:5-6). The first kind of righteousness is the "alien righteousness" of another; it is instilled from without. This is the "righteousness of Christ by which he justifies through faith."[15] The second kind of righteousness is "proper righteousness, not because we alone work it, but because we work with that first and alien righteousness."[16] Proper righteousness involves both the death of the sinful self and the rising up of a new self in Christ. The second kind of "righteousness consists in love for one's neighbor."[17] The focus on serving one's neighbor arises from Luther's doctrine of vocation; Christian baptism is a call, a vocation, to serve others in all stations of daily life.

When we understand Luther's distinction in terms of Christian holiness, we see there are two kinds of holiness. The first is passive holiness, freely received from Jesus Christ as a gift. Christ gives us his own holiness as a gift through the power of the Holy Spirit, mediated through the gospel. It is received in gratitude by faith alone. The second kind is active holiness, activated in the believer by the gospel, which sets a Christian free for good works on behalf of others. This can be described as social holiness, lived out in service to one's neighbors. While Luther had more to say about the Christian life, this twofold understanding of holiness lies at the heart of his teaching.

In the Lutheran tradition, there have been many attempts to interpret further what Luther meant by living out the freedom of the gospel. From the time of the Reformation to the present, there have been distinct attempts to describe more completely the relationship between justification and sanctification, thereby also clarifying the meaning of holiness in the Lutheran tradition.

First, the Third Use of the Law in Philip Melanchthon (1497–1560) and the Formula of Concord (1577)

Philip Melanchthon was a friend and close collaborator with Luther. He provided an additional Lutheran way for understanding Christian discipleship. Melanchthon emphasized "the third use of the law," a theme subsequently included in the Lutheran Confessions. The first use of the law is political; it governs human affairs in society. The second use of the law is theological; it reveals human sinfulness and prepares a sinner to receive the gospel. In its third use, the law functions as a guide for Christian life. In the 1543 edition of *Loci Communes*, Melanchthon explained:

> The third use of the Law pertains to the regenerate. Insofar as the regenerate have been justified by faith, they are free from the Law. . . . Yet in the meantime it must be said that the Law which points

out the remnants of sin, in order that the knowledge of sin and repentance may increase, and the Gospel also must proclaim Christ in order that faith may grow. Furthermore, the Law must be preached to the regenerate to teach them certain works in which God wills that we practice obedience.[18]

There is extensive debate regarding the third use of the law as it relates to Luther's own thought and its standing in Lutheran theology. Nevertheless, the third use became an early and enduring way for understanding sanctification among Lutherans.[19] The third use affirms that believers must receive direction from God's law in order to practice obedience to his commands.

The Formula of Concord (1577), the last of the confessional writings in the Book of Concord, describes the third use of the law as a "guide" for life: "third, after they have been reborn—since nevertheless the flesh still clings to them—that precisely because of the flesh they may have a sure guide, according to which they can orient and conduct their entire life."[20] The article "Concerning the Third Use of the Law" was included in the Formula of Concord because of controversies between Lutheran theologians over legalism and antinomianism.[21] It seeks to answer the question whether the law is applicable to Christians as well as to "unbelievers, non-Christians, and the unrepentant."[22]

Therefore, for both the repentant and unrepentant, for the reborn and those not reborn, the law is and remains one single law, the unchangeable will of God. In terms of obedience to it there is a difference only in that those people who are not yet reborn do what the law demands unwillingly, because they are coerced (as is also the case with the reborn with respect to the flesh). Believers, however, do without coercion, with a willing spirit, insofar as they are born anew, what no threat of the law could ever force from them.[23]

Luther had placed his central emphasis on how the gospel sets Christians free to serve their neighbors as an expression of social holiness. In the Formula of Concord we observe an emerging focus on the quality of Christian life *among* believers, in contrast to those who are not Christians. This is an early indication of how the Lutheran tradition began more fully to address the nature of sanctification or Christian holiness. Although Lutherans have never decreased their emphasis on social holiness, many Lutheran theologians increasingly explore personal holiness in relation to sanctification.

Second, Renovation of Life in Lutheran Orthodoxy and Lutheran Pietism

The seventeenth and eighteenth centuries of Lutheran history are known as periods characterized first by Lutheran Orthodoxy, then by Lutheran Pietism. Lutheran theology became organized according to Aristotelian categories characteristic of medieval scholastic theology. Orthodox theologians stressed "concomitants [corollaries] and conse-quences of justifying faith."[24] These include (1) vocation, (2) illumination (by the Holy Spirit), (3) regeneration and conversion, (4) mystical union, and (5) renovation.[25] These themes relate directly to Christian holiness. According to Lutheran theologian David Hollaz (1648–1713), as cited by Heinrich Schmid, renovation is

> an act of grace, whereby the Holy Spirit, expelling the faults of a jus-tified man, endows him with inherent sanctity. The change that takes place in man consists further in this, that by the influence of divine grace the sin still cleaving to man disappears, more and more, and gives place to an increasing facility for doing what is good. As, how-ever, the sinfulness yet remaining in man yields only through con-stantly repeated struggle against sin, this renovation is not a sudden, but a gradual one, susceptible of constant growth; and as sin never entirely leaves man, it is never perfect, although we are always to strive after perfection. Finally, it is a work of God in man, yet of such a nature that there is a free co-operation on the part of man, who now in conversion has received new spiritual powers.[26]

The emphasis upon renovation was retained and stressed by Lutheran Pietism. Pietists sought to recover the vital relationship between the be-liever and God that Luther had emphasized.

Philipp Jakob Spener (1635–1705) was the central figure in the Pietist renewal of vital Christian faith and practice. He authored the classical 1675 work *Pia Desideria* (Pious Longings), *or Heartfelt Desires for Improve-ment Pleasing to God of the True Evangelical Churches, Including Some Chris-tian Recommendations to That End.*[27] In part 3, Spener offers six proposals for reforming Lutheranism. The first two are drawn from Luther; the last four from Johann Arndt (1555–1621): (1) Bible reading by families in homes and by individuals and reading books of the Bible at church services and in meetings during the week meant for "mutual instruc-tion and edification"; (2) establishing "the spiritual priesthood" of all believers for mutual encouragement and admonition; (3) teaching that the Christian faith means practice, not just knowledge; (4) showing love and praying for unbelievers; (5) reforming the education of pastors; and (6) sermons focused more on forming listeners in faith and love and less on theological erudition.[28]

Other major figures of German Pietism included August Hermann Francke (1663–1727) of Halle and Count Nicolaus von Zinzendorf (1700–1760), Moravian bishop at Herrnhut. Historian of German Pietism Douglas H. Shantz summarizes the contributions made by Lutheran Pietism:

> The genius of Pietism lay in the adjectives it employed: *true* Christianity; *heartfelt, living* faith; a *living* knowledge of God; the *inward* Christ and the *inner* Word. Another set of adjectives expressed Pietist hopes for renewal of humanity and a better future for the church: the *new* man, *born-again* Christianity, the coming *Philadelphian* church. Born-again laypeople became agents of their own spirituality, reading the Bible for themselves and teaching and encouraging one another in non-church settings.[29]

The characteristics of Pietism identified by Shantz parallel those promoted in holiness movements in other Christian traditions. However, an important reservation should be noted. In the Lutheran tradition, the Pietist characteristics rest firmly upon the doctrinal foundation of justification by faith. Subsequent figures influenced by Lutheran Pietism advanced these emphases into the nineteenth and twentieth centuries.

Third, the Work of the Holy Spirit in the Full Communion Agreement between the Evangelical Lutheran Church in America and the Moravian Church in America

The agreement, titled *Following Our Shepherd to Full Communion*, provides a fascinating example of how ecumenical rapprochement can contribute new insights to Lutheran doctrine. The section of the agreement titled "Mutual Complementarities" addresses the topic "The Holy Spirit, the Believer, and the Christian Life." The section affirms that Lutherans and Moravians, a tradition influenced by Lutheran Pietism, share a core commitment to justification by faith apart from works of the law. It offers an example of complementarity between Lutherans and Moravians:

> The Moravian experience of the Spirit in the life of the believer was not shaped by the polemics of the Reformation but by the Brethren's [Moravians] endurance in the Ancient Church, the "period of the

hidden seed," its renewal in Continental Pietism, and its internal struggles to be faithful to the power of the Spirit and the need for witnessing to Christ as individuals and as a community. . . .

Moravians and Lutherans complement each other in agreeing on the point of the need for the Spirit in engendering faith through our central affirmation of justification through grace by means of the Spirit. Lutherans seek to maintain the grace of God bestowed through the Spirit against any shadow of human works and worth. The Unity endeavors to insure that the believer realizes that justification opens a gracious relationship with Jesus by means of the Spirit.[30]

By explicitly focusing on the work of the Spirit as "the source and power of sanctification in the life of the believer," the agreement offers an opportunity for Lutherans to reclaim more fulsomely Luther's own robust understanding of the Holy Spirit; it inseparably connects sanctification to justification.[31] The Moravian emphasis on "the continual presence and activity of the Spirit within the believer . . . calling them to live according to their calling to holiness and eternal life" offers Lutherans a renewed dimension of their own tradition.[32]

Fourth, a Second or Parenetic (Ethical) Use of the Gospel by William H. Lazareth (1928–2008)

Lazareth presented an unconventional proposal. He interpreted Luther as teaching a "second or parenetic use of the gospel."[33] Instead of appealing to the third use of the law, Lazareth understood the gospel as "faith working through love."[34] He proposed a second use of the gospel that depends upon the natural law and the traditional first use of the law:

It goes without saying that the law's sin-related theological and political functions also apply to imperfect Christians insofar as they still remain sinful. However, insofar as they are already righteous, it is rather the gospel's parenetic or ethical function, under the indwelling Holy Spirit's governance, to empower and guide the joyful fulfillment of God's pre-fall and perennial command of dominion-sharing love by God's renewed Christian workers serving as responsible members of church and society.[35]

The operative concept undergirding Lazareth's proposal is *simul justus et peccator*—which means that Christians simultaneously remain saints and sinners. For Christians, the "parenetic [ethical] function of the gospel interpenetrates the political function of God's law for our vocational sanctification in daily life."[36] Lazareth's proposal is not so much a matter of personal holiness as it is public holiness for the sake of serving one's neighbor.

Fifth, Sanctification according to Dietrich Bonhoeffer (1906-45)

Bonhoeffer not only offered his criticism of "cheap grace" (as noted above) but also proposed his own remedy to the problem by calling for "costly grace." *Discipleship* is his manual for the Christian life, written as a commentary on Jesus's Sermon on the Mount (Matt. 5:1–7:29).

Costly grace means the actual death and resurrection of the Christian in conformity with one's baptism; it entails being joined to the death and resurrection of Jesus Christ in a form that issues in a life of radical discipleship. Unlike generations of Lutheran theologians before him, Bonhoeffer discovered that the Sermon on the Mount is not merely a collection of impossible demands functioning as law to drive sinners to justification. Instead, the Sermon on the Mount provides instruction for Christian discipleship. Discipleship as taught by Jesus becomes the *meaning* of holiness and sanctification.

Consistent with Luther, Bonhoeffer insists that justification and sanctification "spring from the same source, namely, Jesus Christ, the crucified one."[37] In baptismal terms, the Christian life involves a daily death to sin and a daily resurrection to Jesus Christ. This entails complete dependence on the righteousness received as a gift by the work of Jesus Christ. Bonhoeffer makes an important distinction between justification and sanctification:

> Both gifts belong inseparably together. However, just because of this connection between them, they are not simply one and the same. While justification appropriates to Christians the deed God has already accomplished, sanctification promises them God's present and future action. Whereas, in justification, believers are being included in the community with Jesus Christ through Christ's death that took place once and for all, sanctification, on the other hand, preserves them in the sphere into which they have been placed. It keeps them in Christ, within the church-community.[38]

Bonhoeffer shifts the focus of sanctification from the individual to the church community. Sanctification is Christ's gift to the communion of saints. Both the communal character of sanctification according to God's holiness (which forms the church as a "contrast community"[39]) and the hiddenness of sanctification are noteworthy: "For the community of saints this implies three things. *First*, its sanctification will manifest itself *in a clear separation from the world*. Its sanctification will, *second*, prove itself through *conduct* that is *worthy* of God's realm of holiness. And, *third*, its sanctification will be *hidden in waiting* for the day of Jesus Christ."[40]

Holiness as lived by the church community is "hidden with Christ in God (Col. 3:3)."[41] Neither individual Christians nor the discipleship community can earn (or even have knowledge of) their sanctification. "Sanctification always relates to the end of time. Its goal is not to pass the test when judged by the world or even by the person being sanctified, but to pass the test before the Lord."[42] Everything belongs to Jesus Christ.

Sixth, the Indwelling Christ by the Finnish School of Tuomo Mannermaa (1937–2015)

The most innovative contemporary treatment of the relationship between justification and sanctification in the Lutheran tradition comes from the Finnish school of Luther scholarship. Its leading figure is Tuomo Mannermaa. The originality in his interpretation of Luther involves a shift away from a forensic (legal) understanding of Christ's justifying work and toward the real presence of Jesus Christ dwelling in Christians to achieve justification and sanctification. Mannermaa says,

> In faith, human beings are really united with Christ. Christ, in turn, is both the forgiveness of sins and the effective producer of everything that is good in them. Therefore "sanctification"—that is, the sanctity or holiness of the Christian—is, in fact, only another name for the same phenomenon of which Luther speaks when discussing the communication of attributes, the happy exchange, and the union between the person of Christ and the believer.[43]

The work being done by Mannermaa and the Finnish school provides a breakthrough in the history of Luther interpretation. Mannermaa makes two critical points regarding Christian holiness: (1) "The holiness of Christians is totally based on 'external signs,' that is, on word and sacraments,"[44] and (2) "Christians' holiness is also not based on their ability to avoid heresies in doctrine or life."[45] This leads Mannermaa to affirm, as did Bonhoeffer, "the hidden holiness of the church."[46]

Thus the Finnish school, following Mannermaa, claims to have resolved the Lutheran dilemma:

Unlike the *Formula of Concord* and later Lutheran theology, Luther does not separate justification and the presence of Christ in the believer. . . .

The idea of Christ's real presence in faith sheds light on the meaning of many of those themes in Luther's theology that have continued to be subjects of controversy among scholars up to the present day. This idea makes apprehensible the Reformer's understanding of the relationships between justification and sanctification, real and declarative righteousness, and the partial and total aspects of the idea of "simultaneously righteous and a sinner."[47]

The convergence in understanding by Bonhoeffer and Mannermaa allows for an informed conclusion about mending the Lutheran Achilles' heel.

Conclusion

Based upon recent Lutheran scholarship, two pivotal convictions can be affirmed for explaining Christian holiness in the Lutheran tradition.

First, all doctrine must be interpreted according to the *centripetal force* of Christology so central to the Lutheran Reformation. Justification by grace through faith in Christ alone centers the universe of Lutheran theology. Holiness, like righteousness in its first form (the "alien righteousness" of Christ by which sinners are justified), is a gift to be received *passively* for Christ's sake. There is no place for Christian "perfectionism" in Lutheran theology. A Christian always remains under the proviso of being saint and sinner simultaneously (*simul justus et peccator*). Sanctification must always be understood as the gift of the indwelling Jesus Christ, for which the believer can only offer thanks and gratitude. Christian life is a generous response to the great thanksgiving of what God has done for the world in Jesus Christ.

Second, the *centrifugal force* of the gospel of Jesus Christ shifts attention away from personal holiness to social holiness. The gospel of Jesus Christ sets the believer free not only *from* the power of sin, death, and the devil but, even more, *for* service to the neighbor in daily life. Holiness, like righteousness in its second form ("proper righteousness," active holiness, activated in believers by the gospel, which sets them free for good works on behalf of others), involves the civil response of neighborliness to others in the arenas of home, work, local community, citizenship, and the world. Luther's doctrine of *vocation* is grounded in baptism as a call to serve others—and creation itself—as our neighbors.[48] Baptismal vocation is foundational for Luther's understanding of the universal priesthood of all believers, one of the Reformation's most significant gifts.[49]

Only a retrieval of Luther's robust understanding of vocation and the universal priesthood of all believers can express the social holiness that is the final goal of Christian life.[50]

6

"To Show Forth the Glory of God"
A Reformed Portrait of Christian Holiness

❖

Robert M. Jack, D.Min.

Robert Jack, honorably retired member of Charlotte Presbytery, Presbyterian Church (USA), served congregations in New Jersey, Maryland, and North Carolina. In 2019 he retired as senior pastor of the Pleasant Hill Presbyterian Church, Charlotte, North Carolina, after leading that congregation for thirty-three years. He is a graduate of Eastern Nazarene College, Princeton Theological Seminary, and Gordon-Conwell Theological Seminary.

❖

The principle of holiness leads to the exhortation, "Be not conformed to this world; but be ye transformed by the renewing of your mind, that ye may prove what is the will of God" [Rom. 12:2]. . . . It means that we may think, speak, meditate, or do anything only with a view to [God's] glory.[1]
—John Calvin

In this chapter we will explore the vocation of Christian holiness as understood within the Reformed theological tradition. The Reformed understanding of Christian faith and practice came to birth principally in the theology of Protestant Reformer John Calvin (1509-64). Geneva,

Switzerland, provided the primary context in which Calvin developed his theology and form of church government. But Reformed roots are planted more deeply in the soil of the evangelistic fervor that characterized the apostolic age as recorded in the book of Acts.

Many Protestant denominations identify as Reformed in theology, including Presbyterians, the Christian Reformed Church, and Reformed Baptist Churches of America. In addition to John Calvin, famous Reformed ministers include Jonathan Edwards, Cotton Mather, and George Whitefield. The number of Reformed theologians is legion; they include J. Gresham Machen, Karl Barth, Letty Russell, and John Piper. Reformed Christians belong to the whole historic Christian family. They recognize that their tradition is but one part of the greater whole that is the body of Christ. Yet humbly, and with a confidence that marked the "ardor and order" of Calvin's theological enterprise, Reformed Christians contribute their own distinct theology and understanding of Christian discipleship to the greater life of the church catholic.[2]

Presbyterians expressed this sentiment in *A Declaration of Faith* (1977). It was crafted by the Presbyterian Church in the United States (antecedent of the Presbyterian Church [USA]) as an effort to express both the breadth and particularity of our heritage as we proclaim the gospel to a needy world. The *Declaration* says in part,

> The church's story with God did not end
>> with the latest events recorded in Scripture.
> Across the centuries the company of believers
>> has continued its pilgrimage with the Lord of history.
> It is a record of faith and faithlessness, glory and shame.
> The church has been persecuted by hostile societies,
>> but it has also known times of privilege and power
>> when it joined forces with dominant cultures.
> It has sought holiness
>> through separation from society,
>> as well as through involvement in the world's affairs.
> It has experienced life-giving reformations.
> It has known missionary expansion throughout the world,
>> but also periods of dwindling resources and influence.
> It has divided into rival orders, sects and denominations,
>> but it has also labored for cooperation and union.
> We confess we are heirs of this whole story.

We are charged to remember our past,
> to be warned and encouraged by it,
> but not to live it again.

Now is the time of our testing
> as God's story with the church moves forward through us.

We are called to live now as God's servants
> in the service of people everywhere.[3]

Understanding how the Reformed tradition views the vocation of Christian holiness requires that it be placed within a larger Reformed theological context focused on God's sovereignty and what it means to live so as to "show forth his glory" in all things. As Calvin declares, "We must take care that God's glory shine through us."[4] My own religious background serves as a point of entry.

My Reformed Journey

As a teenager coming of age in America during the turbulent sixties, with the upheavals of civil rights demonstrations and antiwar protests broadcast on the evening news, I sensed that society was changing faster and in ways much different from what anyone could safely predict. We were raised in the fear of imminent nuclear holocaust, with civil defense drills that regularly sent us scurrying for cover under our school desks. The 1961 Bay of Pigs debacle was soon followed by the Cuban Missile Crisis and then the assassination of President John Kennedy. In 1968, both Martin Luther King Jr. and Robert Kennedy, John's brother, were assassinated. The war in Vietnam evoked generational divisions that made polite conversation difficult, if not impossible.

The adults in my world at the time often spoke in hushed, despairing terms about the apparent end of all they cherished as good and true and certain. By contrast, representatives of the youth culture (often called a counterculture)[5] and some of my close friends saw the same events as harbingers of a new world being born from the ashes of the old. For them, it was either *1984* or *Brave New World*. That was a frightening time!

And yet I do not remember despairing.

I attribute this mainly to active participation in church life and especially to the catechetical instruction I received, along with consistent Bible study in Sunday school. While many of my friends felt the need to go "in search of themselves," either through hallucinogenic drugs or by dropping out of mainstream society and joining communes, I felt no such compulsion and experienced no identity crisis. Why? Because I had been assured from birth and through Christian baptism that I was a precious child of God. The world I lived in made sense because it was the purposeful creation of a sovereign, loving God in whose image humankind is fashioned. I had no need to search for life's meaning, because I had been instructed by the opening question and answer of the Westminster Shorter Catechism. "What is the chief end of man?" (i.e., "What is the purpose of human life?"). The answer: "Man's chief end is to glorify God and to enjoy him forever."[6] That conviction anchored my life and shaped my understating of Christian discipleship.

At an early age, I benefited from being exposed to sound preaching in my home church. The pastor who made the greatest impact on my faith, and who would later direct my thoughts toward preparation for Christian ministry, was strongly influenced by the great English Reformed Baptist preacher Charles Haddon Spurgeon (1834-92). I remember a reference my pastor made to a sermon Spurgeon preached on Esther. Spurgeon stressed that each of us will be chosen, as was the Hebrew queen, "for such a time as this" (Esth. 4:14, KJV). Each of us has a God-given purpose in life, and that purpose will be revealed by the sovereign God, whose wisdom and love upholds and rules all things.

With the aid of such preaching, and through the witness of some of my peers in the church, in my sixteenth year, during worship one Sunday, I made a profession of faith in Jesus Christ. In some traditions, this action marks the day on which I was "saved." In the Reformed tradition, however, the order of salvation begins with election, the recognition that God chose me from "before the foundation of the world" to live so as to bring glory to his name (Eph. 1:4, KJV). Correctly understood, election is not an impersonal mechanical process but is always "in Christ" (see v. 4) and thus very personal. As such, the mark of election is our union with Christ in faith.[7]

In short order my faith would be tested. It was my intention to attend the United States Naval Academy in preparation for a career as a naval officer. This goal was partly achieved when I received an appointment from my congressman. To that end, and perhaps foolishly, I had put "all my eggs in one basket," turning down admissions to several other colleges and universities because I was sure I was navy bound. I remember offering constant and fervent prayer to God, seeking his will, but all the while certain it must be the navy.

Little did I realize that God had other plans! All that remained in the admissions process was for me to pass the physical examination, a thorough forty-eight-hour ordeal of having my body and mind picked, prodded, and scrutinized by a team of doctors and nurses. And I failed! For medical reasons that need not be mentioned here, I was told the appointment would go, not to me, but to the first alternate behind me. I gathered my things and went home, crestfallen, wondering why God would lead me so far in realizing my destiny, only to pass it on to someone else.

My father sensed my despair. He was also an elder in the church and suggested we consult Pastor Steve, who was keenly aware of my situation. I was doubtful at first, and my pain was little assuaged by the prospect. But Pastor Steve had a way of relating all things to Scripture. And I was anxious to see if he could find a biblical context to redeem my ugly predicament. As I explained to him my disappointment with God and my confusion concerning God's plan for my life, Pastor Steve gently referenced Rom. 8:28: "We know that in all things God works for the good of those who love him, who have been called according to his purpose."

Then life-changing words came from my pastor friend: "Bob, I believe God may be calling you to Christian ministry. I've sensed it for some time, but now that one door has been so obviously closed, another door may be opening. Let's pray about it!"

Honestly, I don't remember much of the content of the prayer that followed. But I do recall the confidence with which my pastor prayed, as if he had known all along what God intended for my life. And I remember my father being there and the wondrous experience of having him take part in such a holy moment. It was a "Damascus road" experience; I felt "something like scales" falling from my eyes (see Acts 9:18) and God's calling being placed on my heart.

Helping me reflect on this experience, French Reformed minister and author Jean Cadier (1898–1981) speaks of the need for grounding our faith in a calling beyond preoccupation with one's self:

> I am thinking of the man who said to me a short time ago as he came out of a lecture, "I have been converted through reading the *Institutes*" [John Calvin's chief work (1536-60)]. And when I asked him to tell me what exactly had been the message which had effected this transformation in his life, he replied: "I learnt from reading Calvin that all the worries about health and about the uncertain future which had hitherto dominated my life were without much impor-

tance and that the only things that counted were obedience to the will of God and a care for His glory."[8]

In this spirit I was formed in Christian faith. It indicates the spirit of Reformed theology and the vocation of Christian holiness or "piety" (Calvin's word for genuine spirituality).

"True" Piety: The Vocation of Holiness

John Calvin was a man who seemed destined for a church vocation. Born outside of Paris in the little town of Noyon in Picardy, France, as a young man he was sent by his father to study theology at a strict boarding school. From there he went to the University of Paris, where he came in contact with the ideas of humanism and the teachings of Martin Luther. Sympathetic to the Reformation movement, he was forced to flee from France to Switzerland to avoid persecution. At Basel in 1536, he published the first edition of his *Institutes of the Christian Religion* in Latin. Later that year he was persuaded by a friend, Guillaume Farel, to settle in Geneva to assist in organizing the Reformation there. Apart from a brief subsequent exile in Strasbourg, Calvin spent the rest of his life in Geneva, writing, preaching, teaching, and supervising the articles of evangelical reform that touched on every aspect of life in the church and civil community.

While Calvin and the Reformed tradition have emphasized the sovereign majesty and lordship of the triune God revealed in Jesus Christ, they have just as strongly emphasized a personal and lived faith that exhibits true piety in the world. In numerous ways, Reformed Christians emphasize true piety (Christian holiness) as essential for Christian discipleship. They especially do this in their confessional and catechetical literature, which details expectations placed upon believers to live according to Christ's commandments. As theologian Richard Burnett points out, "Confessions . . . emerge out of persistent conflict over what the Scriptures teach about the Christian faith and living out that faith." Confessions of faith exist, not because Reformed Christians want to say more than the Bible says, but because they don't want to say less.[9]

Although Reformed Christians are not typically noted for their emphasis upon Christian holiness, or the doctrine of sanctification, this is not because of any deficit in their understanding or lack of valuing its importance. In fact, in Calvin's *Institutes of the Christian Religion* there are far more references to "sanctification" than to "predestination"—the doctrine that often popularly identifies the Reformed tradition. The Christian life, Calvin insisted, is one of conforming to God's will. Any form of worship or theology or polity (church government) that does not first glorify God and then lead to a life of holiness must be reconsidered or abandoned.[10] The call includes the whole of life. Indeed, Calvin insisted that the Christian life is not a matter of "the tongue but of the inmost heart," this truth being in "first place" because it is where our faith begins. "It must enter our heart and pass into our daily living, and so transform us into itself," in order that it might bear fruit in the form of true piety or holiness.[11]

Typical of Calvin's teaching on Christian holiness, he insisted that when we speak of "our union with God," we must always remember that "holiness must be its bond." If Christians are to be regarded as "the people of the Lord," we must answer his call to holiness and "dwell in the holy city of Jerusalem." To that end we were "rescued from the wickedness and pollution of the world in which we were submerged."[12]

True to the New Testament, Calvin insisted that Christian holiness has nothing to do with merit, and everything to do with "cleaving" to God in faith, with being "infused with his holiness," and then following him "whither he calls." The goal of Christian holiness is to glorify God in all things. It entails "having no fellowship with wickedness and uncleanness."[13]

Calvin's admonition is summarized in the Westminster Shorter Catechism (1646-47):

Q. 35. What is sanctification?

A. Sanctification is the work of God's free grace, whereby we are renewed in the whole [person] after the image of God, and are enabled more and more to die unto sin and live unto righteousness.[14]

Importantly, the emphasis is upon "more and more to die unto sin and live unto righteousness." Sanctification is a gradual and persistent process in which God's image is increasingly restored in believers. The process of sanctification must be manifest in self-denial, cross bearing, and contemplation on eternal life. Justification by grace through faith initiates the process of sanctification. In conversion, or new birth, following repentance, we are completely forgiven of sin and restored to a right relationship with God. Importantly, for Calvin, forgiveness is *logically* prior to repentance, that is to say, repentance is our response to God's gift of grace, not a condition for receiving it. God's goodness leads to repentance, not the other way around.[15]

Repentance is in two parts: (1) "mortification," or putting to death our "flesh"—that is, our fallen condition dominated by sinfulness, and (2) "vivification," the commitment to live a holy life characterized by God's Spirit dwelling within us.[16] Calvin taught that the object of regeneration (the change in our lives brought about by God) is to bring believers into a "harmony and agreement" between God's righteousness and their obedience, and thus to confirm the adoption they have received as sons and daughters.[17]

In his first Catechism (published in French in 1537 and in Latin in 1538), Calvin used the word "piety" as a kind of shorthand for Christian holiness, for understanding the faith and practice of Christian discipleship:

> True piety does not consist in a fear which willingly indeed flees God's judgment, but since it cannot escape is terrified. True godliness (*pietas*) consists rather in a sincere feeling which loves God as Father as much as it fears and reverences him as Lord, embraces his righteousness, and dreads offending him worse than death. And whoever have been endowed with this godliness dare not fashion out of their own rashness any God for themselves. Rather, they seek from him the knowledge of the true God, and conceive him just as he shows and declares himself to be.[18]

More succinctly, Calvin defined "piety" as "that reverence joined with love of God which the knowledge of his benefits induces."[19] To live with the knowledge of God's constant beneficence toward us is to learn to rely steadily on God, just as children do their parents or as one spouse does the other. Piety means loving God completely and recognizing that he is an active partner in our lives. "God" isn't a formal name that merely refers to an empty concept or a distant deity. Rather, God is intensely personal.

In Calvin's own words, God is "toward us" (Lat., *erga nos*).[20] This is more than a general disposition toward humanity as a whole, although this much is conveyed in Scripture.[21] "Toward us" is much more specific and intimate. It is the unshakable conviction, operative in every true believer, that he or she has received personal salvation in Christ. "Faith is nothing," Calvin insists, "unless we are certainly persuaded that Christ is ours and that the Father is propitious to us in him." Every believer may take comfort in knowing that God's mercy is extended specifically toward her or him and that the benefit is personal salvation.[22]

"Worldly Piety": Holiness in Practice

Calvin, the theologian, is rightly known and referred to as the "father of Reformed theology." If the only things he had accomplished in his professional career in Geneva were his writings in Bible and theology, this would be a prodigious accomplishment. Yet even more than a theologian and biblical commentator, Calvin practiced being a true pastor and friend to his flock. The beauty of his theology and biblical acumen flowed from the pulpit and written page and into the lives of everyday believers, aiding them in living the Christian faith more zealously. Calvin counseled that Christian holiness consists of conforming our lives to Christ. "Because the Father has reconciled us to Himself in Christ, therefore He commands us to be conformed to Christ as to our pattern."[23]

Conforming to this pattern is not merely imitation, as if we have it within ourselves to follow Christ without his aid. Rather, it begins in humble obedience, which is the true imitation of Christ. We must "exhibit the character of Christ in our lives,"[24] Calvin urges, but this comes only through the transforming power of the Holy Spirit. He cites Romans 12:1-2, where the apostle Paul warns us not to conform "to the pattern of this world, but be transformed by the renewing of your mind." Transformation first takes the form of "Self-Denial"[25] (that which pleases God and promotes his glory—self-control, uprightness or righteousness, godliness, respect for others, and seeking the good for others before our own). Second, transformation entails "Patience in Cross-Bearing."[26] Self-denial is challenging, Calvin observes, but bearing the cross is even more demanding. It is more than an adjustment of attitude toward the world and things of the world; it is rather an acceptance that "the hard, difficult, and painful circumstances of life" come from the very hand of God as means by which our lives are conformed to the image of Christ (Rom. 8:29).[27]

In a book that deals with suffering, Reformed theologian John Piper has an insightful chapter titled, "Don't Waste Your Cancer." He reflects on the time immediately after he was diagnosed and the lessons about God's sovereignty he learned during his suffering. "I believe in God's power to heal," Piper observes, "by miracle and by medicine." It is right and good for Christians to pray for both kinds of healing. Cancer is not wasted when God heals a patient, because then God gets the glory (cf. John 9:3). But healing is not always God's plan. What God permits happens as part of his design for our lives. That is how Piper makes the apparently outrageous statement, "You will waste your cancer if you do not believe it is designed for you by God."[28]

Piper's statement cannot be understood properly apart from Calvin's doctrine of providence and its relation to Christian life. By providence he means God's powerful activity in nourishing and maintaining his creation.[29] God is never aloof from his creation but is intimately involved in every aspect of its governance, as illustrated by Jesus's statement that "even the hairs of your head are all numbered" (Matt. 10:30, RSV).[30] Providence means "God's peculiar care over every one of his works."[31]

This was not a topic of idle speculation for Calvin; it came from someone who completely placed his faith in the infinite power and love of God. Calvin's own life was difficult, his body ravaged by serious diseases and his theological and political integrity challenged at every turn. Still, he clung to the belief that God's providence means he cares immediately and continually for everything and every person in creation. Calvin developed his doctrine of providence by reflecting on his conviction that God is a loving Father who cares deeply for his children.[32]

Where do Christians find the strength, the means, to persevere in faith when they are not only confronting the wiles of the devil but also being tested by God's hand? In answer to this question, Calvin devotes the last section of *The Institutes*, book 4, to explaining the church and the sacraments as means of grace. The means of grace are the ways God invites us into communion with him and graciously sustains us. In book 3, chapter 20, Calvin reveals what else has sustained his faith—prayer. He deals with the practice of prayer, not primarily with its doctrine. Once again he reveals himself as a true pastor. Prayer, Calvin counsels, is "the essence of the Christian life" and not an optional or occasional routine or habit.[33]

Persistent prayer should characterize the life of piety. Its regular practice, Calvin observes, is a principal exercise of faith and one way we receive the benefits of faith. In prayer we do not so much petition God to grant our requests as petition him to strengthen our discipleship. The purpose of prayer is to open God's heavenly riches stored up for us in Christ.[34] Still, Calvin urges, because of sin and our tendency toward irreverence, prayer must be governed by discipline. To that end, he prescribes four *rules of prayer* meant to aid in its practice.[35]

The first rule is that prayer should arise from authentic reverence. We should acknowledge that when praying, we are conversing with God and contemplating the benefits he bestows on us through faith. Not only is "devout detachment" from worldly distractions required, but so also is a "discipline" of mind and heart that overcomes our "inertia and dullness." The Holy Spirit must direct and empower us in prayer.[36]

The second rule is that "we pray from a sincere sense of want and with penitence," recognizing the poverty of our condition apart from God's sustaining hand. This doesn't mean, Calvin explains, that we should expect any less from God, for he is omnipotent, but that we must pray penitently in accordance with God's will.[37] We must pray intending to glorify God. The Shorter Catechism is helpful:

Q. 98. What is prayer?

A. Prayer is an offering up of our desires unto God, for things agreeable to his will, in the name of Christ, with confession of our sins, and thankful acknowledgement of his mercies.[38]

The third rule of prayer urges sincere humility and completely placing our trust in God. This entails abandoning all confidence in ourselves and earnestly pleading for pardon. We seek God's mercy in forgiveness of our sins, past and present. By this rule Calvin underscores the importance of true humility and sincerity. He insists that "no heart can ever break into sincere calling upon God that does not at the same time aspire to godliness."[39]

The fourth rule is that we must pray with a confident hope and assurance that our prayers will be answered. Such confidence is produced by the Holy Spirit working in us, not by anything we generate. Because of the covenant Christ makes with us (Reformed theology is often referred to as "Covenantal theology"), prayer is supported by confidence of success. "You may ask me for anything in my name," Jesus proclaimed, "and I will do it" (John 14:14). Therefore, we should approach God boldly and cheerfully, even when we think we cannot pray or when our words seem not to reach past the ceiling. Indeed, there are times when words fail or when our mood is less than generous toward God. But even "defective prayers" still reach the throne of God. In spite of all hindrances, our prayers please God; he will grant our petitions when they are made earnestly and humbly.[40]

The Sphere of God's Sovereignty

Christian holiness involves all aspects of life, religious and secular, for God is sovereign over all. In an inaugural address to the faculty of the Free University in Amsterdam (October 20, 1889), Dutch Reformed theologian and political leader Abraham Kuyper (1837–1920) famously summarized God's sovereignty. He declared, "There is not a square inch in the whole domain of our human existence over which Christ, who is Sovereign over *all*, does not cry: 'Mine!'"[41] This is what Reformed Christians believe about the extent of Christian holiness.

However, such inclusive divine ownership entails that Reformed Christians live with a significant measure of tension: they have an uneasy relationship with their surrounding culture. On the one hand, they participate in it as testimony to God's sovereign providence. On the other hand, in the name and power of Christ, they seek to reform it. Both convictions are imperative. Believing that the tension is entailed by God's sovereign rule, Reformed Christians don't shrink from the mandate. Their commitment to engage in and reform culture by restraining evil and promoting social righteousness distinguishes them from some other Christian traditions.[42]

Presbyterian theologian John Leith (1919–2002) elucidated the relationship between God's sovereignty and the role of Christian piety in the world.[43]

On the one hand, and predominantly, Christians should live each moment recognizing and appreciating God's sovereignty. God is the creator of heaven and earth, he maintains all things in their proper order, and he governs them by his will.[44] God sets the stars and planets in their celestial courses. He cares for the fragile grass of the plains and the lilies of the field (Luke 12:27-28) and attends to the well-being of mortals. He crowns them with glory and honor and grants them dominion over earthly species and systems (Ps. 8:5-8).

If God cares for the creation in this way, should we doubt that humans are any less the object of God's care (Matt. 6:25-34)? Even situations that appear to contradict God's beneficence are, in reality, "just so many proofs of heavenly providence, especially of [God's] fatherly kindness." Even in questionable instances, reasons for rejoicing are given to the godly wise who have ears to hear and eyes to see God's goodness (Matt. 11:15; 1 Cor. 2:9-10). But to unbelievers, the lessons to be learned in this "dazzling theater" of God's sovereignty go unheeded.[45]

On the other hand, recognition of God's sovereignty does not exempt Christians from active and responsible participation in and contribution to God's work in the world, including individual and social reform. According to Calvin, faithfully living this way manifests Christian holiness.[46]

A Godly Death

Discussion of Christian holiness apart from hope for a "godly death" would be incomplete. As pastor of a congregation, I am permitted into the private lives and experiences of my congregants in ways unmatched in most other professions. A typical day might begin with an early morning visit to the hospital for prayer before surgery. Later, in the same hospital, after breakfast in the cafeteria, I might visit a young couple welcoming the birth of their first child. I will offer a prayer of thanksgiving and hope. On my return to the office I will ponder the contents of my approaching Sunday sermon. No sooner do I continue preparing a message of hope from the gospel than the telephone rings. I learn that after a long battle with cancer, an elderly church member has died. Now I must go to offer comfort to the grieving family.

In one day my duties have brought me from the beginning of life, through the cycles of illness and aging, and to death. At each point my presence has been welcomed as one who represents God and the church. I am a gospel messenger, who announces Christian hope for life and death, instead of one who accepts the hopelessness that characterizes so many people and families.

There is nothing new about hopelessness. The Christian gospel came into a first-century Greco-Roman world, where a sense of fate (determinism completely void of ultimate meaning or purpose) ruled most people, whether slave or free. Similarly, fate as an inescapable power continues for many today. As a Christian minister, I often hear this disposition expressed: "It must have been in the cards," or "When your time's up, there's nothing you can do," or "Que sera, sera."

In radical contrast to acceptance of rigid determinism, Christians live and die in sure hope of a resurrection like that of their risen and reigning Lord (2 Cor. 4:14; 1 Thess. 4:13-18). Christian hope is founded on God's sovereign providence. The Father of our Lord and Savior is a loving God who fills our future with hope, joy, and peace (Rom. 15:13). When Christians face death, that "last enemy" (1 Cor. 15:26), they do so knowing that beyond the grave awaits the resurrection (vv. 20-58). Christians are "sanctified in Christ" (1:2), and Christ is in them; he is their "hope of glory" (Col. 1:27).

Members of the Reformed tradition are reminded of God's providential care and their Christian hope by the 1563 Heidelberg Catechism. Although death is an enemy, it is already a conquered enemy. The Catechism asks and answers:

Q. 1. What is your only comfort in life and in death?

A. That I belong—body and soul, in life and in death—not to myself but to my faithful Savior, Jesus Christ, who at the cost of his own blood has fully paid for all my sins and has completely freed me from the dominion of the devil; that he protects me so well that without the will of my Father in heaven not a hair can fall from my head; indeed, that everything must fit his purpose for my salvation. Therefore, by his Holy Spirit, he also assures me of eternal life, and makes me wholeheartedly willing and ready from now on to live for him.

Q. 2. How many things must you know that you may live and die in the blessedness of this comfort?

A. Three. First, the greatness of my sin and wretchedness. Second, how I am freed from all my sins and their wretched consequences. Third, what gratitude I owe to God for such redemption.[47]

Grounded in the certainty of the resurrection, Christians can in hope face the anxiety, even the anger associated with death. As the Catechism affirms, whether in life or death, the Holy Spirit "assures [us] of eternal life," for we are safely in the care of our heavenly Father.

Ad majorem Dei gloriam (to the greater glory of God)!

7

The Pursuit of Holiness in the Anglican Community

❖

Don H. Compier, PhD

The Very Rev. Dr. Don H. Compier is dean of the Bishop Kemper School for Ministry and canon theologian of the Episcopal Diocese of Kansas. He received a PhD in theology, Emory University. Dean Compier has published numerous books, including a coedited volume, *Empire and the Christian Tradition* (Fortress Press, 2007). The Academy of Parish Clergy named the book the best reference book of the year.

❖

And to all thy people give thy heavenly grace, and especially to
this congregation here present; that, with meek heart and due
reverence, they may hear and receive thy holy Word,
truly serving thee in holiness and righteousness
all the days of their life.
—"The Prayers of the People," Holy Eucharist: Rite I,
Book of Common Prayer

The Anglican Communion is the third largest Christian body in the world today. Approximately eighty-five million members in more than 165 countries are part of this branch of the Jesus movement. It is a loose confederation that grants considerable autonomy to its thirty-nine provinces and six "extra provincials" (free standing national or local churches). No wonder, then, that Anglicans are quite a diverse lot, displaying marked cultural, organizational, and theological differences—including definitions of holiness. In fact, disagreements about what constitutes godly living currently threaten to tear the Anglican Communion in two.[1]

My perspective is clearly influenced by my ministry, teaching, and scholarship in the Episcopal Church, just one of the provinces of the global Anglican Communion. We are established in seventeen nations, but the vast majority of our communicants live in the United States.[2] I have deliberately cultivated contacts with Anglicans in other nations, particularly in Latin America, where my fluency in Spanish facilitates communication.

In spite of Anglican diversity, Anglicans mostly agree on what is needed for sanctified living: common prayer. Nearly all assume that worshipping God "in the beauty of holiness"[3] transforms our lives as we grow in the likeness of Christ. Mostly, there is broad Anglican agreement on what human life conformed to Christ through regular encounters with the Holy One ought to look like. The emergence of this consensus over the course of church history offers testimony to God's sanctifying work in the various theological traditions, as well as in individual lives.

The Pursuit of Holiness through Common Prayer

The single most important instrument for the promotion of holiness in the Anglican Communion is the Book of Common Prayer (hereafter BCP). It has undergone considerable revision since the first edition of 1549. It has been translated into many languages and sometimes thoroughly adapted to national cultures. After careful review, new material expressing emerging insights has been included. Some of the variations are theologically significant. They also reflect the constant evolution of human languages.[4] Further revision of the BCP is always a hot topic, as it was at the most recent General Convention of the Episcopal Church in Austin, Texas (July 2018).[5] Matters such as inclusive and expansive language should not be minimized, for reasons to be addressed later. Anglicans can sometimes be quite fussy and even a bit fanatical about liturgical details and preferences. That is an inevitable temptation facing those who acknowledge the importance of right worship as a central tenet of faith and practice.

The basic purpose and form of the BCP has remained remarkably consistent since 1549. Even significant revisions remain in continuity with the Reformation's desire to make the Bible and public worship accessible to all the people in their own language. Throughout Anglican history the BCP has continually called us to regular communal adoration of God and to transforming encounter through Word and Sacrament.

Archbishop Thomas Cranmer (1489–1556) was the chief author and compiler of the first BCP and hence the principal architect of Anglicanism.[6] His preface to the first BCP clearly makes the connection between prayer and the pursuit of holiness. Referring to the fathers of the Christian church, he insisted that the "good purpose" of "common prayers" is "a great advancement of godliness" as the people are "inflamed with the love of [God's] true religion." Cranmer's strategies for pursuing these lofty goals have endured.

Let's consider the governing principle first. Anglicanism remains committed to *common prayer.* Cranmer sought "but one use" for "all the whole realme."[7] The BCP promotes communal, not merely individual, formation in sanctity. Doing research at the Bodleian Library in Oxford during the summer of 1994, I examined first editions of the 1549 and 1552 BCPs. They are large books intended for pulpit use. Cranmer assumed the populace would gather in their local church building twice a day, every day. Over time, this ideal became impractical; smaller formats of prayer for home use proliferated. Yet all were encouraged to follow the same written liturgies and use the same lectionary (portions of the Bible assigned for reading) of the Bible. Even when praying alone, an Anglican engages in a communal act.

Anglicans are often criticized for saying rote prayers, engaging in "vain repetitions." Certainly spiritual attention demands that we do more than repeatedly mouth the same words. When rightly practiced, however, common prayer constantly reminds us of the essential sociality of Christian faith. Frequent repetitions of set prayers, canticles, responses, and so on, mostly drawn from the Holy Scriptures, engrave their message on our hearts. The words seep into our subconscious and form our religious dispositions beyond mere intellectual apprehension. They engage our whole being.

Shared prayers can promote the vital spiritual virtue traditionally known as obedience. If we are to grow in holiness, we must surrender our will to God and commit ourselves to the good of the whole beloved community. We accept the words authoritatively selected and offered to all and abandon our willful desire for unique and isolated religious experience.

111

Moreover, precisely because the words are established, they can serve as platforms for launching into profound contemplation. To use a musical analogy, jazz artists only achieve improvisational heights when the scales, chords, keys, time signatures, and shared melodies are thoroughly first absorbed. Anglican poets like George Herbert attest to the rich inner spiritual life that can be realized by those who follow the pattern set out in the BCP.[8]

In harmony with this normative understanding of spirituality, the BCP urges the pursuit of concrete paths that foster holiness. For most of Anglican history the principal form for advancement in godliness has been the daily office. Derived from the ancient monastic practice known as the hours, the daily office is meant to provide a regular pattern for constant prayer every day. At set times participants read psalms, hear readings of passages of the Bible, and say the Lord's Prayer and other petitions. Before the late twentieth-century ecumenical revival influenced revisions of the BCP, on most Sundays, morning prayer was the chief office. Many value Sunday evening evensong that includes the oft-glorious choral version of evening prayer. The practice of weekly Eucharist became common for most Anglicans less than a half century ago.

In his preface to the 1549 BCP, Cranmer clearly assumed the centrality of the daily office. His chief aim was to assure "that all the whole Bible (or the greatest parte thereof) should be read over once in the yeare." Cranmer wanted nothing used in prayer but "the very pure worde of God, the holy scriptures, or that whiche is evidently grounded upon the same."[9] The BCP continues the practice of *lectio divina*, carefully listening to the ancient texts of Holy Scripture and believing that God's Spirit still speaks directly to us today in this way.[10] Holy life can be realized only by intentional daily attention to God's living Word.

Cranmer's contribution to monastic spirituality was revolutionary. It consisted of his insistence that the benefits of praying the hours should be available to all members of the commonwealth, not to monks and nuns alone. The rules for prayer, therefore, should be "plain and easy to be understood."[11] Only two books were needed: the Bible and the BCP. Cranmer surely knew that ordinary people could not follow the monks and nuns in praying seven or eight times daily. So he prescribed only daily morning and evening prayer. The 1979 BCP and other results of liturgical renewal also include short rites (set orders of service) for noonday prayer and compline (prayers before retiring for the night).

Like many Anglicans, I regularly observe the daily office. We teach students preparing for lay or ordained ministry to do the same. Allow me to offer a brief account of how ordered daily prayer can foster Christian holiness.[12]

Each of the four offices (morning prayer, noonday prayer, evening prayer, and compline [prayer before retiring for the night]) begins by placing participants in the presence of God, which evokes praise. Sometimes confession and remission of sins is a precondition. That option is included at the outset in morning prayer, evening prayer, and compline. Spiritual directors often recommend this penitential practice on Fridays and during Lent. When ready to come before the divine throne, worshippers at various points make repeated use of the ancient *Gloria*: "Glory to the Father, and to the Son, and to the Holy Spirit: as it was in the beginning, is now, and will be for ever. Amen."[13] An "alleluia" may be added in all seasons except Lent. At morning and evening prayers additional hymns of praise and thanksgiving, mostly drawn from the Bible, follow. They are interspersed with the reverent reading of Holy Scripture. Selections from the Psalms always come first, in accordance with monastic tradition. Many recognize, as Dietrich Bonhoeffer reminded us, that the Psalms comprised the prayer book of Jesus of Nazareth. So we pray along with our Lord.[14]

After immersion in *lectio divina* (reading Scripture, meditation, and prayer) according to the prescribed lectionary reading for the daily office, we recite the Apostles' Creed. This is done in the morning and evening. This statement of trust is accepted at baptism and invoked at Christian burial. The creed reminds participants of *who* they are: citizens of the reign of God, members of the body of Christ. More importantly, participants recall *whose* they are: persons "marked as Christ's own forever."[15]

In the second part of the daily office, Anglicans offer their prayers of thanksgiving and intercession to God. In agreement with the principle of obedience, worshippers always begin by praying the Lord's Prayer. Set responses and collects (written prayers that "collect" us all in prayerful unity) follow. They include multiple references to sanctified living. For instance, responses after the Lord's Prayer ask God to "create in us clean hearts" and "keep us from all sin today."[16] Collects hope that we may do God's "will with cheerfulness during the day"; remind us that "to know [God] is eternal life and to serve [God] is perfect freedom"; and plead that "in all we do" we may be "direct[ed] to the fulfilling of [God's] purpose."[17]

A collect for mission must always be said. We pray for the whole church's faithfulness in fulfilling its vocation, for the worldwide expansion of God's reign, and for the care of all persons in all conditions. We pray that we may share in the work of Christ crucified so "that we, reaching forth our hands in love, may bring those who do not know you to the knowledge and love of you."[18] Only after this orientation and formation of our desires and affections may we offer our own petitions and expressions of thanksgiving.

Morning and evening prayers draw to a conclusion with two prayers, the second being "A Prayer of St. Chrysostom."[19] The vocation of holiness finds clearest expression, however, in the "General Thanksgiving," whose original form may well be a private prayer of Queen Elizabeth I (r. 1558–1603).[20] In its words we pray that we may "giv[e] up our selves to your service . . . walking before you in holiness and righteousness all our days." Finally, worshippers bless the Lord, and in the morning and evening they are sent forth through one of three Scripture texts that praise God and urge faithful living. The selection from Ephesians 3:20-21, for instance, glorifies God who "working in us, can do infinitely more than we can ask or imagine."[21]

Recovery of regular Eucharistic observance in the Anglican Communion is commendable. But unfortunately it has unintentionally tended to obscure the lasting importance of the daily office. Parishioners must receive regular reminders that the whole and holy purpose of the BCP cannot be realized if the hours are neglected. We need daily formation. Sundays alone do not suffice!

Holy Communion (the Eucharist) is now regularly celebrated each Sunday in most Anglican congregations. In some places, such as theological schools, Holy Communion may even be offered several times a week. In versions of the BCP that followed liturgical renewal (e.g., the Episcopal Church's 1979 edition), various Eucharistic prayers may be used. The number of options is increasing as inclusive and expansive language alternatives are authorized.[22] The Anglican Communion has not developed a definitive position on the long-debated question of the mode of Christ's presence in the elements of bread and wine.[23] Consequently, Anglicans hold diverse theological concepts about the nature, operation, and fruits of the Lord's Supper.

Once we approach the Eucharist with an interest in holiness, however, we once again find there has been remarkable consistency since 1549.

Anglicans believe Holy Communion both symbolizes and is an actual occasion for transformative encounter and exchange. Language used in the BCP and other authorized liturgies clearly demonstrates the central emphasis upon holiness in Anglicanism: believers become holy by being *conformed* to Christ, changed into his image and likeness to do his work in the world. Each person at the Lord's Table is made a member of Christ, knit into his one body.

Let's examine some passages in the 1979 BCP that clearly illustrate the emphasis on holiness in the Eucharist. Rite I's anaphora (the extended prayer the celebrant says prior to the Lord's Prayer and administration of Communion) culminates in language originating in Cranmer's 1549 edition. We offer "our selves, our souls and bodies" as a "reasonable, holy, and living sacrifice" to God. By doing this we receive Christ's very life, "the most precious Body and Blood of thy Son Jesus Christ." In this sacred exchange we are "made one body with him, that he may dwell in us, and we in him."[24]

The more modern versions of Rite II offer two options for the post-Communion prayer. Both stress that communicants have become "living members" of Jesus Christ. They are now sent out to love and serve God. The second variant asks God to "send us out to do the work you have given us to do . . . as faithful witnesses of Christ our Lord."[25]

Accounts abound of conversion while participating in the Eucharist in an Anglican setting. Permit a personal testimony. In 1988 the Eucharist drew me to be confirmed in the Episcopal Church. I was raised in a "low church" (nonliturgical) tradition that celebrated the Lord's Supper once a month and stressed the "memorial" understanding of the Lord's Supper, and covenant renewal. I had never experienced anything like the Anglican celebration of the Eucharist. But once tasted, I yearned for the envisioned Eucharistic encounter with Christ at least weekly. Consequently, I am deeply grateful for the good fruits of the ecumenical liturgical reform movement of the twentieth century. I understand why the Eucharist was always cherished by great minds and souls in the Anglican tradition and why it now occupies such a central place in Episcopal piety. As a teacher and writer, I stress the sanctifying power of grace expressed through the effectual symbols of Holy Communion.[26]

As always, however, we need to be cautious lest even the Eucharist become an idol, an end in itself. The Eucharist is by no means the only vehicle the BCP provides for cultivating holiness. In addition to the daily office, the BCP includes additional ways to teach us how God blesses and calls us at every juncture of life: from birth (infant baptism and thanksgiving for the birth or adoption of a child) through conscious commitment to the way of Christ (confirmation). The junctures also include marriage, sickness, and death (last rites and burial). And when we stray from the way, reconciliation is always available through confession, penance, and absolution.[27] God might call us to special ministries as lay leaders, deacons, priests, and bishops. At the proper time and setting, the community gathers in set liturgies to solemnize these holy occasions.[28]

Holiness is also promoted through a much more robust observance of the seasons of the Christian year. They are linked to *The Revised Common Lectionary*'s three-year cycle. The seasons are Advent, Christmas (twelve days!), Epiphany, Lent, Holy Week, the Easter Season, Pentecost, and the "ordinary time" after Pentecost. These Christian seasons sanctify by drawing communicants into a yearly retelling and reliving of the great history of salvation.[29] Pulpits, altars, and clergy are customarily decorated with vibrant colors, appropriate to each season, as aesthetic means of formation in holiness. They include penitent purple or anticipatory blue for Advent (always purple for Lent) and celebratory white for Christmas and Easter. Others are blazing red for Pentecost (and any occasion of the Spirit's fiery blessing, such as confirmations and ordinations), and the green of growth for Epiphany and the season after Pentecost. A sparing use of the black of mourning on Good Fridays and sometimes at funerals (where resurrection white may be more appropriate) is striking.

The fact that green is used more than half of the year points to the importance of growing in holiness. The fruit of all God's saving work in Christ and the sending of the Spirit are lives increasingly set apart to do God's work in the world. "Ordinary time" in the liturgical year is actually extra-ordinary; in it we proclaim the incredible good news that we humans, with all our shortcomings, are divinely called to become participants and even coauthors of the sacred story. We are participants in salvation history. According to one of Anglicanism's best-known authors, C. S. Lewis, all people are invited to share in the glory revealed at Christ's transfiguration. That means no time is ordinary and neither is any person.[30]

Regular devotion to worship of the Holy One is in itself a major part of any proper definition of holiness. In its various forms, Anglican common prayer expresses the invitation extended to everyone to commune with the Holy Trinity in everlasting life. We are called to love God with our whole being. We are also called to love our neighbors as ourselves (Mark 12:29-31). The devotions commended in the BCP plant the Word of God in us. But as the Epistle of James reminds us, listening to the Word is not enough. We must also "do what it says" (1:22). At the end of every worship service, Anglicans are sent out to engage in God's mission in the world. In the words of Rite I's post-Communion prayer, we ask for God's help so that we may "do all such good works as thou hast prepared for us to walk in."[31]

Now let's consider what some of those "good works" are.

Holy Praxis in Anglicanism

"Praxis" is a useful term derived from Latin American liberation theology. It indicates that we strive not to perform a good deed here and there but to form holistic Christian lifestyles that anticipate dwelling in God's reign.[32] Anglican clergy often deliver sermons based on Micah 6:8:

He has shown you, O mortal, what is good.

And what does the LORD require of you?

To act justly and to love mercy

and to walk humbly with your God.

Walking humbly with God spells out in practice the devotion discussed in the previous section. Anglicans generally believe that just and merciful actions must include more than personal purity or charitable giving. Holy living seeks to sanctify the whole world so that it will increasingly conform to God's reign of peace and justice.

Personal morality is not neglected. Cultural differences persist, but in Western nations Anglicans tend to practice moderation. They strive to avoid being judgmental and exclusive. After some struggle, Anglicans accepted birth control.[33] Sexual promiscuity is strongly discouraged. The sanctity of marriage is upheld, for instance, by requiring premarital counseling. Yet divorced and remarried persons can be members in good standing. After proper consideration by a bishop in accordance with the canons (laws) of the church, they may even serve as clergy.[34] There is zero tolerance for child abuse, sexual harassment, predatory sexual behavior, clergy adultery, and the like.[35] Anglicans have long permitted moderate use of alcohol. But policies have been strengthened that strongly oppose alcoholism and driving while drunk.[36]

Anglicans have always been encouraged to practice charity. Archbishop Cranmer associated gifts for the poor with the Eucharist. Justin Martyr (AD 100–165) did also.[37] In 1547 Cranmer issued regulations placing "the poore mennes [men's] boxe" near or even attached to the altar.[38] The BCP of 1549 urged congregants to come forward to deposit their offerings in the coffer, "every one accordynge to his habilitie and charitable mynde."[39] Today Anglicans operate and support a variety of organizations that feed the hungry, aid refugees and migrants, and provide relief for those affected by natural disasters. They provide pastoral care for prisoners, support schools, care for neglected children by organizing foster parenting, adoption, and orphanages. Anglicans also encourage economic development in poorer nations.

Holy praxis also entails promoting peace and justice in society, understood as striving to usher in God's reign. This dimension of Christian holiness developed slowly in Anglican history. Ours was, after all, the established Church of England and its overseas colonies. Even in the United States, as any visit to a historic Anglican church building will attest, the Episcopal Church was often preferred by the rich and powerful. They could fund superb architecture, works of art, and organs. They paid for splendid vestments, candlesticks, and liturgical utensils.

Hence for centuries, few Anglicans recognized any conflict between their religious profession and perpetuating marked class differences and economic inequality. As in society at large, women were usually relegated to inferior roles. Anglican clergymen accompanied and blessed colonizers and imperialists; they accepted the assumed superiority of Western culture and European ethnicity.[40] In the United States, priests regularly owned slaves.[41] In the Jim Crow era of forced racial segregation, Episcopal churches were often segregated. Separate ecclesial jurisdictions were created for African American communicants.[42] Even at the Lord's Table whites and blacks could not partake together.[43]

Demands for social justice were never absent in Anglicanism. In the seventeenth century, Archbishop William Laud (1573–1645) and Bishop Robert Sanderson (1587–1663) spoke up for peasants driven off the common grazing lands by agricultural entrepreneurs who bribed judges to manipulate land titles.[44] And evangelicals in the Church of England waged a fifty-year campaign to peacefully abolish slavery in the British Empire.[45]

So Anglicans did address what they considered gross abuses. But none of them envisioned a fundamental reorientation of society. The great majority of Anglicans readily endorsed the now suppressed third verse of the beloved hymn "All Things Bright and Beautiful," which declared,

> The rich man in his castle,
> The poor man at his gate,
> God made them high and lowly,
> And ordered their estate.[46]

Changes in the larger society—such as the growing strength of labor and anti-colonial, women's, and civil rights movements—often spurred needed repentance and reorientation in the church. "Incarnation" has been a leading theme in modern Anglican theology. It refers not only to Christ's coming in the flesh but also to God's continuing operation in, through, and with creation and history. The Holy Spirit is also active outside the church! God may call us to deepened holiness through any means, however unexpected.[47]

Holiness as a Work in Progress

As is true of all parts of Christ's church, the pursuit of holiness in the Anglican Communion is a work in progress. With the advantage of historical hindsight, we can look back over our history and give thanks for how God has been sanctifying the entire Anglican Communion.[48]

One notable mark of progress is found in the BCP's baptismal liturgy. Cranmer's 1549 rite stresses baptismal regeneration, salvation from sin and the devil. The interrogation prior to baptism required only a desire to "forsake the devil"; "the vaine pompe, and glory of the worlde, with all the covetouse desyres of the same"; and "the carnall desyres of the flesh."[49]

Today's baptismal liturgies don't neglect baptismal regeneration. But they add to it by encouraging a broader understanding of holiness. In the 1979 BCP, for instance, the first set of questions generally covers the same territory Cranmer's did. But now there is more emphasis on the generous lordship of Jesus Christ. Those baptized (or in the case of infants, their parents and godparents) promise to "put [their] whole trust in [Christ's] grace and love" and to "follow and obey him as [their] Lord."[50]

The whole congregation is then invited to renew its baptismal vows. This part of the liturgy is also used on other occasions, such as the installation of a new pastor. After reciting the Apostles' Creed, a robust Christian life is affirmed. All those present promise regularly to participate in the sacramental life, prayers, and companionship of the apostolic community. This includes repentance when needed. All those present pledge to participate in evangelism by "proclaim[ing] by word and example the Good News of God in Christ."[51] Charity is commended: "Seek and serve Christ in all persons."[52]

A final baptismal question best demonstrates the expanded understanding of holiness Anglicanism has embraced: "Will you strive for justice and peace among all people, and respect the dignity of every human being?"[53] The baptismal service summarizes this holistic approach to sanctification by declaring that all the baptized "share in the royal priesthood of Jesus Christ."[54] As is also expressed in the Eucharist, holy persons are those now being conformed to Christ, including doing all our Lord did on the world's behalf.

The church, consisting of the baptized, is correctly called "the extension of the Incarnation."[55] This means that the call to holiness requires that the church and all its members grow ever more into the image and likeness of our Lord, in harmony with all dimensions of Christ's life and ministry.

Sexism, racism, colonialism, neglect of children and the poor, and all kinds of oppression, discrimination, and abuse are simply incompatible with how Jesus welcomed everyone and affirmed the dignity and worth of every person. These "enfleshed" values of God's reign have the highest moral authority. This is why women are now ordained and eligible for the episcopacy in many (not yet all) parts of the Anglican Communion. Representatives from the Global South now form the majority at international gatherings. The Anglican Communion has embraced the Millennium Development Goals of the United Nations, advocating for the elimination of poverty in all the world.[56]

Legislation approved by the recent General Convention of the Episcopal Church demonstrates that we are willing to become quite specific in defense of human dignity. The bishops and deputies, for instance, called for comprehensive immigration reform, demanded an end to political gerrymandering and voter suppression, and deplored scapegoating in political discourse. They called for education about how the church was complicit in the physical and cultural genocide of Native Americans and insisted on the human rights of Palestinians. The General Convention also appropriated millions of dollars to advance racial justice and reconciliation with the goal of eliminating racism. These are not merely eloquent sentiments. Through the permanent presence of representatives at the United Nations and the United States Congress, and through mobilization of support through instruments such as the Episcopal Policy Network, these values are consistently and vigorously promoted.[57]

Conclusion

We Anglicans are painfully aware that we do not yet fully live up to our commitment to pursue Christian holiness in all aspects of life. For example, the Episcopal Church still overwhelmingly consists of persons of European origin,[58] and it is mostly led by males.[59] Moreover, our baptismal covenant does not yet include commitments to care for creation as God requires (Gen. 1:26). But in spite of our failures, we embrace an understanding of and commitment to living in full conformity to Jesus Christ. We are committed to being a continuation of God's incarnation in Jesus of Nazareth in the world.

8

Christian Holiness in the Baptist Tradition

❖

Harold Segura, PhD and David Wheeler, ThD

Harold Segura is a Colombian Baptist pastor and theologian, currently serving as director of Faith and Development for Latin America, World Vision International, in San José, Costa Rica. Formerly, he was rector of the Seminario Bautista International in Cali, Colombia.

David L. Wheeler is adjunct professor of theology, Palmer Theological Seminary, St. Davids, Pennsylvania. For fourteen years he served as professor of theology and ethics, Central Baptist Theological Seminary, Shawnee, Kansas. For eleven years he served as senior pastor, First Baptist Church, Portland, Oregon.

❖

As he who called you is holy, be holy yourselves in all your conduct; for it is written, "You shall be holy, for I am holy."
—1 Peter 1:15-16, NRSV

This chapter discusses Christian holiness as expressed in the Baptist tradition. The international family of Baptists[1] comprises some forty million believers. They reside in most countries. There are more than thirty self-identified Baptist groups in the United States and Canada alone.[2] Many Baptists understand themselves to be evangelicals. Others, perhaps most, simply define themselves as theologically, culturally, and politically conservative. But at the same time, there are others who declare themselves "progressives"[3] in these areas.

Across this wide spectrum, there are generally applicable "Baptist distinctives." They include (1) an emphasis on a personal relationship with Christ, often arising from an experience of being "born again"; (2) a strong view of biblical authority; (3) "soul liberty" in the interpretation of Scripture and other matters of conscience; (4) congregational autonomy; and (5) in most times and places, separation of church and state.

Fully describing the "Baptist view" of Christian holiness would take us on an overly long journey across several centuries and multiple cultures. So we need to establish limits.

We will examine a variety of doctrinal perspectives. We will not include (1) a theology of holiness at the origins of modern Baptist life in England and among English expatriates in the Netherlands at the turn of the seventeenth century; (2) the rapidly growing Baptist movement on the "western frontier" of the United States during the nineteenth century; and (3) global Baptists today. We will discuss Baptist leaders and theologians from the end of the nineteenth century to the present in the United States, Canada, and Latin America. And we will do this from the perspective of Christian holiness in Scripture, faith, and practice. In addition to English-speaking Baptists, we will include significant contributions by the growing Spanish-language Baptist tradition in the Americas.

Christian Holiness

Speaking of holiness as a quality of character and aspiration is not common among Baptists. The term "holiness" is seldom used. For example, the Baptist Association of Argentina (ABA) employs the term "holiness" only once in its eight-page confession of faith. The term is used in relation to the extent of God's grace:

> We believe that God, in his infinite mercy, expresses his grace for every person. He invites everyone who calls upon the name of the Lord to receive salvation in Jesus Christ. The work of grace in the life of the redeemed is comprehensive, given that it frees the believer from the power of Satan, pardons their sins, transforms their character and enables their progress toward maturity and holiness.[4]

Sanctification

Southern Baptist theologian Dale Moody stressed the importance of balance between the past, present, and future in the process of sanctification. "The lack of balance between the past, present and future in the process of sanctification has led to false ideas of Christian perfectionism."[5] His emphasis is typical among Baptists. Instead of "Christian holiness," Baptists more commonly speak of the process of "sanctification." The word comes from the Latin term *sanctus*, which means "holy," or, more literally, "holification." Sanctification is situated in a constellation of biblical terms that represent moments or phases of Christ's work in believers. Terms such as "regeneration," "new birth," "justification," and "reconciliation" are all construed as punctual, immediate, and decisive. They are relatively instantaneous changes of standing before God through Christ's intervention.

Christian sanctification is the lifelong process, superintended by the Holy Spirit, by which progress toward maturity and holiness is achieved. Over time we *become what we are* in Christ; our renewed standing before God unfolds through the development of spiritual gifts and Christian character. This is the "fruit of the Spirit" (Gal. 5:22-23, NRSV) that makes Christians more and more like Christ the Redeemer. Theologian and ethicist James William McClendon says sanctification is the "process of [the] gradual acquisition of holiness or moral purity, [and] growth in grace in contrast to justification."[6] Dale Moody adds that "progressive" sanctification has been characteristic of the broader Augustinian-Calvinist tradition so influential in Baptist life.[7]

From the moment of regeneration, God works to purify our bodies, which are the "temple of God" (see 1 Cor. 6:19), and our spirits. The book of Hebrews urges Christians to "strive for peace with all men, and for the holiness without which no one will see the Lord" (12:14, RSV).[8] In this regard, Dale Moody quotes John Calvin who says that "the Lord is daily at work in smoothing out wrinkles and cleansing spots"[9] American Baptist theologian and twentieth-century evangelical leader Carl F. H. Henry adds, "To be sure, the New Testament excludes the notion of sinless perfection in this life, of a state of righteousness possible to the people of God that exempts them here and now, even for a moment, from total dependence for salvation on the Savior's substitutionary work."[10]

But Christ's work in Christians through the Holy Spirit is not simply "promissory" or future. The Bible distinguishes sanctification from merely forensic justification (Rom. 8:1-17), on the one hand, and future glorification (v. 23), on the other. In the interim, we must "walk by the Spirit" until the final transformation when we are fully conformed to Christ's image (Gal. 5:16; 1 John 3:2-3).

These Baptist emphases derive not only from the Lutheran and Calvinist Reformation of the sixteenth century but also from seventeenth-century German Pietism. The importance of personal piety left an indelible mark on Baptists. This is not always recognized. Samuel Escobar, a Peruvian Baptist, comments, "It is a shame that the term 'pietist' has acquired a negative connotation." He adds that "taking into account history and human necessity, we need to recover this dimension of our faith and recognize that intense personal piety must by no means be divorced from serious theological reflection, or social commitments and missionary action."[11]

The importance of Pietism is notable in Latin American Baptist life, where, along with Anabaptist ideas and principles, it has gained major influence. We will see how this plays out in a Baptist understanding of Christian holiness.

Spiritual Formation

The process of sanctification is the clearest Baptist similarity to language about holiness as used in some other Christian traditions. However, recently new language and practices have entered Baptist life: the disciplines of spiritual formation. American Baptist theologian Molly T. Marshall, president of Central Seminary in Kansas, is a strong advocate of spiritual disciplines, traditionally associated with Roman Catholics. Marshall notes that "today in the Free Church context, attending to one's *spiritual formation* is considered as important as learning biblical exegesis, homiletical skills, theological and liturgical history and pastoral care."[12] Perhaps her observation here is most applicable to clergy education. But it is also more generally applicable. Followers of Jesus, in obedient faith, can be active participants in the process of sanctification. Sanctification is initiated and empowered by God, but not without our assent. "A bruised reed he will not break, and a dimly burning wick he will not quench" (Isa. 42:3, NRSV).

Marshall asks, "How does God's work of transformation occur in our lives?" She answers that we should consider spiritual formation as God's "unfinished business. As John's first epistle puts it, 'it does not yet appear what we shall be' (1 John 3:2), but we have traces, inchoate longings, the welling up of hope, all of which are crafting our grace-full participation in the ways of Christ."[13]

Much of Baptist life in Latin America originated from evangelism and church planting by predominately conservative Baptist missionaries from the United States. The Baptist presence expanded among nominal Roman Catholics. It actually fed off of opposition to the Catholics by many missionaries. But ironically, the strong residual Catholicism of many Latin American Baptists has furnished a fertile soil for encouraging spiritual formation.

In Latin American countries, one of the most important factors for understanding and practicing the spiritual disciplines has been the work of Richard J. Foster, a North American of Quaker background. Foster presents twelve spiritual disciplines, arranged in three groups: inward, outward, and corporate. All three are well known as traditional spiritual practices. The inward disciplines are meditation, prayer, fasting, and study. The outward ones are simplicity, spiritual retreats, submission, and service. The corporate disciplines are confession, worship, counseling, and joy. Together they can lead Christians from superficiality to the depths of the Christian life.

Foster agrees with Latin American Baptists that God who authors transformation gave the disciplines as ways to receive his grace. Through the spiritual disciplines, Jesus's disciples open themselves to transformation. Christians are similar to farmers; they can't produce grain but must provide the conditions needed for its production. One who practices the disciplines "sows to the Spirit" (Gal. 6:8, NKJV). This is the path *of* "disciplined grace." Practice of the disciplines has helped promote a spirit of ecumenism that seeks to overcome traditional conflicts between Latin American evangelicals and Catholics.[14]

God's Holiness

Most often, when language about holiness is used in Baptist circles, the reference is to God´s holiness. God's holiness is defined as (1) otherness from created reality; (2) moral perfection; (3) unlimited being, power, and wisdom; and (4) the maximum presence of love, mercy, and justice. God's holiness is the foundation and starting point for talking about Christian holiness. The strong Baptist tradition of practical piety quickly applies language about God's holiness—his very being—to practical ends.

Baptist theologian Stanley Grenz said, "'God is holy' means that God is completely upright, fair, just and righteous in treatment of creatures. Not only is God morally perfect, he is the standard for morality."[15] To the extent that human holiness can be attained, preserved, and exercised, it is a function of divine holiness. It is never preserved and effective outside of relationship to the holy God. Grenz continues, "Our participation in the divine image affects us in the present. Even now we are being transformed into the image of Christ (2 Cor. 3:18). This renewal carries implications for how we should live: we must 'put on the new self, created to be like God in true righteousness and holiness (Eph. 4:24; cf. Col. 3:9-10)."[16]

Personal and Corporate Holiness

Baptists have most often thought of holiness as *personal* holiness. Retired Texas Baptist pastor Jerry L. Ervin says, "We live in a world that is increasingly ungodly and wicked."[17] In such a world, "we are set apart for God's service and work [1 Pet. 1:14]."[18] This entails avoidance of vulgar language, adultery, same-sex relationships, and other evils. When we are surrounded and beset by these, we must "pray without ceasing" (1 Thess. 5:17, KJV), knowing that we were "chosen . . . in him before the foundation of the world, that we should be holy and without blame" (Eph. 1:4, KJV).[19]

This moral content of Christian holiness is strongly emphasized by Latin American Baptists. Neo-Calvinist[20] Miguel Núñez, pastor of the International Baptist Church in Santo Domingo, Dominican Republic, and president and founder of Integrity and Wisdom Ministries, is one of its strongest proponents. A gifted preacher, Núñez frequently teaches about Christian holiness. He says it is difficult "to watch television, go to the movies, stroll down the street or use social media without exposing ourselves to different expressions of sin so frequently that the great majority of these dangerous exposures go unnoticed." His preaching frequently includes controversial topics such as homosexuality, abortion, and the empowerment of women in society (the so-called ideology of gender).[21]

On the other hand, in North and South America, among Baptists there is a strong tradition of communal or corporate holiness. This emphasis is rooted in the Old Testament prophets and in Jesus's kingdom teaching. At the height of the Civil Rights movement, in his "Letter from a Birmingham Jail" (1963), Baptist minister Martin Luther King Jr. explained to Birmingham's white clergy why he was there. He was present because injustice was present. He was confident that in his opposition to forced segregation and its abuses, he stood in the lineage of Old Testament prophets such as Amos and Micah, who, in the Lord's name, traveled from their hometowns to expose and condemn the exploitation of the poor. He also believed he was following the apostle Paul, who left

Tarsus to proclaim the gospel of liberation in Roman cities and towns. Dr. King was keenly aware of the systemic nature of injustice. Injustice anywhere, he believed, spreads injustice everywhere.[22]

Decades earlier, Baptist pastor and theologian Walter Rauschenbusch gained notoriety as "father of the social gospel." Beginning as pastor of a German Baptist congregation in Hell's Kitchen, New York City, Rauschenbusch became a highly influential teacher and writer. Although he was often accused by conservative critics of replacing evangelism with social work, roots of his social consciousness lay in his personal experience with Jesus Christ. "I am a Baptist," he said, "because in our church life we have a minimum of emphasis on ritual and creed, and a maximum of emphasis on spiritual experience."[23]

Through his own experience, Rauschenbusch understood that no one forms his or her character in isolation. For twenty years he met with three other Baptist pastors in Hell's Kitchen for prayer, for mutual encouragement, and to read devotional classics by Augustine, Thomas à Kempis, John Bunyan, and others.[24] Consequently, he knew that personal holiness and corporate holiness are indissolubly connected. While experiential knowledge of God is vital, it must open out into passionate social engagement and ethics. Rauschenbusch insisted that "decline [in] our spiritual life, if it lasted long enough, brought in its train a corresponding decline in our moral vigor."[25]

Holiness, Reason, and Ethics

With respect to both personal and communal holiness, Baptists of all stripes are consistent in construing holiness—or (more often) a Christian lifestyle—primarily in ethical terms. A team of influential African American Baptists addressed this topic in *American Baptist Quarterly*: "African-American spirituality is unembarrassed by displays of sincere emotion, but it is also related to faith and action in the world. The Holy Spirit moves, therefore, in the world of everyday life, in the sanctuary and in the realm of secular affairs."[26]

Baptist faith and practice also evidence the strong influence of reason. Disciplined study of Scripture yields a plan of salvation and guidelines for holy living. These principles can be extracted inductively from Holy Scripture. E. Y. Mullins, president of The Southern Baptist Theological Seminary (Louisville, Kentucky) from 1899 until his death in 1928, gave classic expression to this strand of Baptist DNA in his 1908 book,

The Axioms of Religion: A New Interpretation of the Baptist Faith. "Truth," Mullins taught, "apprehended and obeyed is the way of God's Kingdom in making men holy. 'Sanctify them through thy truth, thy word is truth' was the prayer of Jesus."[27] Mullins identified seven "Spiritual Laws of the Kingdom" which "must be respected in any and every ecclesiastical polity which can lay any claim to biblical warrant."[28] His seventh principle is the "Law of Holiness": "This implies that all the means adopted in the church must be adjusted to the ends of personal and social holiness, and not merely ceremonial righteousness and empty orthodoxy."[29] Mullins's "Law of Holiness" reflects the influence of Dutch Calvinists on early English Baptists. That influence continues in Baptist considerations of holiness.

The role of reason in understanding and applying Scripture to holy living is combined with an intense Jesus piety widely characteristic of Baptists. Christian life is often simply described as "following Jesus." But what does this mean? Does it look more like the personal holiness described above by Jerry Ervin? Or does it look more like intervention on behalf of the oppressed as described by Martin Luther King Jr.? For Baptists, "following Jesus" includes both.

In Latin America, a group of noted Baptist theologians, among them C. René Padilla, Samuel Escobar, Rolando Gutiérrez, and the late Orlando Costas, have since the late 1970s advocated a view of holiness closely associated with social ethics. They form part of the Fraternidad Teológica Latinoamericana (FTL; "Latin American Theological Fraternity"), organized in 1970 in Cochabamba, Bolivia.[30] Their position appears in the final document of the Lausanne Covenant (1974)[31] in the section titled "Christian Social Responsibility." The statement has been quite influential in Latin America. It states, "The message of salvation implies also a message of justice, opposing every form of alienation, oppression and discrimination, and we should never be afraid to denounce evil and injustice wherever they exist."[32]

The statement appeared during a debate about the influence of the theology of liberation in Latin America. The Baptist theologians insisted that evangelization should be united with social transformation, thus overcoming the necessity of political revolution. "When persons receive Christ, they are born again into his kingdom and should seek not only to exhibit but to propagate the justice of his kingdom in the midst of a sinful world. The salvation that we claim to have should be transforming us in the totality of our personal and social responsibilities. Faith without works is dead."[33]

Following Jesus Freely

Christian holiness entails establishing a clear trajectory of goals and actions. Jesus said, "If any want to become my followers, let them deny themselves and take up their cross daily and follow me" (Luke 9:23, NRSV). Human freedom is an essential part of being created in God's image (Gen. 1:26-31). The decision to follow Jesus is freely taken. God continues to take the risk of honoring our freedom (cf. Josh. 24:14-15; Isa. 42:1-3; Rev. 3:20). In Jesus's own ministry, some said yes to his invitation (Matt. 4:18-22; 9:9) while others refused (19:16-22). E. Y. Mullins included essential human freedom among his "Spiritual Laws": "Christian liberty is limited only by the spiritual environment. But the inner impulse to personal and social development under Christ is like an endless spring fixed in the machinery of man's faculties and uncoiling itself through the centuries in ever-increasing vigor and power."[34]

But we are not left to achieve Christian holiness on our own. We rely upon the power of Jesus, mediated through the Holy Spirit (Rom. 8:9-11; Gal. 5:16-26). Outside of our relationship with Christ, we can neither establish nor pursue godly goals. Molly Marshall counsels that "the knowledge of glory is delivered in Jesus (2 Cor. 4:6). The saving deeds of Jesus make known the mystery of Glory, hidden from the ages past, to all the nations (Rom. 9:23). Incorporation into Christ transfers glory to the believer."[35]

The Holy Spirit and Christian Holiness

In their faith and practice, Baptists have tended to understate the role of the Holy Spirit.[36] But a survey of Scripture displays the breadth of the Holy Spirit's role in creation and redemption. There is a harmony between the saving work of Christ and the transforming work of the Spirit. The Spirit is the wind and breath of God present at creation (Gen. 1:1-2; 2:7) and the divine power and insight that moved heroes and prophets (Judg. 15:14-15; Isa. 61:1-4). The Holy Spirit is present and active at the beginning of Jesus's ministry (Luke 3:21–4:15). To his disciples, Jesus promises the coming of the Holy Spirit to continue Jesus's ministry (John 14:16-18; 16:13-15; Acts 1:4-8).

In *Spirit of the Living God*, Dale Moody surveys the Holy Spirit's activity in transforming believers. He concentrates on the Epistle to the Romans, especially chapter 8. Following Paul, Moody emphasizes that the indwelling Spirit "of the one who raised Jesus from the dead" will also be the agent of "our overcoming of death" (see Rom. 8:9-11).[37] Living according to the Holy Spirit rather than "according to the flesh" leads to a life and to the status of children of God who are set free from fear (vv. 10-17, NRSV). "When we cry, 'Abba! Father!'" the Holy Spirit is "bearing witness . . . that we are children of God" (vv. 15-16, NRSV). And if we are children, then we are heirs, "heirs of God and joint heirs with Christ" (v. 17, NRSV). The Spirit gives us hope as we wait for the eschatological transformation of the entire wounded creation (vv. 18-25). The Spirit intercedes for us as we pray in a way that transcends our own awareness and intentions (vv. 26-27).[38]

Carl Henry echoes Moody: "The Spirit fashions a new mindset for those who were formerly hostile to God (Rom. 8:5-7), a mindset that prizes God´s truth, and stimulates whole-hearted obedience to his will. The Spirit, moreover, provides the dynamic for defying sin and its temptations."[39]

A small number of Latin American Baptists favor a broader understanding of the Spirit's work in the process of sanctification. The Holy Spirit, they maintain, acts not only in the spiritual realm but also in the material. He is active on the stage of human history and in all creation. These Baptists relate Christian holiness to ecology, politics, and all other human interests. For example, Ecuadorian-Argentine Baptist theologian René Padilla insists that "the action of the Spirit in connection with matters that the majority of Christians consider merely secular forms a basis to, at the very least, ask ourselves at what point is it justified to limit the work of the Spirit to the sphere of redemption and the church."[40]

Christian Holiness: "Already" and "Not Yet"

As we noted earlier, for Baptists, sanctification has typically been understood as growth in the image of Christ and, more recently, as spiritual formation. Both expressions refer to the initial realization of the new humanity Christ gives his disciples in the event of regeneration, or new birth. But a full realization of Christ's image does not happen in the present age. Sin remains universally present for individual Christians. The apostle Paul speaks of the ongoing struggle between the old and the new for believers (Rom. 7:14-25). But sin is also *structural*. It pervades social systems, political parties, economic systems, and family relationships. These realities require a current and ongoing Spirit-powered "project" of transformation and a confident hope in God's present and future provisions for us.

American Baptist ethicist Emilie Townes speaks from the context of dreams deferred and justice denied in the African American experience. She ponders the distinction between our present fullness in Christ and the incompletion still to be overcome as we work to "stare down the interior life of the cultural production of evil." "Live your life deeply," she says. "This is not a quest for perfection, but for what we call in Christian ethics the everydayness of moral acts."[41]

Sanctification is *eschatological,* which means that having been initiated, it proceeds toward completion at Christ's return. The divine promise of completion draws our present into God's future. Believing that the process can be completed now makes us vulnerable to self-righteousness. It threatens to short-circuit an unceasing pursuit of the holiness God made humanly real in Christ Jesus (Heb. 12:14; 1 Pet. 1:14-16). The influential Baptist theologian Augustus H. Strong (1836–1921) explained that "although in regeneration the governing disposition of the soul is made holy, there still remain tendencies to evil which are unsubdued (Rom. 8:12). . . . Thus the existence of these two opposing principles gives rise to a conflict which lasts through life" (cf. Gal. 5:17; 1 Tim. 6:12).[42]

Stanley Grenz puts it this way:

Although we enjoy a foretaste in the present, our full participation in the divine image lies ultimately in the future. Conformity to Christ . . . is the glorious destiny that awaits us when Jesus returns (Rom. 8:29). . . .

. . . Therefore, being created in the divine image is a process which begins in conversion and continues until the great future day when God brings us into full conformity with the divine goal for us.[43]

This typical Baptist understanding of sanctification as an unending process in this life joins with the theme of following Jesus. As far back as Walter Rauschenbusch, on the one hand, traditional Baptists criticized the "social gospel" for placing "worldly concerns" ahead of what really matters: our eternal destiny. On the other hand, "progressive" Baptists criticized what they saw as an "otherworldly faith" that left injustice unchallenged. Baptists need not choose one or the other. Jesus proclaimed God's new world order, the kingdom of God. He accompanied his proclamation of the kingdom with deeds of power, casting out demons, healing the sick, feeding the hungry, and announcing "the year of the Lord's favor" (Luke 4:19, NRSV). He challenged his followers to do the same (Matt. 25:31-46).

In 1 Cor. 3:10-15, Paul compares the Christian life to a building project. Christ is the foundation, received as God's gift of grace through Christ. But Christians can build either well or poorly upon Christ the Foundation. The day of judgment will test that work. Following Jesus, modeling our lives after his, we are now building relationships, priorities, and values that will carry over into the life everlasting.

Conclusion

The contrasting emphases in the theology and practice of Christian holiness among Baptists that we have discussed are present among most evangelicals. Conversations among Baptists about the relationship between Christian holiness viewed as personal piety, on the one hand, and social transformation, on the other, can perhaps serve as a model for other Christian traditions. Both dimensions of holiness are present in the teaching and ministry of Jesus, and they are widely present in other parts of Scripture. Our hope in Christ is comprehensive, and it motivates every dimension of our lives. "Brethren, I count not myself to have apprehended: but this one thing I do, forgetting those things which are behind, and reaching forth unto those things which are before, I press toward the mark for the prize of the high calling of God in Christ Jesus" (Phil. 3:13-14, KJV).

9

The Vocation of Christian Holiness according to the Wesleyan Tradition

T. Scott Daniels, PhD

T. Scott Daniels is the senior pastor of the College Church of the
Nazarene and Pastoral Scholar in Residence, Northwest Nazarene
University, Nampa, Idaho. He served as dean of the School of Theology,
Azusa Pacific University, Azusa, California.

❧

Finish then Thy new creation;
  Pure and spotless let us be.
Let us see Thy great salvation,
  Perfectly restored in Thee:
Changed from glory into glory,
  Till in heav'n we take our place,
  Till we cast our crowns before Thee,
  Lost in wonder, love, and praise![1]

The Wesleyan theological tradition is that understanding of Christian
faith and practice initially authored by John Wesley (1703-91) and
Charles Wesley (1707-88). It has been refined by Wesleyan theologians
and the denominational bodies that compose it. The Wesleyan tradition
is firmly rooted in and formed by the Scriptures and historic Christian
faith and doctrine. It is immediately indebted to Anglicanism, its parent,

but is also shaped by the sixteenth-century Protestant Reformation, the Roman Catholic Church, Orthodoxy, and eighteenth-century Pietism.

Institutionally, the Wesleyan tradition is represented by the eighty Methodist, Wesleyan, and related Uniting and United Churches in 138 countries that compose the World Methodist Council. The council represents the 40.5 million members of the bodies that constitute it.

John Wesley and the Methodists

John Wesley was an ordained Anglican minister who served as a missionary, was an Oxford fellow, and (with his brother Charles and colleague George Whitefield) became the founder of Methodism. Initially, Methodism was not a denomination but an order Wesley birthed within the Anglican Church in hopes of renewing and reviving believers in Britain and the American colonies. Ever the organizer, Wesley formed Methodist societies that met weekly in gatherings called "classes" and "bands" that provided small accountability groups and settings for promoting holy living. Itinerant ministers—both men and women—were also trained and sent out to support the Methodist societies. The pursuit of the holy life for those early Methodists was not only personal but also social. Wesley and the Methodist societies created schools and orphanages for children and advocated on behalf of prison reform and the abolition of slavery.[2]

Wesley was a prolific writer. He wrote sermons, biblical notes or commentaries, hymns, letters, and a series of journals that spanned nearly fifty years of his life. Although sometimes critiqued by scholars and historians for not being a systematic theologian, Wesley chose instead to write and speak "plain truth for plain people: Therefore, of set purpose, I abstain from all nice and philosophical speculations; from all perplexed and intricate reasonings; and, as far as possible, from even the show of learning."[3] His plainspoken, pastoral methodology was designed not only for better understanding by the masses but also to protect those under his care from "formality, from mere outside religion, which has almost driven heart-religion out of the world."[4]

Consistent with the Protestant Reformers, who came two centuries before him, Wesley emphasized justification and salvation of believers by faith in Christ alone. There are, however, three unique doctrines or theological themes or emphases for which he and the theological tradition that carries his name are usually known.

The first is the rejection of the Calvinist or Reformed doctrine of pre-destination. In the theological world of his day, Wesley found himself between a convictional rock and a hard place. On the one hand, like his Reformed brothers and sisters, Wesley affirmed the total depravity of humankind after the fall of Adam and Eve. Apart from grace, no good thing could come from the human person, and certainly salvation could come only as a gift of God's grace. The problem was that this led Reformed thinkers to affirm a limited atonement and the unconditional election of some by God. These doctrines contrasted sharply with Wesley's more inclusive Arminian convictions. On the other hand, the way Roman Catholics and many Eastern Orthodox theologians avoided this problem was to insist that depravity was not total. For Wesley, this, too, was problematic, because it not only underestimated the impact of sin but also opened the door to thinking that a person might be saved—or even become morally good—apart from grace.

The solution to this conundrum, for Wesley, was the doctrine of prevenient grace. Prevenient grace is given to all persons. It precedes conversion (it pre-vents) and draws persons toward Christ. It makes possible a universal response to God's love and mercy–to moral responsibility—and the love of others. Prevenient grace also makes possible an ability (however limited) to reason and reflect to others (even if in marred ways) the nature of divine love.[5]

The second theological emphasis for which Wesley and the Methodists are widely known is the personal nature of salvation. This is particularly connected to the continuing witness of the Spirit in a believer's life.

As is often pointed out by critics of Wesleyan-Arminianism, the potential danger of abandoning the doctrine of election is the possibility that one might slip back into forms of works righteousness because of a lack of assurance for one's salvation. But for Wesley, neither works righteousness nor fear of losing one's salvation need happen to a believer. Salvation (and sanctification) is always a gift of grace, a grace that requires response but not "meritorious works." The opposite of eternal security need not be eternal insecurity. For Wesley, one can live deeply and freely *in* and *because* of the witness of the Spirit.

Drawing upon Romans 8:16—"The Spirit himself testifies with our spirit that we are God's children"—Wesley argued that although people are created and called to love God with their whole selves, a person cannot love God or neighbor fully until a person knows he or she has been born anew. Wesley explained,

> By the testimony of the Spirit, I mean, an inward impression on the soul, whereby the Spirit of God immediately and directly witnesses to my spirit, that I am a child of God; that Jesus Christ hath loved me, and given himself for me; that all my sins are blotted out, and I, even I, am reconciled to God.[6]

The third emphasis for Wesley—the primary focus of this chapter—is his conviction that although the work of God's grace in conversion is fundamental, God's decisive grace does not stop there. Using terms such as "sanctification," "holiness," and "Christian perfection," Wesley articulated a radical optimism in the power of God's grace to bring believers into a deeper renewal of God's image. Although Wesley's language about sanctification—especially the term "Christian perfection"—can be easily misunderstood, he saw this doctrine not only as explicitly biblical but also as the *telos* (Gk., "goal" or "purpose") of Christian faith.

To explore more fully Wesley's understanding of Christian holiness, let's begin by recounting a biblical story of deeply committed faith.

A Biblical Model

If I have a hero in Scripture (other than Jesus), it is Stephen. In Acts 6, Stephen is seized and brought in for interrogation before the Sanhedrin. They produce false witnesses against him, testifying that he was part of a plot to destroy the temple and damage the customs and laws of Moses.

In Acts 7, Stephen mounts his defense. His sermon to the high priest and the entire body of the Sanhedrin rehearses the history of Israel's rebellious ways toward God, and God's consistently gracious response. After generations of rejecting Moses and many other divinely commissioned prophets, God in his grace sends "the Righteous One" (v. 52). Once more the religious leaders not only reject the Lord's messenger but also kill him. (Like many of my favorite sermons, this one concludes by offending nearly everyone.)

Rather than receiving vindication for his remarks, Stephen is condemned, dragged out of the Sanhedrin, and stoned to death. Luke describes the event this way:

> But Stephen, full of the Holy Spirit, looked up to heaven and saw the glory of God, and Jesus standing at the right hand of God. "Look,"

he said, "I see heaven open and the Son of Man standing at the right hand of God."

At this they covered their ears and, yelling at the top of their voices, they all rushed at him, dragged him out of the city and began to stone him. Meanwhile, witnesses laid their coats at the feet of a young man named Saul.

While they were stoning him, Stephen prayed, "Lord Jesus, receive my spirit." Then he fell on his knees and cried out, "Lord, do not hold this sin against them." When he had said this, he fell asleep.

And Saul approved of their killing him. (Acts 7:55–8:1)

Several things tug at my heart and conscience each time I encounter this story of the first Christian martyr.

First, there is Stephen's vision. He sees heaven open. In his last moments he glimpses the heavenly throne room—the realm of God's reign. It isn't far away. It is, rather, nearby. Luke narrates Stephen's vision, not as a telescopic glimpse of a faraway place but, like the opening of C. S. Lewis's wardrobe,[7] as a peek into a kingdom not only close but also coming fully in all its glory.

Most significant in Stephen's vision, however, is not its location, but its content. He sees Jesus standing at the right hand of God. This always strikes me as eschatological language. Jesus's followers are not waiting for the day when their Lord will finally take his rightful place at the Father's right hand. He is already there. The kingdom of God and the reign of Christ as the world's true ruler are not just future expectations for Stephen; they are a present reality.

Second, Stephen's vision—this new creation reality—changes Stephen. Earlier in the story, Luke describes Stephen's appearance as "like the face of an angel" (Acts 6:15). During the stoning, however, his appearance does not change. But his vocation does. Before the Sanhedrin, Stephen assumes the role of a prophet. At his death, Stephen takes up the cross of Christ and assumes the vocation of witness (literally in the Gk., *martys* [martyr]). Those who are casting stones refuse to look at the open door into heaven that Stephen desperately wants them to see. But in his death—especially in his response to their persecution—Stephen became a reflection (an image) of the heavenly kingdom he has seen. Maybe Luke's inclusion of Saul's presence is his way of showing not just what a despicable persecutor of the church Saul-Paul was prior to his conversion but also that Saul's conversion actually begins with his haunting observation of the Christ-reflecting Stephen.

This leads to a third observation. What Stephen reflects from the open door of heaven is love. His final words, spoken in prayer, are more than a plea for the Lord to receive his spirit. He also prays that the sins of his persecutors not be held against them. Stephen's prayer echoes Jesus's words spoken from the cross: "Father, forgive them, for they do not know what they are doing" (Luke 23:34). Stephen's prayer, like the prayer of his crucified and resurrected Lord, reflects the love and mercy Jesus extended to his own persecutors and executioners.

Finally, Stephen's martyrdom impresses me by how it invites us to reassess the nature of the individuals and the principalities and powers present in the story. When one reads the narrative of Stephen's martyrdom with the three previous observations in mind, one certainly has sympathy for Stephen. Martyrdom, especially being killed by stoning, is a horrible way to die. However, sympathy for Stephen is short lived because we realize that Stephen is, before his death, already living into the kingdom of God. He already reflects the new creation. A faith-filled reader has not only sympathy for Stephen but also empathy for the misguided religious leaders and their followers who fail to realize they are no longer living in a world where they have to throw rocks at their enemies.

Stephen's witness is profound and filled with meaning. It should not be surprising that someone immersed in the Wesleyan theological tradition, as I am, has such affection for the Stephen story. In important ways it reflects beautifully the vocation of Christian holiness according to the Wesleyan tradition.

Let's examine the Wesleyan view of Christian holiness and its implications as observed in the Stephen story. A Wesleyan understanding of holiness ought to begin at the end of the Christian story (with eschatology) rather than at the beginning (with the creation and fall).

I begin by reflecting on John Wesley's view of the new creation already breaking into the world through the life, death, and resurrection of Jesus and through the gift of the Holy Spirit poured out on the Christian community at Pentecost.

Second, I will examine the change Wesley believes this inbreaking of the new creation makes in the life of believers. Like Stephen, this change, this transformation, this sanctification, is the work of God that forms people into a reflection or image of Christ.

Third, I will examine what may be the key Wesleyan distinctive connected with Christian holiness—namely, that at its core, holiness is a life lived in holy love.

Finally, let's think about what Wesley sees as the fundamental brokenness or fallenness of creation in light of his understanding of salvation (soteriology) and sanctification. In robust Wesleyan theology, holiness is not simply the solution to a universal problem but also a call or vocation taken up by those who have placed their trust in Jesus and who have been filled by his Spirit.

The Inbreaking of the New Creation

In more recent decades, Wesleyan scholarship has increasingly paid attention to how the inbreaking of the kingdom of God, through the life, death, and resurrection of Jesus, shapes the hopes and expectations of Wesley's theology.[8] For Wesley, Jesus's proclamation of the kingdom is not just a future event but also a present reality. The kingdom of God is indeed at hand. Israel's hope and expectation that God would move to bring about "a new heaven and a new earth" (Rev. 21:1) is initiated in the incarnation, the crucifixion, and most especially in the resurrection of Jesus.

For Wesley, although the resurrection is certainly significant as a validation by God the Father of everything Jesus the Son said and did during his ministry, it has a much deeper significance. Jesus's resurrection means more than just his return from the dead (or the place of the dead), although that, too, is significant. Other people in Scripture returned from the dead. Elijah raised the widow's son (1 Kings 17:17-24). Jesus raised Jairus's daughter (Luke 8:40-42, 49-56) and Jesus's beloved Lazarus (John 11:1-44) from the dead. Each of these, however, died again. What is uniquely transformative about Jesus is that he *resurrected* from the dead. Death no longer has dominion over him. To quote the great hymn of Charles Wesley:

> *Lives again our glorious King. Alleluia!*
> *Where, O death, is now thy sting? Alleluia!*
> *Dying once, He all doth save. Alleluia!*
> *Where thy victory, O grave? Alleluia!*
>
> *Love's redeeming work is done. Alleluia!*
> *Fought the fight, the battle won. Alleluia!*

Death in vain forbids Him rise. Alleluia!
Christ has opened paradise. Alleluia![9]

In the resurrection of Jesus, what was supposed to happen at the end of time—the resurrection of the dead and the restoration of all creation—has now broken (in part) into the middle of time. "Therefore, if anyone is in Christ, the new creation has come: The old has gone, the new is here!" (2 Cor. 5:17).

The heirs of Wesley's theological tradition have been more explicit than Wesley himself in connecting the resurrection of Jesus with the beginnings of the new creation. But in numerous places Wesley expresses optimism that even now God's grace makes a real change in a Christian's life. This can happen because of the new reality, the new life ushered in through Jesus's conquest over sin and the grave. For example, in his sermon "The General Spread of the Gospel," Wesley proclaims,

> All unprejudiced persons may see with their eyes, *that He is already re-newing the face of the earth*: And we have strong reason to hope that the work he hath begun, he will carry on unto the day of the Lord Jesus; that he will never intermit this blessed work of his Spirit, until he has fulfilled all his promises, until he hath put a period to sin, and misery, and infirmity, and death, and re-established universal holiness and happiness, and caused all the inhabitants of the earth to sing together, "Hallelujah, the Lord God omnipotent reigneth!" "Blessing, and glory, and wisdom, and honour, and power, and might, be unto our God for ever and ever!" (Rev. vii. 12).[10]

Like Stephen, who sees the kingdom of God already at hand, Wesley is convinced "we have a strong reason to hope"[11] that because Christ has been raised from the dead, "he who began a good work in you will carry it on to completion until the day of Christ Jesus" (Phil. 1:6).

But what does this foretaste of the new creation look like in a believer's life? Without doubt, for Wesley it looks like the renewal of the image of Christ.

Renewal of the Image of Christ

In contrast to the deists[12] of his day, who tended to identify the image of God in humanity as the human ability to reason, Wesley understood the image of God relationally. For him, human beings are uniquely created to be relational reflections or representations of God, first in their love back to God, but also in their love for others (the neighbor), creation, and themselves. Wesley likely borrowed this conviction from the Eastern fathers. They used the metaphor of humanity as a "mirror." In their view, humans were created to reflect or mediate back into the world the grace, love, and life they have received from God.[13]

In his sermon "The New Birth,"[14] Wesley describes human beings as imaging or reflecting God in three ways: the natural image, the political image, and the moral image. The first of these includes all those qualities that make humans uniquely capable of responding in relationship to God. Wesley's articulation of the natural image in humans is close to the views of his Enlightenment colleagues. He affirmed that God gave to human beings reason (Wesley preferred "understanding"), freedom (or liberty), and will (or volition). Without these qualities, a relationship with God (and with one another) would be impossible. These gifts make it possible to love and glorify God freely and voluntarily. However, the gifts can be used for destruction, sin, and violence. Theodore Runyon observes, "It is evident that these capacities are gifts given to enable human beings to carry out their calling to image and reflect their Creator, gifts that flourish when used in ways consistent with the will of the Giver, but gifts that also are easily distorted when turned to serve the selfish interests of the creature."[15]

The second aspect of God's image—the political image—includes gifts that make it possible for humans to reflect the Creator in their dominion or caretaking of the world. This means that God holds people responsible not only for how they care for what God has formed but also for all they have "created" as cocreators with God. The wheat God created is "good" and should be cared for. Additionally, human creative activity (as God's imagers) that results in bread is also "very good." However, not all human creativity benefits nature and other humans. Thus the political image in humankind can be either a source of blessing or a curse.

The final characteristic of the image of God is the moral image. "This is the chief mark of the human relationship to God, according to Wesley, but also the one most easily distorted."[16] Whereas the natural image of God relates to the human capacity to reflect God's being, and the political image relates to human work and responsibility, the moral image involves human character, created by God as a reflection (a mirror) of God as well. Wesley tells us in his sermon "The New Birth,"

In this [moral] image of God was man made. "God is love:" Accordingly, man at his creation was full of love; which was the sole principle of all his tempers, thoughts, words, and actions. God is full of justice, mercy, and truth; so was man as he came from the hands of his Creator. God is spotless purity; and so man was in the beginning pure from every sinful blot; otherwise God could not have pronounced him, as well as all the other work of his hands, "very good" (Gen. i. 31). . . . If we suppose an intelligent creature not to love God, not to be righteous and holy, we necessarily suppose him not to be good at all; much less to be "very good."[17]

This beautiful picture of humankind's unbroken relationship with God in being, purpose, and in moral, holy love is not a picture of how things currently are. Broken relationship is how Wesley understood the fall. The image of God has not been lost, but it has been marred and fractured by sin. Yet, as Tim Crutcher points out about Wesley's view of salvation, "Wesley does not begin with the idea of how sinful humanity is now; he starts with the glorious creatures God created them to be. . . . Over and over again throughout his sermons, Wesley articulates his view of salvation and redemption as the restoration or renewal of the image of God in human beings. What God does in salvation is intimately connected to what God did in creation."[18] And I would add, original creation is intimately connected with God's purposes in new creation.

As Stephen views the inbreaking of the kingdom of God (the new creation), to those around him Stephen becomes an image, a reflection or mirror of the One who is seated on the throne.

Holy Love

If the primary work of salvation is the renewal of the moral image of God in humanity, what does this look like? For Wesley, it looks like a heart reborn in the holy love of God and love for others.

Renewal of the believer's moral life (and then consequently the political and natural dimensions) requires, for Wesley, that sanctification (making holy) of the believer follow as an inseparable complement to justification. For Wesley, it isn't enough to hope for release from the penalty of sin only. Scripture, for him, testifies to deliverance, by God, from the plague of sin as well. At its core, sanctification is restoration of fallen humanity to fellowship with the Creator and to faithful stewardship of God's creation. Wesley often used the term "Christian perfection" to describe this restored, new creation life. The term meant Christian life contains a goal or *telos* (as noted earlier, Gk., "design," "purpose," or "goal") of complete perfection or restoration in the image of God (this does not mean sinless perfection or being flawless). Though decisive in character, Christian perfection is also a lifelong process. "Perfecting" the image of Christ begins by grace through faith at justification, regeneration, or the new birth.

For Wesley, sanctification carries negative and positive implications. The negative side usually raises most of the questions and poses most of the challenges for Wesleyans. Holiness seems to imply freedom from sin. But just how free can one expect to be from the power and dominion of sin in this life? Although Wesley refused to use the term "sinless perfection,"[19] he did hold out the possibility that a sanctified believer might be released from conscious transgressions against the known law of God. Although this understanding of sin is admittedly narrow, individualistic, and rationalistic, it still remains important. By renewal of the image of God in a believer, the weight of sin can be set aside so that a Christian can be clothed with the new creation.

Future generations of Wesleyan theologians have attempted to broaden the definition of sin without forfeiting Wesley's optimism of grace. It is safe to say that for Wesley one can continue to confess sin while also setting it aside. Although one may never claim "sinlessness," one can certainly, by grace through faith, be set free from the dominion of sin (Rom. 6:17-18; 8:12-17).

Emphasis should be placed on the positive dimension of the holy life, not on the negative. Once by grace the life of sin has been set aside, one can through the Spirit take up a life constantly renewed in holy love. Growth in holiness is always part of the holy life; as one lives into love, there are no limits.

Repeatedly Wesley speaks of sanctification, perfection, and holiness as love—love for God and one's neighbor. For relationship God created us. That was lost, damaged in the fall. For Wesley, restoration of that relationship is the goal of new birth and sanctification. Timothy Crutcher says, "God wants to fully heal our diseased will so that it is driven by nothing but love, nothing but a desire for God and for the good of everyone else around us. The full reorientation of that will would then be worthy of being called entire sanctification."[20]

Renewal of and in love doesn't happen in one's own strength. It is the work of Christ through the Holy Spirit in an obedient believer. Through obedient faith, renewal in love is decisive and also a continuing work of the Holy Spirit through the various means of grace. Although Wesley is open to other signs (or gifts) that evidence the indwelling Holy Spirit, he would affirm with Paul in 1 Corinthians 13, although one might have a number of spiritual gifts, unless he or she has love, no other gifts matter.

Again, Stephen is exemplary. Filled with the Spirit, Stephen "[gives] over [his] body to hardship" (1 Cor. 13:3). But it is not just his martyrdom that witnesses to the new creation. His Spirit-enabled love in the form of forgiveness also witnesses to the renewal of God's image in him and to the presence of the new creation.

The Vocation of the Faithful

If it is obvious that the renewal of love in the heart of the believer is the goal of God's redemptive work, then the Christian vocation is also obvious. As individuals and as members of God's renewed people—the church—Christians are to live lives of holy love. For Wesley and the Methodists, this was not abstract theory, but physical and practical. It entailed finding tangible ways to love the poor and marginalized.

Wesley's sermons were often preached within the tension between exhorting the church to be a community that loved and cared for one another and finding ways to love and care for those outside the church. Although achieving balance between "inside" and "outside" the church, between "spiritual" and "physical" priorities, and between "temporal" and "eternal" needs could often be difficult, Wesley's Methodists were not permitted to choose one or the other. Love for God compels us to try to be "all things to all people" (1 Cor. 9:22).

In one of his sermons treating the Sermon on the Mount, Wesley encourages his congregation to feed the hungry and clothe the naked, not as an evangelistic strategy, but simply in obedience to God. Like Stephen who bore witness in peaceful faith, the vocation of Christian holiness is to remain faithful. "It is your part to do as you are commanded: the event is in the hand of God."[21]

Positives of the Wesleyan View of Holiness

As our Christian vocation, there is much about the Wesleyan view of holiness to admire and emulate. I will mention three aspects that are important for me: a therapeutic understanding of sin as a disease that needs healing, an optimism of grace, and sanctification as holy love.

We children of the Reformation have often received a judicial or juridical view of sin rather than a therapeutic one. A judicial or juridical view tends to see sin primarily as an offense against God, God's justice, and God's honor. By this view, as Savior, on the cross Christ must successfully satisfy God's justice or honor. Although there may be important biblical aspects of this view, the weight of Scripture treats sin less as an offense against God's honor and more as breaking a relationship between Father and children, or between a ruler-shepherd and his people-flock. Wesley seems to intuit the relational or therapeutic aspect of sin and salvation as being at the heart of the gospel.

Wesley's optimism of grace is encouraging and consistent with the hopes proclaimed in the Scripture. There is something deeply true about a theology convinced that in Christ, God refuses to let darkness and sin have the dominant or final word *in this life, not just* in the life to come.

Most importantly, I value Wesley's emphasis on love as the heart of the holy life. One cannot love as God intends if bound by the devastating effects of sin and corruption. But as Paul so beautifully states in 1 Corinthians 13, if one has all kinds of gifts and makes all kinds of commitments but has not love, it amounts to nothing.

Critiques of the Wesleyan View of Holiness

Although I believe there is much to affirm in Wesley's theology, there are features that deserve critique and work. I will briefly mention one critique of Wesley and another of his heirs.

Wesley, in part, as an heir of the Enlightenment, has an overly individualistic and shallow conception of sin. Although there are hints of an understanding of corporate and systemic sin in his writings, he is mostly concerned with individuals. A serious contemporary holiness theology must do much better than did Wesley. Sanctification must not only deal with individuals but also with structural evil, with principalities and powers that continue to "squeeze us into their molds."

As a child of the Holiness Movement, I have observed that many of Wesley's heirs neglect the means of grace through which believers are restored in the power of the Holy Spirit. It is interesting that some children of a theological parent committed to methods or practices of holiness (a "Methodist") could pay such little attention to formative liturgies and spiritual disciplines during corporate worship and beyond. Too often this has been true for many of Wesley's offspring. Holiness takes practice(s).

Wesley had an ecumenical spirit. His preaching and teaching on holiness was not broadly embraced by Anglicans. He would be deeply pleased that today a strong interest in holiness is playing an important and broad role in the theological traditions represented in this book.

10

The Path to Holiness
Trajectories in Pentecostalism

❖

Glen W. Menzies, PhD

Glen W. Menzies is the president of Simple Ear, a hearing aid company. Previously, he taught biblical studies for twenty-seven years at North Central University, Minneapolis, Minnesota, and was dean of North Central's Institute for Biblical and Theological Studies. He has also served as research projects coordinator for the Museum of the Bible, Washington, DC. He is an ordained minister of the Assemblies of God.

❖

The Pentecostal Movement is a river with many currents flowing in it. It has no single, unified position on sanctification. Sanctification was the primary doctrinal engine that propelled the nineteenth-century Holiness Movement, and it was the Holiness Movement that gave birth to Pentecostalism.[1] But sanctification does not hold the position of importance among Pentecostals it has held for its theological parent. Baptism in the Spirit, understood as an empowering for witness, became the star of Pentecostal theology; sanctification has stood in its shadow. Despite this, the two parts of the Christian family have much in common. They emphasize the importance of spiritual experiences, that faith is more than assent to doctrine. Both share a restorationist impulse.[2] The Protestant Reformation was largely an attempt to restore New Testament doctrine to the church. The Holiness Movement and Pentecostalism aimed for more: a restoration of New Testament experience and practice.[3]

What Is Pentecostalism?

The most recent statistical table of global Christianity published annually by the *International Bulletin of Mission Research* reports that in mid-2018, of the slightly more than 2.5 billion Christians in the world, 682,731,000 of them are members of Pentecostal, charismatic, or independent charismatic groups.[4] Diversity within this Pentecostal-charismatic family is immense. It includes African indigenous churches, a variety of Chinese house churches, and a host of other traditions and movements. The range is too great to discuss here. We will limit our consideration to classical Pentecostalism,[5] which comprises about 120 million people worldwide, or a little more than one-sixth of the larger total.

Classical Pentecostalism emerged from the Holiness Movement at the beginning of the twentieth century. Historians of Pentecostalism have proposed three slightly different accounts of its origin. The oldest story, which the earliest Pentecostals embraced, associates it with events that took place on January 1, 1901, shortly after midnight at a watch-night service held in Topeka, Kansas, to usher in the New Year. The key name in this account is Charles Parham (1873–1929). A second account places the beginning of the Pentecostal Movement at the Azusa Street revival that began a little over five years later in Los Angeles. The key figure there was William Seymour (1870–1922), an African American preacher who led the fully integrated, multiracial Azusa Street revival. The third account describes multiple, simultaneous and independent outpourings of the Spirit that occurred in India, Korea, North America, and elsewhere. While all three accounts have evidence in their favor, I believe the first account is the most helpful.[6]

Classical Pentecostals divide into three categories: (1) Pentecostals influenced by John Wesley who speak of three definite religious experiences: salvation, [entire] sanctification, and baptism in the Holy Spirit;[7] (2) Finished Work Pentecostals, who speak of two definite experiences: conversion (or the new birth) and baptism in the Holy Spirit as an empowering for witness;[8] and (3) Oneness or Jesus' Name Pentecostals, who reject the doctrine of the Trinity.[9] On the topic of sanctification, Oneness Pentecostals stand firmly within the Finished Work camp.[10] Therefore, we need only explore the views of Wesleyan Pentecostals and Finished Work Pentecostals.

The term "finished work" requires additional explanation because it is used in more than one way. The preceding paragraph used the phrase in its broader sense, as a catchall, describing groups that teach only the new birth and baptism in the Holy Spirit as definite experiences. It also has a narrower sense, precisely describing the theology of William H. Durham (1873–1912), the first Pentecostal who rejected the Wesleyan approach to sanctification. Durham used Jesus's cry from the cross, "It is finished" (John 19:30, KJV), to name his new teaching, which asserted that the new birth included the elimination of original or inborn sin. This effectively collapsed the new birth and the Wesleyan doctrine of entire sanctification into one experience. However, today most Finished Work Pentecostals—using the term in its broader sense—explain sanctification differently than Durham did.

While in America Pentecostalism is fairly evenly divided between the Wesleyan and Finished Work wings, worldwide Finished Work Pentecostalism is the much larger branch.[11]

All classical Pentecostals believe the gifts of the Spirit described in the New Testament, including the oral gifts (e.g., prophecy, words of knowledge, words of wisdom, tongues, and the interpretation of tongues) and the gifts that manifest supernatural power (e.g., healing and miracles) continue today.[12] They consider baptism in the Holy Spirit to be primarily a charismatic empowerment for witness. The experience is distinct from conversion or the new birth. Classical Pentecostals do not believe baptism in the Holy Spirit makes them more holy or superior to other Christians.

The earliest Pentecostals tended not to identify themselves by the term "Pentecostal," although they did not object to it. It was simply confusing because parts of the Holiness Movement claimed the term. To illustrate, from the time of its formation in 1907, the Church of the Nazarene called itself the Pentecostal Church of the Nazarene.[13] When in 1919 it dropped "Pentecostal" from its name, it did so to avoid confusion with groups that spoke in tongues.

In the first decade of the twentieth century, the most common self-designator Pentecostals used was "Apostolic Faith," although they also used "Full Gospel" to identify themselves. After Pentecostalism fractured in 1916 between Trinitarian Pentecostals and Oneness Pentecostals, increasingly the Oneness Pentecostals claimed the designation

"Apostolic Faith" and the Trinitarians from both the Wesleyan and the Finished Work wings avoided using it.[14]

Classical Pentecostalism is a little over a century old. When considering religious movements, this makes it rather young. What Pentecostals believe about sanctification is not their distinctive feature. Their beliefs about this topic are diverse and often confusing. The truly distinctive contribution of Pentecostalism resides in its doctrine of baptism in the Holy Spirit, understood as an empowering for witness.

Most of what Pentecostals do believe about sanctification has been borrowed from earlier movements and integrated into the larger fabric of Pentecostal theology in creative ways.

The Pentecostal Altar: My Journey

I grew up during the 1960s and early 1970s in a Pentecostal home in the Ozark Mountains of southwest Missouri. We attended church three times a week, Sunday morning, Sunday night, and Wednesday night, unless the church was having revival services. Then we attended church every night. We lived in Springfield, the headquarters city of the Assemblies of God. My father taught first at a Bible institute and later at a Christian college. To say that church was at the center of our lives is an understatement. It was the hub around which everything else turned.

Church services usually lasted about two hours, although they could go much longer. In many ways, congregational singing and the sermon were preliminaries preparing the way for the altar call and time around the altar. This was the climax of the service when the important spiritual work took place. Sunday night meetings were the liveliest, often of the hellfire and brimstone variety, with apocalyptic overtones. "If you were to die tonight, would you be ready to meet your Maker?" "The Lord is coming soon to gather up his church. It will happen in a moment, in the twinkling of an eye. Will you be ready?"

I remember many moments of great terror, as awareness of my sins danced before my eyes. I was a Christian; I had first professed faith at the age of five or six, and I had reaffirmed my commitment many times. But I was certainly not free from sin. And the preachers always pushed for a response to this problem in my life, but not always in the same way. The solutions they offered came in three varieties, and these solutions offer insights into conflicting Pentecostal approaches to sanctification and Christian holiness.

The first solution was that my sins had separated me from God. I had backslidden and could no longer properly be counted as a Christian. I needed to be "saved" once more.

The second solution was less dire. It did not claim I was no longer a Christian, although it did not deny that the situation was grave. "You think that sin is your problem. Well, it's only a symptom of a larger problem. You are not 'sold out' to God. Jesus is not the Lord of your life.[15] You are an 'unclean vessel' that God cannot use. You must surrender everything in your life to Christ." This solution required two things of me: repentance for my sins, and reconsecration of my life to God. Then God would forgive me and again be willing to use me for his service. I would experience an internal awareness of his forgiveness and a sense of peace. In this type of appeal in my Finished Work Pentecostal context, the words "sanctify" and "sanctification" were rarely used. Nevertheless, these exhortations were about sanctification.

If I had grown up in the Wesleyan wing of Pentecostalism, I would have been presented with a very similar solution, although it would usually have included the words "sanctify" and "sanctification." Similarly, two things would have been asked of me: repentance for my sins, and reconsecration of my life to God. But God's response would have been framed differently: he would forgive me, and he would sanctify me. Then I would become conscious of both his forgiveness and the definite work of sanctification he had performed in me.

The third solution was much like the second. It did not say I had lost my salvation. The main difference was its greater stress on the role of the Spirit in bringing me to increased spiritual maturity. "The Christian life is a struggle between the flesh and the Spirit. We naturally gravitate toward the flesh and toward sin. But by inviting the Spirit to guide us at every moment, we can live an 'overcoming life' and develop spiritual power."

The two latter "solutions" to sin after conversion, and the understandings of sanctification they support, form much of the present Pentecostal tapestry.

To explain Pentecostal approaches to sanctification more fully, it is necessary first to explore struggles earlier in church history over what sanctification means and how it occurs. We will highlight elements of the Protestant Reformation, the teachings of John Wesley, and innovations in the Keswick or Higher Life Movement.

The Incomplete Heritage of the Protestant Reformation

The prevailing consensus is that the central topic of debate in the Protestant Reformation was justification. So it is puzzling to some Protestant observers that the main practices and teachings that prompted this splintering of the church—penance, indulgences, and purgatory— did not deal with how to enter the Christian life (justification), but rather, how to deal with acts of sin in those who already claimed to be Christian (sanctification).

Luther's slogan *simul justus et peccator* (Lat., "at the same time justified and a sinner") summed up the core of Protestant theology. Through faith by grace, individuals could be declared righteous before God on the basis of the righteousness of Christ, but original sin remained in them following justification. The original sin that remained (also known as "inward sin," "inborn sin," "inbred sin," or "concupiscence") was inherited from Adam and Eve and had destroyed the original righteousness of the human nature with which Adam and Eve were originally created. Adam and Eve's fall from righteousness had also marred the image of God, which their descendants bore. The damage to human nature caused by original sin left every person, even those who had been justified, with a propensity or inclination to sin. This propensity was not a compulsion, but it was still a persistent problem. Luther had written about the "bondage of the will" that characterized people prior to justification and kept them from turning to God on their own. Those who had been justified were no longer separated from God by such bondage, but an inclination to sin still remained within them.

The Contribution of John Wesley to Pentecostal Theology

For John Wesley (1703-91), Christian holiness, perfect love, Christian perfection, or entire sanctification involved the elimination of not only "outward sin" but also original or internal sin. While Wesley disagreed with the Catholic position that every justified person is free from original sin, he thought it *was possible* to find that freedom at some moment following conversion and justification.

For Wesley, Christian perfection implied not only healing from the sickness of original sin but also the formation of perfect love. Wesley envisioned this healing to be a gradual process, but he also taught the possibility of a decisive religious experience, experienced in this life by God's grace, that would bring entire sanctification, or Christian perfection as love made perfect (not to be confused with "sinless perfection"), to completion in a momentary event. Entire sanctification did not exclude lifelong transformation into the image of Christ. Rather, entire sanctification fostered such growth. Both the process of sanctification and the consummating crisis experience happened following conversion.

As mentioned above, the Wesleyan wing of Pentecostalism embraced Wesley's doctrine of entire sanctification. The Finished Work wing did not.

Whatever position Pentecostals hold about sanctification, they follow Wesley in his Arminianism (that salvation is meant for all persons and that salvation can later be forfeited), his insistence on concupiscence or original sin as humankind's universal inheritance of a corrupted nature, his belief that guilt is not inherited from Adam and Eve, and his conviction that true faith entails a "new birth" that surpasses mere assent to right doctrine.

The Contribution of Keswick (KEHZ-ik) Theology

The American Holiness Movement began in the 1830s when Phoebe Palmer (1807-74) and her sister, Sarah Lankford, began holding a weekly meeting—the Tuesday Meeting for the Promotion of Holiness—in the Palmers' New York City home. The primary purpose of these meetings was to promote a renewed emphasis on Wesley's doctrine of entire sanctification, which had faded in prominence. Palmer represents the Wesleyan wing of the Holiness Movement.

Then in the last quarter of the nineteenth century, a series of conventions began in Great Britain that quickly spread to North America.[16] Their emphasis was also on Christian holiness, but with a slightly different twist from that of John Wesley. The movement drew its name from Keswick, the place in northern England where it began.[17] It was also called the Higher Life Movement, based on the name of the book published in 1858 by William Boardman, *The Higher Christian Life*, which had a great impact on many Keswick leaders.[18]

Like Wesleyan theology, Keswick theology taught that God provides a second work of grace, a definite experience of sanctification available to all believers.[19] The important difference between the Wesleyan doctrine of entire sanctification and the Keswick understanding is that the latter did not teach sanctification involves eradicating the sinful nature or indwelling sin. Instead, sin is "overcome" or "counteracted" by the power of the Holy Spirit.[20] If a person will consecrate his or her life completely to God, then God will sanctify in response.

An important innovation in much of Keswick teaching was the widespread use of imagery and language from the Acts 2 account of the Spirit's outpouring on the day of Pentecost (the Feast of Weeks). Particularly important was use of the term "baptized in the Holy Spirit."[21]

Although Pentecostals reached different conclusions, they read Acts in much the same way as did Keswick holiness people.[22] Both parties applied a common hermeneutic (way of interpreting) to the study of Acts. It made the descent of the Spirit at Pentecost normative for the post-Pentecostal era. It provided a paradigm for separating the reception of the Spirit from the reception of Christ in conversion.[23]

By the end of the nineteenth century, there were two wings of the Holiness Movement. One sailed closer to the course set by John Wesley. The other embraced the newer Keswick theology. When Pentecostalism erupted at the beginning of the twentieth century, it began in the Wesleyan wing of the Holiness Movement. But within about a decade, a less Wesleyan stream of teaching about sanctification also emerged. Many of those who embraced this new approach had Keswick roots, particularly in the Christian and Missionary Alliance founded by A. B. Simpson (1843–1919), but there were other influences as well.

A Changed Vision of the Empowering Work of the Spirit

Acts 1:8 states, "But you shall receive power when the Holy Spirit has come upon you; and you shall be witnesses to Me in Jerusalem, and in all Judea and Samaria, and to the end of the earth" (NKJV). Pentecostals understand this statement to be the major theme of Acts. They read "you shall receive power" as meaning primarily "you shall receive *power for witness*." The text of Acts often links inspired speech, such as bold proclamation, prophecy, and speaking in tongues with Pentecost.

The earliest Pentecostal leaders, such as Charles Parham, William Seymour, J. H. King, Charles Mason, G. B. Cashwell, and J. A. Tomlinson, belonged to the Wesleyan wing of the Holiness Movement before becoming Pentecostals. Like Wesley, they believed in entire sanctification as a second definite work of grace. When they discovered baptism in the Holy

Spirit as an empowering for witness, they simply added it as a third step or a third experience.[24]

However, a major controversy erupted in 1910 when William H. Durham,[25] the pastor of the North Avenue Mission in Chicago, who was also ministering in Los Angeles, began preaching against the doctrine of sanctification as a second work of grace. Instead, Durham taught the "finished work of Calvary." The phrase did not originate with him.[26] He explained that the new birth and sanctification are a single work of grace, not two. Applying Christ's "finished work of Calvary" to one's life through faith meant a complete salvation. Nothing needed for salvation was left for later. This teaching intentionally rejected the doctrine of sanctification as taught by Wesley and the Keswick advocates.[27]

Durham claimed to have developed his position based upon his study of Scripture. But pastoral experience sometimes also molds theology. Durham reported that "hundreds" of new converts had received their Spirit baptisms without any awareness of a preceding experience of sanctification.[28]

In 1911 Durham proclaimed his Finished Work theology at the Azusa Street Mission. Because the mission taught that entire sanctification happens subsequent to the new birth, Durham was barred from the Azusa Street Mission pulpit. In response, he led supporters to a new meeting location at the Women's Christian Temperance Union facility.

Durham strongly opposed the organization of Pentecostal denominations. Nevertheless, when the Assemblies of God was organized in 1914, following Durham's sudden death in 1912, many Finished Work Pentecostals joined the new fellowship. If there was any doubt about what the new fellowship's position on sanctification would be, it was removed when during the organizing General Council, Mack M. Pinson delivered an address titled "The Finished Work of Calvary."[29]

Although the Foursquare Church was organized in 1923, nine years after the organization of the Assemblies of God, the impact of Durham on its theology of sanctification was perhaps greater even than his impact on Assemblies of God theology. Aimee Semple (later Aimee Semple McPherson) (1890–1944), founder of the Foursquare Church, and her first husband, Robert Semple, had in 1909 been ordained by Durham in Chicago. They had ministered with him in Chicago and on evangelistic trips through northern America and Canada.[30] Sister Aimee became a committed proponent of Finished Work theology, as did the denomination she founded.

Various explanations have been proposed for why Durham's subversion of the then-standard Pentecostal theology of sanctification proved so popular. Robert Mapes Anderson argued that those who came to Pentecostalism from non-Wesleyan backgrounds, such as Reformed or Baptist churches, had never been particularly convinced of sanctification as a second definite work of grace. When they found an opportunity to combine an emphasis on baptism in the Holy Spirit as an empowering for witness with their former approach to sanctification, they took it.

D. William Faupel has made a slightly different argument, based on reports of personal experiences. Many experienced baptism in the Holy Spirit with the outward evidence of speaking in tongues without having had an earlier definite experience of sanctification. The testimony of Clara Fisher provides an example. One Sunday in 1906 or 1907, she heard a sermon at the Azusa Street Mission on baptism in the Spirit. When someone approached her after the sermon and asked, "What do you think?" she replied, "I have that." The response was, "You can't. You're a Baptist." Because Baptists did not seek or testify to experiences of entire sanctification, this person assumed she was ineligible. In fact, Fisher had been speaking in tongues for several years, although she was not sure what it meant.[31]

Today, the term "finished work" is often used in a broader sense than the way Durham used it. Today, most Finished Work Pentecostals don't believe original sin is eradicated at conversion. In the 1910s and 1920s, the term became a catchall designating Pentecostals who rejected sanctification as a step preceding baptism in the Holy Spirit. We can describe Finished Work Pentecostals as two-step Pentecostals, while Wesleyan Pentecostals proclaim three steps.

Trajectories of Sanctification in Pentecostalism

The Pentecostal Movement began as the twentieth century dawned. This essay has traced the roots of Pentecostal views of sanctification to earlier discussions about sanctification that took place mainly in the eighteenth century (John Wesley) and nineteenth century (the Keswick Movement). It has also outlined the tensions that soon developed among Pentecostals over divergent theologies of sanctification.

The next portion of this chapter will explain how Pentecostal views of sanctification have been changing over the past one hundred years. The most concise way to tell this story is to speak of trajectories that have emerged and continue. Five such trajectories will be considered.

The first trajectory is a general decline in emphasis on sanctification in Pentecostal churches. For the first generation of Pentecostals, sanctification was a hot-button issue. It was widely preached and discussed with great passion. Differences over how it should be taught caused divisions. Since then there has been a long period of gradual decline. Today, no one in the Pentecostal world suggests Christian holiness is unimportant, but there are no longer spirited debates about how it comes about.

The second trajectory might be best described as a fifty-year decline, followed by a sharp plunge. The belief that acts of sin committed after one's conversion—what Wesley called "outward sin"—places one in eternal jeopardy was once commonly taught in Pentecostal circles. But over the past fifty years this has almost disappeared. While it was once common for Pentecostals to "get saved" and "resaved" several times a year, today this is viewed as erroneous.[32] Pentecostals do believe that a person can forfeit his or her salvation and that neglect of one's discipleship can gradually have the same result. But this doesn't mean each commission of sin amounts to apostasy.

The third trajectory is a decreased emphasis on markers of outward holiness. Because claims of spiritual experience are inherently subjective, and the observable conduct of some individuals who claimed to be sanctified did not always comport with their claims, the presence of "real sanctification" or holiness was often judged by behavioral codes. Catalogs of outward markers of holiness were often framed as vices and disapproved behaviors. These included the use of tobacco or alcohol, dancing, playing cards, going to movies, the use of makeup, and men and women swimming together. The list of acceptable and unacceptable behaviors changed along with changing social mores. Sometimes the codes or "standards" seemed determined more by social conservatism than by authentic holiness. Sermons directed against smoking, drinking, or dancing are today quite uncommon. Particularly in urban areas, dancing is routine at Pentecostal wedding receptions, as is quiet drinking in moderation.

A fourth trajectory is located in the Wesleyan wing of Pentecostalism. Wesleyan Pentecostals still consider the pursuit of Christian holiness an essential part of Christian discipleship. But a clear trajectory now minimizes the Wesleyan doctrine of entire sanctification as a second definite work of grace. It also minimizes sanctification as removal of original or inborn sin prior to death and glorification. Now, with the focus on consecration and complete surrender to Christ, many "Wesleyan" Pentecostals sound positively Keswickian. That is, the possibility of living a "higher life" is proclaimed, but it is less common to hear of the eradication of inborn sin.

Three examples will illustrate this trajectory. The Official Declaration of Faith of the Church of God (Cleveland) commits to "sanctification subsequent to the new birth" and "baptism with the Holy Ghost subsequent to a clean heart," but it does not mention original sin or inborn sin.[33] Similarly, the more elaborate Statement of Faith of the Church of God in Christ (COGIC) is notable for the absence of Wesleyan language about sanctification. It affirms, "We believe in the sanctifying power of the Holy Spirit, by whose indwelling the Christian is enabled to live a holy and separated life in the present world."[34] Finished Work Pentecostals could affirm this statement. And surprisingly, in the Articles of Religion of the COGIC (approved in 1972), sanctification is described as a "gracious and continuous operation of the Holy Ghost."[35] Nevertheless, the Articles of Religion also affirm that sanctification is a prerequisite to baptism in the Holy Spirit.[36] In contrast, in its official statement of faith, the Pentecostal Holiness Church continues to affirm clear Wesleyan doctrine. It describes sanctification as "a definite, instantaneous work of grace," which, among other things, is a "cleansing or taking away of the sin principle."[37] Still, this emphasis has lessened in the pew.

The fifth trajectory is located in the Finished Work branch of Pentecostalism. It is a movement away from the original "finished work of Calvary" theology as taught by William Durham and toward a more Reformed position of gradual growth in sanctification, to be completed at death and glorification.

Durham taught that the inclination to sin inherited from Adam is completely removed when a person is converted, justified. As noted earlier, this belief collapsed entire sanctification into the new birth. While sin after conversion remains possible, it is a willful choice not influenced by a fallen nature. This left two definite experiences remaining: conversion and baptism in the Spirit, understood as empowering for witness.

But even within Finished Work Pentecostalism, Durham's view did not long prevail. Although not embracing the full Keswick notion of a second definite work, calls for those already converted to consecrate their lives fully to Christ became common. This, of course, amounted to a mild repudiation of Durham's doctrine. At one time, calls for consecration subsequent to conversion were extremely frequent and prominent. While today they are less frequent and often more muted, they are still fairly common.

In a major shift, today very few Finished Work Pentecostals affirm that original or inborn sin is eradicated at conversion. They expect a gradual growth in holiness and do not expect this process to be completed until death or at the second coming of Christ. Sanctification will be completed by glorification. Although growth in Christian holiness is not inevitable, and while most Christians encounter valleys in their progression, the normal Christian pattern is ever-increasing growth in conformity to the image of Christ.

When Christian discipleship is discussed, it is often framed as either living *according to the flesh* or *according to the Spirit*. Walking in, and being led by, the Spirit is the way to overcome the flesh, which is identified with original sin. In a Keswickian sense, it can be overcome, although not completely. As in a ball game, one team may be winning, but final victory is not accomplished until the game is over. In the Christian life, the battle between the flesh and the Spirit is constant and ongoing. Spiritual growth is possible, as is greater sanctity, but the fleshly tendency and the possibility of failure in discipleship do not disappear before death or glorification at Christ's return. To state this another way, most Finished Work Pentecostals accept the Reformation theme *simul justus et peccator* (at the same time justified and a sinner), even though they rarely quote this Latin phrase or its English translation. Just as justification results in the nonimputation (not charging) of sin *against* us and the imputation (crediting) of Christ's righteousness *for* us, so, too, by relying upon Christ's righteousness, we remain righteous before God after postconversion acts of sin.

I am a Finished Work Pentecostal who leans toward the Reformed view of sanctification. Since the Reformation, Protestants have struggled with how to describe the enduring effects of a human nature damaged by sin. After justification, Christians are no longer enslaved to sin and alienated from God, as they were prior to justification. But neither have they completely escaped sin's deleterious effects. This is an issue not only of soteriology (the doctrine of salvation) but also of eschatology (completion of God's kingdom) and salvation history. In this life, Christians struggle with the dual nature of God's kingdom: It has come, and it remains still to come.[38] Jesus's parables of the mustard seed (Matt. 13:31-32) and the leaven (v. 33) contrast the more limited beginnings of the kingdom with the immensity of its consummation. Our lives are microcosms of this tension. Through Christ's atonement we have been freed from sin's bondage, yet daily we struggle with sin. We await God's refining fire that one day will make us entirely holy.

Even so, Lord, come quickly!

Notes

❖

Foreword

1. Paul VI, "The Universal Call to Holiness in the Church," in *Lumen gentium* [Light of the Nations], Vatican Website, November 21, 1964, chap. 5, para. 39, http://www.vatican.va/archive/hist_councils/ii_vatican_council/documents/vat-ii _const_19641121_lumen-gentium_en.html.

2. Irenaeus, *Against Heresies*, in *Ante-Nicene Fathers*, vol. 1, *The Apostolic Fathers, Justin Martyr, Irenaeus*, ed. Alexander Roberts and James Donaldson (1885; repr., Christian Classics Ethereal Library [CCEL]), bk. 5, preface, https://ccel.org/ccel /irenaeus/against_heresies_v/anf01.ix.vii.i.html.

3. Athanasius, *On the Incarnation of the Word*, chap. 8, sec. 54, CCEL, https://ccel .org/ccel/athanasius/incarnation/incarnation.ix.html.

Introduction

1. "Torah" means God's "instruction" or "guidance." It refers to large bodies of authoritative instruction found in the Old Testament. For an extended explanation of Torah, see Walter Brueggemann, *Reverberations of Faith: A Theological Handbook of Old Testament Themes* (Louisville, KY: Westminster John Knox Press, 2002), 217-20.

2. Ibid., 235-38.

3. Abraham Joshua Heschel, *God in Search of Man: A Philosophy of Judaism* (New York: Farrar, Straus and Giroux, 1955), 384. Citations refer to paperback edition, first printed 1976.

4. See Frances R. Havergal, "Let It Make Thee Whole" (1874), Hymnary.org, https://hymnary.org/text/precious_precious_blood_of_jesus.

5. Fleming Rutledge, *The Crucifixion: Understanding the Death of Jesus Christ* (Grand Rapids: Eerdmans, 2015), 105. Citations refer to paperback edition, first printed 2017.

6. N. T. Wright, *The Day the Revolution Began: Reconsidering the Meaning of Jesus's Crucifixion* (New York: HarperCollins, 2016), 357.

7. John Calvin correctly instructed that "whatever we obtain from the Lord is granted on the condition of our employing it for the common good of the Church." John Calvin, *On the Christian Life*, trans. Henry Beveridge (Calvin Translation Society, 1845; Grand Rapids: Christian Classics Ethereal Library, 2005), chap. 2.5, https:// www.ccel.org/ccel/calvin/chr_life.i.html.

Chapter 1

1. Tattoos play a symbolic role in this chapter. Mention of tattoos is in no way meant to pass judgment on them as such or on persons who have them. By themselves, tattoos have no necessary religious or moral importance and may have nothing to do with a person's relationship to God.

2. Flannery O'Connor, "Parker's Back," in *Flannery O'Connor: The Complete Stories* (New York: Farrar, Straus and Giroux, 1971), 520. Parker and his tractor had been circling inwards, coming closer and closer to the tree—the cross.

3. Ibid., 510-30. When reading O'Conner, one must be constantly alert to her subtly intentional use of biblical images and terms. The reflection of Christ that Parker saw in the mirror and Parker's subsequent transformation are references to the apostle Paul's use of "mirror" in 2 Corinthians 3:18: "And all of us, with unveiled faces, seeing the glory of the Lord as though reflected in a mirror, are being transformed into the same image from one degree of glory to another; for this comes from the Lord, the Spirit" (NRSV). Initiated transformation is what happens to Parker. O'Conner has Parker make clear he wants nothing to do with "cheap grace." The tattoo artist offers to cut the cost of the intricate Jesus tattoo by providing only an outline and some of Jesus's features. Parker responds, "Just like it is or nothing" (522).

4. Ibid., 528.

5. Two "grotesque" characters dominate O'Connor's most famous short story, "A Good Man Is Hard to Find." One is the grandmother, a superficial Christian quite prepared to deny Jesus's resurrection and label evil good if her life depends on it. The other grotesque character is the wantonly murderous Misfit, who, even though he cannot answer his own agonizing question about Jesus's resurrection, realizes that if Jesus did in fact rise from the dead, "then it's nothing for you to do but throw away everything and follow Him, and if He didn't, then it's nothing for you to do but enjoy the few minutes you got left the best way you can." Perceptive readers know that O'Conner has boldly placed the resolute words of the apostle Paul (1 Cor. 15:32) on the lips of the Misfit, who, ironically, was closer to the kingdom of God than was the superficial "Christian" grandmother. Suspended in uncertainty, he is a "Misfit." *Flannery O'Connor: The Complete Stories*, 117-33.

6. Augustine, *The Confessions of St. Augustine*, trans. Albert C. Outler (Philadelphia: Westminster Press, 1955; Grand Rapids: Christian Classics Ethereal Library [CCEL]), bk. 1, chap. 1.1, http://www.ccel.org/ccel/augustine/confessions.pdf.

7. The words "image" (□elem) and "likeness" (děm□t) mean the same in Hebrew.

8. Being in the image of God includes "entering into communion with other persons" and by grace into "a covenant with his Creator, to offer him a response of faith and love that no other creature can give in his stead." *Catechism of the Catholic Church*, pt. 1, sec. 2, chap. 1, par. 6.1.357, http://www.vatican.va/archive/ENG0015/__P1B.HTM.

9. Abraham Joshua Heschel, *God in Search of Man: A Philosophy of Judaism* (New York: Farrar, Straus and Giroux, 1955), 289-90. The Torah, Heschel says, "is primarily *divine ways* rather than *divine laws*. . . . No image of the Supreme may be fashioned, save one: our own life as an image of His will. Man, formed in His likeness, was made to imitate His ways of mercy. He has delegated to man the power to act in His

stead. We represent Him in relieving affliction, in granting joy. . . . Jewish law is, in a sense, *a science of deeds*. Its main concern is not only how to worship Him at certain times but how to live with Him at all times" (288, 290, 292). Having been created in the likeness of God, humans are "called upon to re-create the world in the likeness of the vision of God" (323). The topic of what it means to be human "can never be treated in isolation but only in relation to God." "The Bible is God's anthropology rather than man's theology" (412).

10. N. T. Wright, *The Day the Revolution Began: Reconsidering the Meaning of Jesus's Crucifixion* (New York: HarperCollins, 2016), 77.

11. Ibid., 78-79.

12. "The unredeemed state of the world," observes Joseph Ratzinger (Pope Benedict XVI), "consists precisely in the failure to understand the meaning of creation, in the failure to recognize truth." Joseph Ratzinger (Pope Benedict XVI), *Jesus of Nazareth, Part Two: Holy Week: From the Entrance into Jerusalem to the Resurrection* (San Francisco: Ignatius Press, 2011), 193.

13. C. John Collins, *Genesis 1–4: A Linguistic, Literary, and Theological Commentary* (Phillipsburg, NJ: P. and R. Publishing, 2005), 172-73. "Man is," says Abraham Joshua Heschel, "meaningless without God. . . . Liberty is an empty concept. . . . There is no freedom except the freedom bestowed upon us by God; there is no freedom without sanctity." *God in Search of Man*, 169-70. *The Catechism of the Catholic Church* says the "tree of the knowledge of good and evil" symbolizes the "moral norms that govern the use of freedom." Pt. 1, sec. 2, chap. 1, par.7.3.396, http://www.vatican.va/archive /ENG0015/__P1C.HTM.

14. Joseph Ratzinger (Pope Benedict XVI), *Jesus of Nazareth* (New York: Doubleday, 2007), 138.

15. Collins, *Genesis 1–4*, 174.

16. John H. Walton, *The Lost World of Genesis One: Ancient Cosmology and the Origins Debate* (Downers Grove, IL: IVP Academic, 2009), 135. N. T. Wright says Genesis means to tell us that "something has gone badly wrong. Something is deeply amiss with creation, and within . . . humankind itself." N. T. Wright, *Paul in Fresh Perspective* (Minneapolis: Fortress Press, 2005), 24.

17. Augustine, describing sin as misdirected love, observes that it is "an abandonment of that which has supreme being for that which has less." *The City of God*, in series I, vol. 2, *Nicene and Post-Nicene Fathers*, ed. Philip Schaff (1885; Grand Rapids: CCEL), bk. XII, chap. 8, https://www.ccel.org/ccel/schaff/npnf102.pdf. Martin Luther employs the concept, but not the same phrase. As a result of the fall, Luther says that humans have "a propensity toward evil." It is "a nausea toward the good, a loathing of light and wisdom." Martin Luther, *Luther's Works, Volume 25: Lectures on Romans* (Saint Louis: Concordia, 1972), 299.

"There is," said Abraham Heschel, "a suffocating selfishness in man which only holiness can ventilate." *God in Search of Man*, 169.

18. Heschel, *God in Search of Man*, 90.

19. N. T. Wright says the primary human problem Paul notes in Romans 1:18 "is not 'sin,' but 'ungodliness.' It is a failure not primarily of behavior (though that follows), but of worship. Worship the wrong divinity, and instead of reflecting God's

wise order into the world you will reflect and then produce distortion: something out of joint, something 'unjust.'" *Day the Revolution Began*, 268.

20. A recent illustration is the arrival of "technological secularism," or "techno-secularity." This is a belief that through advanced technology, globalization, individualism, and urbanization, humankind has created a space in which religious commitments are optional. Technology has displaced religious belief in civic life. Supposedly it provides an ethic, a theology, and a spirituality that replace traditional religion. Willem B. Drees, "Techno-Secularity and Techno-Sapiens: Religion in an Age of Technology" (February 2013), *Zygon: Journal of Religion and Science*, http://zygonjournal.org/technology.html.

21. This passage in Genesis is called the protoevangelium (first gospel): the first announcement of the Messiah and Redeemer.

22. Wright, *Paul in Fresh Perspective*, 23. See chapter 2, where Wright discusses the inseparable relationship between creation and covenant in the Old Testament and in the apostle Paul. See the song of the vineyard in Isaiah 5:1-7 and the parable of the vineyard in Luke 20:9-19.

23. The coming together of creation and covenant "has taken the form of an actual event . . . which has already happened, an event which consisted, surprisingly and shockingly, of the shameful and cruel death by crucifixion of the one who has thus fulfilled the double divine purpose" of covenant faithfulness and judgment against covenant faithlessness, against idolatry. Ibid., 27-28.

24. The Hebrew word for "steadfast love" is ☐esed. It also means "loving-kindness," "mercy," and sometimes "loyalty." British Old Testament scholar Norman Snaith said, "The word stands for the wonder of God's unfailing love for the people of his choice." His "steadfast love" "passes beyond human comprehension." *A Theological Word Book of the Bible*, ed. Alan Richardson (New York: MacMillan, 1951), 136-37. The nearest New Testament equivalent to ☐esed is *charis* (grace).

25. "The incidents recorded in the Bible to the discerning eye are episodes of one great drama: the quest of God for man; His search for man, and man's flight from Him." Heschel, *God in Search of Man*, 197.

26. Wright, *Day the Revolution Began*, 1-6.

27. New Testament scholar Michael J. Gorman takes us deep into this affirmation. For Paul, God's actions are "self-revelatory, the expression of God's essence or character." "*Christ crucified both reveals and redefines God.* . . . In Christ, Paul does not know a God of power *and* weaknesses but the God of power *in* weakness. God is cruciform." The "kerygmatic paradox" of 1 Cor. 1:18–2:5 "declares boldly that 'Christ [is] the power and wisdom of God' (1:24). . . . Traditional divine attributes—wisdom and power—are turned topsy-turvy by being associated with the foolishness and weakness of crucifixion." "The cross reveals the *holiness of God* (attribute, essence), just as it reveals the wisdom and power of God." For crucifixion to become the criterion of God's holiness is the "supreme scandal." Here we are not dealing with a "normal" deity. *Inhabiting the Cruciform God: Kenosis, Justification, and Theosis in Paul's Narrative Soteriology* (Grand Rapids: Eerdmans, 2009), 118-19.

See also N. T. Wright, *How God Became King: The Forgotten Story of the Gospels* (New York: HarperOne, 2012), 207.

28. Gorman says, "A fundamental category for understanding Paul [is] 'participation' [which] means participation in Christ, his crucifixion and resurrection, his story, and/or his present life." This understanding of "in Christ" spirituality and theology "is now widely accepted." *Inhabiting the Cruciform God*, 3.

29. Here in brief is N. T. Wright's explanation of what Paul means when he says God "put forth" (*hilastērion*) his Son (Rom. 3:25; cf. Heb. 9:5). Astonishingly, the faithful, living God comes into his world to do for Israel and the world what they could not do for themselves. In Jesus of Nazareth, God incarnate becomes the place of meeting between the Creator and his human creatures. The word *hilastērion* (Gk.), *kappōret* (Hebr.), refers to the covering, the lid of the ark of the covenant—the "mercy seat" (Exod. 25:17; 30:6; 31:7). The *kappōret* or *hilastērion* was the specific place of meeting between Israel and Yahweh as they came together in solemn mutual relation. Here purification was made. It was sprinkled with the blood of the sacrificed animal on the annual Day of Atonement. The blood of the sin offering acted as a ritual detergent to purify the sanctuary, so that the place where the divine Glory came to dwell might be kept pure (Exod. 40). The divine Glory appeared in a cloud.

The ark of the covenant was the acacia-wood box, overlaid with gold. It contained the tablets of the Torah (Exod. 25:17-22, 10-16).

The cross of Christ is where the Passover event was heading all along—to establishing the unbreakable bond between God and his people and to new creation (the symbolic re-creation of Eden). The cross is the place where God cleanses Israel from sins so that he and his people can meet and the true worship that replaces faithlessness and idolatry can be restored. Wright, *Day the Revolution Began*, 299-317.

30. Ibid., 2-3.

31. Ibid., 34.

32. Gorman says that according to the apostle Paul, through enablement by the Holy Spirit, "God's justified, holy, Spirit-led people" are to become so completely identified with and participants in the God revealed in Christ crucified that "the gospel of God reconciling the world to himself becomes" their defining story in the world. Gorman, *Inhabiting the Cruciform God*, 8.

33. Gorman says the apostle Paul understood Christian holiness as "theosis," which means "transformative participation in the kenotic [self-emptying], cruciform character and life of God through Spirit-enabled conformity to the incarnate, crucified, and resurrected/glorified Christ, who is the image of God." Ibid., 7, 125, 162. Earlier Gorman makes clear this means "the triune God, Father, Son, and Spirit." Ibid., 2.

34. Wright, *Day the Revolution Began*, 147.

35. Ibid., 385.

36. Ibid.

37. Ibid., 358.

38. Ibid., 384.

39. Ibid.

40. Ibid., 357.

41. Ibid.

42. Ibid., 356-57.

43. Eugene Peterson, *Reversed Thunder: The Revelation of John and the Praying Imagination* (New York: HarperCollins, 1988), 3.

44. Frances Ridley Havergal (1836-79), composer of "Take My Life and Let It Be," cautions that Christian discipleship "is not a religiously selfish thing. If it sinks into that it ceases to be discipleship." We are redeemed "not for ourselves, but for Jesus; not for our own safety, but for God's glory; not for comfort, but for God's joy; not for our own leisure, but that Christ may see the travail of His soul accomplished in us." We are redeemed "for Christ's sake, for His will and work, redeemed so that no other lord will have dominion over us. We should desire, and will have, all God's privileges that come with being fully given to Him. But the lower is included in the higher. If the love of Christ constrains us, our controlling aim will be far beyond our own interests." *Kept for the Master's Use* (Philadelphia: Henry Altemus, 1895; repr., Grand Rapids: CCEL), chap. 1, http://www.ccel.org/ccel/havergal/keptuse.txt.

45. "The joy of the gospel fills the hearts and lives of all who encounter Jesus. Those who accept his offer of salvation are set free from sin, sorrow, inner emptiness and loneliness. With Christ joy is constantly born anew." Francis, *Evangelii gaudium* [The Joy of the Gospel], Vatican Website, November 24, 2013, introd., sec. 1, https://w2.vatican.va/content/francesco/en/apost_exhortations/documents/papa-francesco_esortazione-ap_20131124_evangelii-gaudium.html.

46. Australian New Testament scholar David Peterson, commenting on 2 Corinthians 3:18, says, "All believers under the New Covenant can have an uninterrupted vision of the glory of God, and the 'boldness' of approach enjoyed by Moses. There is no place for any spiritual elite in the New Testament." *Possessed by God: A New Testament Theology of Sanctification and Holiness* (Grand Rapids: Eerdmans, 1995), 123.

47. Martin Luther, *On the Freedom of a Christian* (1520), Modern History Sourcebook, Fordham University, http://sourcebooks.fordham.edu/halsall/mod/luther-freedomchristian.asp.

48. R. J. Snell, "On Having Enemies to Love," The Catholic Thing, July 6, 2017, https://www.thecatholicthing.org/2017/07/06/on-having-enemies-to-love/. This is strongly recommended for reading and reflection.

49. O'Connor, "Parker's Back," 528.

Chapter 2

1. The term is Richard Hays's in *Reading Backwards: Figural Christology and the Fourfold Gospel Witness* (Waco, TX: Baylor University Press, 2014).

2. John E. Hartley, *Leviticus*. Word Biblical Commentary 4 (Dallas: Word, 1992), lvi.

3. Philip Jenson, "Holiness in the Priestly Writings of the Old Testament," in *Holiness: Past and Present*, ed. Stephen C. Barton (London: T and T Clark, 2003), 104.

4. Andy Johnson, *Holiness and the Missio Dei* (Eugene, OR: Cascade Books, 2016), 7.

5. Timothy C. Tennent, *The Call to Holiness: Pursuing the Heart of God for the Love of the World* (Franklin, TN: Seedbed, 2014), 13.

6. Johnson, *Holiness and the Missio Dei*, 8.

7. Christopher J. H. Wright, *The Mission of God: Unlocking the Bible's Grand Narrative* (Downers Grove, IL: InterVarsity Press, 2006), 257.

8. Won Keun Oh, "Holiness of Abraham in Genesis and in the Rewritten Bible" (PhD Thesis, University of Manchester, 2007), 75–77.

9. "Blameless" is not the same as "flawless."

10. Wright, *Mission of God*, 367.

11. Johnson, *Holiness and the Missio Dei*, 16.

12. Jo Bailey Wells, *God's Holy People: A Theme in Biblical Theology*, Journal for the Study of the Old Testament Supplement Series 305 (Sheffield, UK: Sheffield Academic Press, 2000), 28.

13. James E. Robson, "Forgotten Dimensions of Holiness," *Horizons in Biblical Theology* 33, no. 2 (2011): 133.

14. Ibid.

15. Ibid.

16. Wells, *God's Holy People*, 28.

17. Dwight Swanson, "Leviticus and Purity," in *Purity: Essays in Bible and Theology*, eds. Andrew Brower Latz and Arseny Ermakov (Eugene, OR: Wipf and Stock, 2014), 38.

18. Wright, *Mission of God*, 372.

19. Wells, *God's Holy People*, 60.

20. Mary Douglas, "Justice as the Cornerstone: An Interpretation of Leviticus 18–20," *Interpretation* 53 (1999): 348.

21. Ibid., 349.

22. Wright, *Mission of God*, 373.

23. Tennent, *The Call to Holiness*, 20.

24. Jonathan Sacks, *Not in God's Name: Confronting Religious Violence* (New York: Schocken Books, 2015), 209.

25. Lawson Stone, "7 Keys to Understanding Violence in the Book of Joshua," September 2, 2013, Seedbed, https://www.seedbed.com/7-keys-to-understanding-violence-in-the-book-of-joshua.

26. Sacks, *Not in God's Name*, 186. The problem of violence in the Christian sacred text remains. It must never be used by those whose vocation is to be holy to justify any violence against wickedness. God's purposes are life giving, not death. Ultimately, the story of God deconstructs the human story of division, domination, and violence. For Christians, only a rereading of the narrative, understood in the light of the life, death, resurrection, and ascension of the Messiah who absorbs rather than perpetuates violence, will challenge what Sacks (101) calls "altruistic evil: evil committed in a sacred cause, in the name of high ideals." For further discussion, see Kent Brower, "Holiness and Purity in a Post-Christian Age," in *The Journal of Wesleyan Thought* 1, no. 1 (November 2018), https://www.acwr.edu.au/journal-of-wesleyan-thought.

27. Sacks, *Not in God's Name*, 236.

28. Johnson, *Holiness and the Missio Dei*, 32.

29. Wells, *God's Holy People*, 136.

30. Marcus J. Borg, *Conflict, Holiness, Politics in the Teaching of Jesus* (London: Continuum, 1984), 67.

31. Ibid., 66.

32. The view is controversial. See James M. Scott, ed., *Exile: A Conversation with N. T. Wright* (Downers Grove, IL: InterVarsity Press, 2017).

33. Borg, *Conflict, Holiness, Politics*, 71.

34. Ibid., 67.

35. Alex R. G. Deasley, *The Shape of Qumran Theology* (Carlisle, UK: Paternoster, 2001), 214.

36. Borg, *Conflict, Holiness, Politics*, 73.

37. The literature on Messiah(s) is vast. See, for instance, Stanley E. Porter, ed., *The Messiah in the Old and New Testaments* (Grand Rapids: Eerdmans, 2007).

38. While "son of god" [υ□ο□ θεο□] in Mark 1:1 is disputed on textual grounds, a strong case can be made for reading it on literary grounds.

39. Arseny Ermakov, "The Holy One of God in Markan Narrative," in *Horizons in Biblical Theology* 36, no. 2 (2014), 159-84.

40. See Brian K. Gamel, *Mark 15:39 as a Markan Theology of Revelation: The Centurion's Confession as Apocalyptic Unveiling*, Library of New Testament Studies 574 (London: T and T Clark, 2017).

41. Richard A. Burridge, *What Are the Gospels? A Comparison with Graeco-Roman Biography*, 2nd ed. (Grand Rapids: Eerdmans, 2004); Richard Bauckham, ed., *The Gospels for All Christians: Rethinking the Gospel Audiences* (Grand Rapids: Eerdmans, 1998).

42. For a detailed discussion, see Kent E. Brower, *Mark: A Commentary in the Wesleyan Tradition*, New Beacon Bible Commentary (Kansas City: Beacon Hill Press of Kansas City, 2012).

43. Ibid., 116.

44. See J. Patrick Mullen, *Dining with Pharisees* (Collegeville, MN: Liturgical Press, 2004); Craig L. Blomberg, *Contagious Holiness: Jesus' Meals with Sinners*, New Studies in Biblical Theology 19 (Downers Grove, IL: InterVarsity Press, 2005).

45. See Mi Ja Wi, *The Path to Salvation in Luke's Gospel: What Must We Do?*, Library of New Testament Studies 607 (London: T and T Clark, 2019).

46. See Jenson, "Holiness in the Priestly Writings."

47. See Stephen C. Barton, "Dislocating and Relocating Holiness: A New Testament Study," in *Holiness: Past and Present*, 193-213.

48. Ibid., 197.

49. Johnson, *Holiness and the Missio Dei*, 103.

50. Ibid., 70.

51. See Gabi Markusse, *Salvation in the Gospel of Mark: The Death of Jesus and the Path of Discipleship* (Eugene, OR: Pickwick, 2018).

52. See Michael J. Gorman, "'You Shall Be Cruciform for I Am Cruciform': Paul's Trinitarian Reconstruction of Holiness," in *Holiness and Ecclesiology in the New Testament*, ed. Kent E. Brower and Andy Johnson (Grand Rapids: Eerdmans, 2007), 148-67.

53. Johnson, *Holiness and the Missio Dei*, 116.

54. See Luke Bretherton, *Hospitality as Holiness: Christian Witness amid Moral Diversity* (Aldershot, UK: Ashgate, 2006); Christine D. Pohl, *Living into Community: Cultivating Practices That Sustain Us* (Grand Rapids: Eerdmans, 2011).

55. See, for example, Brian Brock, *Wondrously Wounded: Theology, Disability, and the Body of Christ* (Waco, TX: Baylor University Press, 2019); Amos Yong, *The Bible,*

Disability, and the Church: A New Vision of the People of God (Grand Rapids: Eerdmans, 2011); Thomas E. Reynolds, *Vulnerable Communion: A Theology of Disability and Hospitality* (Grand Rapids: Brazos Press, 2008). Parts of the church have always seen service among the marginalized as the vocation of holiness. The L'Arche communities epitomize this outlook. This service has to be set alongside the appalling stain on the church from its legacy of the abuse of the vulnerable.

56. John Wesley, *Explanatory Notes upon the New Testament* (1755; repr., Kansas City: Beacon Hill Press of Kansas City, 1981), comment on 1 Tim. 1:5.

57. For further details, see Brower, "Holiness and Purity."

58. Robert W. Wall, "Acts," in vol. 10 of *The New Interpreter's Bible* (Nashville: Abingdon, 2002), 26.

59. Ibid., 271.

60. See Svetlana Khobnya, *The Father Who Redeems and the Son Who Obeys: Consideration of Paul's Teaching in Romans* (Eugene, OR: Pickwick, 2013).

61. See Gorman, "You Shall Be Cruciform."

62. The translation is that of Markus Bockmuehl, *The Epistle to the Philippians*, Black's New Testament Commentaries (London: A and C Black, 1997), 97.

63. Johnson, *Holiness and the Missio Dei*, 152.

64. Michael J. Gorman, *Cruciformity: Paul's Narrative Spirituality of the Cross* (Grand Rapids: Eerdmans, 2001), 349, cited by Johnson, *Holiness and the Missio* Dei, 127.

65. Barton, "Dislocating and Relocating Holiness," 206, his italics.

66. Ibid., 208.

67. See G. J. Thomas, "The Perfection of Christ and the Perfecting of Believers," in *Holiness and Ecclesiology in the New Testament*, 293-310.

68. See Shively T. J. Smith, *Strangers to Family: Diaspora and 1 Peter's Invention of God's Household* (Waco, TX: Baylor University Press, 2016); Daniel L. Smith-Christopher, *A Biblical Theology of Exile*, Overtures to Biblical Theology (Minneapolis: Fortress Press, 2002).

69. Ibid., 42.

70. Joel B. Green, "Living as Exiles: The Church in the Diaspora in 1 Peter," in *Holiness and Ecclesiology in the New Testament*, 322.

71. Smith, *Strangers to Family*, 165.

72. For a reading that reflects the tension between Paul and his Corinthian converts, see Hans Frör, *You Wretched Corinthians! The Correspondence between the Church in Corinth and Paul* (London: SCM Press, 1995).

73. See Gordon J. Thomas, "A Holy God among a Holy People in a Holy Place: The Enduring Eschatological Hope," in *Eschatology in Bible and Theology: Evangelical Essays at the Dawn of a New Millennium*, ed. Kent E. Brower and Mark W. Elliott (Downers Grove, IL: InterVarsity Press, 1997), 53-69.

74. Dean Flemming, "On Earth as It Is in Heaven: Holiness and the People of God in Revelation," in *Holiness and Ecclesiology in the New Testament*, 347-48.

75. Ibid., 353.

76. Ibid., 358, citing N. T. Wright, "Paul's Gospel and Caesar's Empire," in *Paul and Politics: Ekklesia, Israel, Imperium, Interpretation*, ed. R. A. Horsley (Harrisburg, PA: Trinity Press International, 2000), 182-83.

77. Ibid., 358.

78. These conclusions are a revision of Brower, "Holiness and Purity."

Chapter 3

1. The Russian Orthodox Church sent missionaries to Alaska, then a Russian territory, in 1793. The mission expanded into the lower forty-eight and included most Orthodox Christians. After the Bolshevik Revolution in 1917, Orthodoxy in America was cut off from the Russian church. The different ethnic Orthodox groups went under their own patriarchs in the old countries, and Orthodoxy in America was fragmented into many ethnic jurisdictions. The original mission became the "Orthodox Church in America" in 1970. See *Orthodox America 1794–1796: Development of the Orthodox Church in America*, ed. Constance J. Tarasar and John H. Erickson (Syosset, NY: Orthodox Church in America, Dept. of History and Archives, 1975).

2. Alexander Schmemann, *The Historical Road of Eastern Orthodoxy*, trans. Lydia Kesich (Crestwood, NY: St. Vladimir's Seminary Press, 2003), 199.

3. Georges Florovsky, "Patristic Theology and the Ethos of the Orthodox Church," in *Aspects of Church History*, vol. 4 of *The Collected Works of Georges Florovsky, Emeritus Professor of Eastern Church History, Harvard University*, ed. Richard S. Haugh (Belmont, MA: Nordland, 1987), 13-14, 30.

4. "Afterfeast" refers to a period of time following certain major feasts of the Christian year during which the feast continues to be celebrated.

5. Saint Macarius the Egyptian (AD 300–386), Homily 34.3, in *Fifty Spiritual Homilies of St. Macarius the Egyptian*, by A. J. Mason (London: Society for Promoting Christian Knowledge, 1921; repr., London: Forgotten Books, 2012), 245.

6. "Likeness" is the potential to become one with God. *The Philokalia*, trans. Constantine Cavarnos (Belmont, MA: Institute for Byzantine and Modern Greek Studies, 2008), 96.

7. LXX is the abbreviation for the Greek translation of the Old Testament, called the Septuagint. It is the official Bible of the Orthodox Church.

8. Mother Mary and Archimandrite Kallistos Ware, eds., *The Festal Menaion* (1969; repr., South Canaan, PA: St. Tikhon's Seminary Press, 1998), 278.

9. Saint Macarius, Homily 15.32, in *Fifty Spiritual Homilies*, 122.

10. Saint Macarius, Homily 15.36, in *Fifty Spiritual Homilies*, 123.

11. Saint Gregory Palamas, *The Homilies*, ed. and trans. Christopher Veniamin (Waymart, PA: Mount Thabor Publishing, 2009), 518.

12. Saint Ephrem the Syrian, *Hymns on Paradise*, trans. Sebastian Brock (Crestwood, NY: St. Vladimir's Seminary Press, 1990), hymn 1.8-9, pp. 51, 91, 95.

13. Ibid., hymn 3.1, p. 90.

14. Saint John of Damascus, *An Exact Exposition of the Orthodox Faith*, 2.11, in vol. 94 of J. P. Migne, *Patrologiae Graecae* (Turnholti Belgium: Typographi Brepols Editores Pontificii, n.d.), col. 913AB.

15. For example, *The Lenten Triodion* (Church Services of Great Lent), trans. Mother Mary and Archimandrite Kallistos Ware (London and Boston: Faber and Faber, 1984), 199.

16. Saint Macarius, Homily 15.35, in *Fifty Spiritual Homilies,* 123.

17. St. Maximus the Confessor, "Second Century on Love," secs. 78, 82, in *The Philokalia* II, 78, 79.

18. Saint Ephrem the Syrian, *Hymns on Paradise,* hymn 3, pp. 90-96.

19. Discussed in Hieromonk Damascene, *Christ the Eternal Tao,* 7th ed. (Platina, CA: Valaam Books, 2017), 217-21, 279-85.

20. Wisdom of Solomon 1:2-4, LXX: "The LORD will be found only of them that do not tempt Him. He shows Himself only to those who do not distrust Him. Crooked thoughts separate from God, for into a malicious soul Wisdom will not enter nor dwell in the body that is subject to sin" (trans. author).

21. St. Diadochos of Photiki, "On Spiritual Knowledge," sec. 25, in vol. 1 of *The Philokalia: The Complete Text Compiled by St. Nikodimos of the Holy Mountain and St. Makarios of Corinth,* ed. G. E. H. Palmer, Philip Sherrard, and Kallistos Ware (London and Boston: Faber and Faber, 1990), 259.

22. Damascene, *Christ the Eternal Tao,* 219-20.

23. See Saint Maximos the Confessor, "Fifth Century of Various Texts," secs. 84, 83, in *Philokalia,* vol. 2, 280.

24. Mary and Ware, *Festal Menaion,* 376.

25. Saint Macarius, Homily 15.39, in *Fifty Spiritual Homilies,* 125.

26. Saint Maximos, "Second Century on Love," sec. 93, in *Philokalia,* vol. 2, 81.

27. Ibid.

28. Saint Diadochos of Photiki, "On Spiritual Knowledge," sec. 3, in *Philokalia,* vol. 1, 253; *Sources Chretiennes* (Paris: Les Éditions du Cerf, 2011), 86.

29. "First Century of Various Texts," sec. 33, in *Philokalia,* vol. 2, 172.

30. Saint Macarius, Homily 15.48, in *Fifty Spiritual Homilies,* 130.

31. Saint Macarius, Homily 11.11, in *Fifty Spiritual Homilies,* 85.

32. Saint Maximos, "Second Century on Love," sec. 93, in *Philokalia,* vol. 2, 81.

33. Saint Macarius, Homily 30.8, in *Fifty Spiritual Homilies,* 227.

34. Saint Macarius, Homily 15.35, in *Fifty Spiritual Homilies,* 123.

35. Tuesday Matins, Tone 5, in *The Octoechos. The Hymns of the Cycle of the Eight Tones for Sundays and Weekdays,* vol. 3, trans. Isaac E. Lambertsen (Liberty, TN: St. John of Kronstadt Press, 1999), 37.

36. Mary and Ware, *Festal Menaion,* 174-75.

37. That the Theotokos is the Temple of God foreshadowed in the Old Testament is indicated by Saint Luke. He records the word of the archangel to the Holy Virgin: "The Holy Spirit will come upon you, and the Power of the Most High (the Holy Spirit) will overshadow you [from the verb *episkiazō*]" (Luke 1:35, trans. author). "Overshadow," *episkiazō,* is the verb used of the glory of the Lord, the Holy Spirit, overshadowing the "moving temple" or the tent of meeting (Exod. 40:35).

38. The feasts are the Nativity of the Theotokos, September 8; the Entry of Virgin Mary into the Temple, November 21; the Entry of the Lord into the Temple, February

2; the Annunciation of Virgin Mary, March 25; and the Dormition of the Theotokos, August 15.

39. Mary and Ware, *Festal Menaion*, 101.

40. From the *Octoechos*, a prayer sung to the Theotokos at a weekday Matins service.

41. Mary and Ware, *Festal Menaion*, 107.

42. Ibid., 376-77, 383.

43. It is confirmed in the church's liturgical texts—for example, "The place of the Skull has become Paradise; as soon as the wood of the Cross was planted there, at once it bore the Fruit of Life." Friday Matins, Tone 5.

44. From the *Octoechos*, Tone 2, for Friday Matins.

45. *Lenten Triodion*, 656. See also *The Ascetical Homilies of Saint Isaac the Syrian* (Brookline, MA: Holy Transfiguration Monastery, 1984), 142.

46. The ascetic disciplines of prayer, fasting, and almsgiving or deeds of mercy are central to Orthodox spirituality. They are the concrete form of the cross Christ commands his followers to take up if they would follow him. By them, they master their desire and submit themselves to Christ in the voluntary obedience of love.

47. *Lenten Triodion*, 230.

48. Mary and Ware, *Festal Menaion*, 133.

Chapter 4

1. "But if there is no resurrection of the dead, then Christ has not been raised; if Christ has not been raised, then our preaching is in vain and your faith is in vain" (1 Cor. 15:13-14, RSV).

2. "For the glory of God is a living man; and the life of man consists in beholding God." Saint Irenaeus (AD 130–202), *Against Heresies*, bk 4, chap. 20.7, New Advent, http://www.newadvent.org/fathers/0103420.htm.

3. "Why do you call me good? No one is good but God alone" (Mark 10:18, RSV).

4. "A holy life is not primarily the result of our efforts, of our actions, because it is God, the three times Holy (cf. Is. 6:3) who sanctifies us, it is the Holy Spirit's action that enlivens us from within, it is the very life of the Risen Christ that is communicated to us and that transforms us." Benedict XVI, *The Holiness*, Vatican Website, April 13, 2011, http://www.vatican.va/content/benedict-xvi/en/audiences/2011/documents/hf_ben-xvi_aud_20110413.html.

5. The Epistle to the Hebrews begins, "In the past God spoke to our ancestors through the prophets at many times and in various [fragmented] ways, but in these last days he has spoken to us by his Son, whom he appointed heir of all things, and through whom also he made the universe" (1:1-2).

6. Devine, Arthur, "State or Way (Purgative, Illuminative, Unitive)," in vol. 14 of *The Catholic Encyclopedia* (New York: Robert Appleton Company, 1912), New Advent, <http://www.newadvent.org/cathen/14254a.htm>. Primary source is Reginald Garrigou-Lagrange, *The Three Ages of the Interior Life: Prelude of Eternal Life*, trans. Sister M. Timothea Doyle (St. Louis: B. Herder Book, 1948). Originally published as *Les Trois Ages de la Vie Interieure* (1938).

7. Saint Thomas Aquinas (1225-74), *Opusculum 57, in festo Corporis Christi* (Feast of the Body and Blood), lect. 1-4. See "Saint Thomas Aquinas on the Feast of Corpus

Christi (Feast of the Body and Blood),"Agape Bible Study, http://agapebiblestudy .com/documents/St.%20Thomas%20Aquinas%20on%20the%20Feast%20of%20 Corpus%20Christi.htm.

8. "For lo, he who forms the mountains, and creates the wind, and declares to man what is his thought; who makes the morning darkness, and treads on the heights of the earth—the LORD, the God of hosts, is his name!" (Amos 4:13, RSV).

9. Saint Philip Neri, *The Maxims and Sayings of St. Philip Neri: Daily Meditations* (Potosi, WI: St. Athanasius Press, n.d.), 6, https://tinyurl.com/yckfeg9t.

10. "What no eye has seen, nor ear heard, nor the heart of man conceived, what God has prepared for those who love him" (1 Cor. 2:9, RSV).

11. "Do not hold me, for I have not yet ascended to the Father; but go to my brethren and say to them, I am ascending to my Father and your Father, to my God and your God" (John 20:17, RSV).

12. In an Advent sermon, Pope Leo the Great (r. 440-61) explained that representing the church, Mary Magdalene hastened to approach and touch Jesus. In his response to Mary (John 20:17), Jesus was saying to Mary and the church, "I would not have you come to Me as to a human body, nor yet recognize Me by fleshly perceptions: I put you off for higher things, I prepare greater things for you: when I have ascended to My Father, then you shall handle Me more perfectly and truly, for you shall grasp what you cannot touch and believe what you cannot see." Leo the Great, Sermon 74, "On the Lord's Ascension, II," sec. 4, New Advent, http://www .newadvent.org/fathers/360374.htm.

13. "We look not to the things that are seen but to the things that are unseen; for the things that are seen are transient, but the things that are unseen are eternal" (2 Cor. 4:18, RSV).

14. The Lord has ascended, exulted Pope Leo the Great, "so, dearly-beloved, let us rejoice with spiritual joy, and let us with gladness pay God worthy thanks and raise our hearts' eyes unimpeded to those heights where Christ is. Minds that have heard the call to be uplifted must not be pressed down by earthly affections, they that are fore-ordained to things eternal must not be taken up with the things that perish; they that have entered on the way of Truth must not be entangled in treacherous snares, and the faithful must so take their course through these temporal things as to remember that they are sojourning in the vale of this world, in which, even though they meet with some attractions, they must not sinfully embrace them, but bravely pass through them." "On the Lord's Ascension, II," sec. 5.

15. "I have been crucified with Christ; it is no longer I who live, but Christ who lives in me; and the life I now live in the flesh I live by faith in the Son of God, who loved me and gave himself for me" (Gal. 2:20, RSV).

16. For example, the Gospel account of the multiplication of loaves is revisited, prefiguring the first Mass on Holy Thursday. We are reminded of the Bread of Life discourse (John 6:22-59) that foreshadows and confirms a literal interpretation of the words of Jesus during the Last Supper, "This is my body."

17. "In this sacramental dispensation of Christ's mystery the Holy Spirit acts in the same way as at other times in the economy of salvation: he prepares the Church to encounter her Lord; he recalls and makes Christ manifest to the faith of the as-

sembly. By his transforming power, he makes the mystery of Christ present here and now. Finally the Spirit of communion unites the Church to the life and mission of Christ. The Holy Spirit prepares for the reception of Christ." *Catechism of the Catholic Church,* pt. 2, sec. 1, chap. 1, art. 1.3.1092, http://www.vatican.va/archive/ENG0015/__P2X.HTM.

18. From the Penitential Rite of the Catholic Mass.

19. Implicit in the words of Christ—cf. Matthew 12:32.

Chapter 5

1. "Canon within the canon" refers to those portions of the Scriptures that provide a particular biblical foundation for a given Christian tradition.

2. The classic treatment is Regin Prenter, *Spiritus Creator: Luther's Concept of the Holy Spirit* (Philadelphia: Fortress Press, 1953).

3. Martin Luther, "The Third Article: On Being Made Holy," *The Small Catechism,* in *The Book of Concord: The Confessions of the Evangelical Lutheran Church,* ed. Robert Kolb and Timothy J. Wengert (Minneapolis: Fortress Press, 2000), 355-56.

4. Cf. Luther, "The Second Article: On Redemption," *The Small Catechism,* 355.

5. The Book of Concord is a collection of authoritative writings used in the Lutheran tradition to interpret and standardize Christian teaching.

6. "The Augsburg Confession," in *The Book of Concord,* 41 [art. 4, Concerning Justification].

7. Martin Luther, "The Smalcald Articles," in *The Book of Concord,* 301 [pt. 2, art. 1].

8. For example, Carl E. Braaten, *Justification: The Article by Which the Church Stands or Falls* (Minneapolis: Fortress Press, 1990).

9. Gerhard Forde, "The Lutheran View," in *Christian Spirituality: Five Views of Sanctification,* ed. Donald L. Alexander (Downers Grove, IL: InterVarsity Press, 1988), 13.

10. Dietrich Bonhoeffer, *Discipleship,* eds. Geffrey B. Kelly and John D. Godsey, trans. Barbara Green and Reinhard Krauss (Minneapolis: Fortress Press, 2001), 53. The earlier translation of Bonhoeffer's book was titled *The Cost of Discipleship.*

11. Martin Luther, "The Freedom of a Christian," in *Luther's Works,* vol. 31, *Career of the Reformer I,* ed. Harold J. Grimm (Philadelphia: Fortress Press, 1957), 344.

12. Ibid., 346.

13. Ibid., 351.

14. Ibid., 365.

15. Martin Luther, "Two Kinds of Righteousness," in *Luther's Works,* vol. 31, *Career of the Reformer I,* 297.

16. Ibid., 299.

17. Ibid.

18. Philip Melanchthon, "The Use of the Law," in *Loci Communes* (1543), trans. J. A. O. Preus (St. Louis: Concordia, 1992), 74.

19. See Scott R. Murray, *Law, Life, and the Living God: The Third Use of Law in Modern American Lutheranism* (St. Louis: Concordia, 2002). Murray has provided an important survey of the third use of the law in American Lutheranism from 1940–2000. His research documents how the third use of the law remains highly contested

among American Lutheran theologians. Those who reject the third use of the law do so primarily to avoid the reintroduction of a new legalism into Lutheran theology. Those who defend the third use of the law do so to ward off antinomianism in the form of "Gospel reductionism." "Supporters of the third use of the Law warned that by denying it the church would fall into moral laxity." According to this view, a third use of the law is necessary to hold in check the sinner as self. There remains an open question whether Luther himself can be cited as an authority for a third use of the law and therefore whether it is a useful constructive category, even though it was clearly affirmed by Melanchthon and in the Formula of Concord. The danger is that the dictates of the law might displace the centrality of justification by faith in Christ alone. Those who shun the third use place their central focus on the freedom of the gospel as the fulcrum between the doctrine of justification and Lutheran ethics.

20. *Formula of Concord*, in *The Book of Concord*, 502 [art. 6.1, Concerning the Third Use of the Law].

21. "Legalism" in the Lutheran tradition is a term used to describe attempts to satisfy God's expectations through human efforts. "Antinomianism" in the Lutheran tradition is a term used to describe attempts to reject the value of following the law by Christians.

22. *Formula of Concord*, in *The Book of Concord*, 503 [art. 6, Negative Theses: False and Contrary Teaching].

23. Ibid, 503 [art. 6.6, Concerning the Third Use of the Law].

24. Heinrich Schmid, *The Doctrinal Theology of the Evangelical Lutheran Church: Exhibited and Verified from the Original Sources*, trans. Charles A. Hay and Henry E. Jacobs, 4th ed. (Philadelphia: Lutheran Publication Society, 1899), 424-41.

25. Ibid., 441-91.

26. Ibid., 486-87.

27. Philipp Jakob Spener, *Pia Desideria*, trans. Theodore G. Tappert (Philadelphia: Fortress Press, 1964).

28. Summarized from Douglas H. Shantz, *An Introduction to German Pietism: Protestant Renewal at the Dawn of Modern Europe*, foreword by Peter C. Erb (Baltimore: Johns Hopkins University Press, 2013), 89-91.

29. Ibid., 284.

30. *Following Our Shepherd to Full Communion: Report of the Lutheran-Moravian Dialogue with Recommendations for Full Communion in Worship, Fellowship, and Mission* (Chicago: Evangelical Lutheran Church in America, 1998), 30.

31. Ibid., 28.

32. Ibid., 31.

33. William H. Lazareth, *Christians in Society: Luther, the Bible, and Social Ethics* (Minneapolis: Augsburg Fortress, 2001), 199.

34. Ibid., 205.

35. Ibid., 224.

36. Ibid., 234.

37. Ibid., 259.

38. Ibid.

39. Cf. James L. Bailey, *Contrast Community: Practicing the Sermon on the Mount* (Eugene, OR: Wipf and Stock, 2013).

40. Bonhoeffer, *Discipleship,* 261.

41. Ibid., 252.

42. Ibid., 276.

43. Tuomo Mannermaa, *Christ Present in Faith: Luther's View of Justification*, ed. Kirsi Stjerna (Minneapolis: Fortress Press, 2005), 49 (italics removed).

44. Ibid., 84.

45. Ibid., 85.

46. Ibid., 85-86.

47. Ibid., 87-88. Mannermaa introduces the Orthodox understanding of "divinization" to characterize Luther's position, a theme not taken up in this chapter. See also Tuomo Mannermaa, *Two Kinds of Love: Martin Luther's Religious World*, trans. and ed. Kirsi Stjerna (Minneapolis: Fortress Press, 2010).

48. In the Affirmation of Baptism rite, the baptized promise "to live among God's faithful people, to hear the word of God and share in the Lord's Supper, to proclaim the good news of God in Christ through word and deed, to serve all people, following the example of Jesus, and to strive for justice and peace in all the earth." *Evangelical Lutheran Worship* (Minneapolis: Augsburg Fortress, 2006), 236.

49. Gustaf Wingren, *Luther on Vocation*, trans. Carl C. Rasmussen (Philadelphia: Muhlenberg Press, 1957).

50. See Craig L. Nessan, "Universal Priesthood of All Believers: Unfulfilled Promise of the Reformation," in *Reflecting Reformation and the Call for Renewal*, ed. Claudia Jahnel (Neuendettelsau, Ger.: Erlanger Verlag für Mission und Ökumene, 2018).

Chapter 6

1. John Calvin, *Golden Booklet of the True Christian Life*, trans. Henry J. Van Andel (Grand Rapids: Baker Books, 1952), 25.

2. John T. McNeill, *The History and Character of Calvinism* (New York: Oxford University Press, 1967), 109-18.

3. *A Declaration of Faith* (1977), Presbyterian Church (U.S.A.), https://www.pcusa .org/site_media/media/uploads/theologyandworship/pdfs/decoffaith.pdf.

4. John Calvin, *Institutes of the Christian Religion*, ed. John T. McNeill, trans. Ford Lewis Battles, Library of Christian Classics, vols. 20 and 21 (Philadelphia: Westminster Press, 1960), 3.6.3.

5. One of the best analyses of the youth phenomenon of that time is still Theodore Roszak, *The Making of a Counter Culture* (Garden City, NY: Doubleday, 1969), esp. 42-83.

6. *Westminster Shorter Catechism*, question 1, https://prts.edu/wp-content/uploads /2013/09/Shorter_Catechism.pdf.

7. Richard D. Phillips, "Election and Reprobation," in *John Calvin: A Heart for Devotion, Doctrine, and Doxology*, ed. Burk Parsons (Orlando, FL: Reformation Trust, 2008), 152.

8. Jean Cadier, *The Man God Mastered*, trans. O. R. Johnston (London: Inter-Varsity Press, 1960), 178; quoted in Iain H. Murray, foreword to *John Calvin: A Heart for Devotion, Doctrine, and Doxology*, xiii-xiv.

9. Richard Burnett, "Who Needs Confessions of Faith? A Reformed and Ecumenical Response," *Theology Matters* 23, no. 2 (Spring 2017): 1.

10. John H. Leith, *Introduction to the Reformed Tradition* (Atlanta: John Knox Press, 1977), 76.

11. Calvin, *Institutes*, 3.6.4.

12. Ibid., 3.6.2.

13. Ibid.

14. "The Shorter Catechism," in *The Constitution of the Presbyterian Church (USA), Part I: Book of Confessions* (Louisville, KY: Office of the General Assembly, 1999), 178 (altered by author to reflect gender inclusiveness).

15. Calvin, *Institutes*, 3.3.4. See also James B. Torrance, *Worship, Community and the Triune God of Grace* (Downers Grove, IL: InterVarsity Press, 1996), 54.

16. Calvin, *Institutes*, 3.3.3, and Donald K. McKim, *Introducing the Reformed Faith: Biblical Revelation, Christian Tradition, Contemporary Significance* (Louisville, KY: Westminster John Knox Press, 2001), 244n56.

17. Calvin, *Institutes*, 3.6.1 (gender inclusiveness added).

18. John Calvin, "Catechism," quoted in Ford Lewis Battles, *The Piety of John Calvin: An Anthology Illustrative of the Spirituality of the Reformer* (Grand Rapids: Baker Book House, 1978), 13; translation altered slightly in I. John Hesselink, *Calvin's First Catechism: A Commentary* (Louisville, KY: Westminster John Knox Press, 1997), 46.

19. Calvin, *Institutes*, 1.2.1.

20. Ibid., 3.2.7.

21. See especially John 3:16; 2 Corinthians 5:19.

22. Edward A. Dowey Jr., *The Knowledge of God in Calvin's Theology*, rev. ed. (Grand Rapids: Eerdmans, 1994), 182, quoting Calvin, *Commentary on Romans*, 8:34.

23. Calvin, *Golden Booklet*, 18; quoted in Jerry Bridges, "The True Christian Life," in *John Calvin: A Heart for Devotion, Doctrine and Doxology*, 222.

24. Calvin, *Golden Booklet*, 19.

25. Ibid., 25-46.

26. Ibid., 47-66.

27. Bridges, "The True Christian Life," 227.

28. John Piper, "Don't Waste Your Cancer," in *Suffering and the Sovereignty of God*, ed. John Piper and Justin Taylor (Wheaton, IL: Crossway Books, 2006), 207.

29. Calvin, *Institutes*, 1.16.1.

30. Ibid., 1.17.6.

31. John H. Leith, *John Calvin's Doctrine of the Christian Life* (Louisville, KY: Westminster John Knox Press, 1989), 110.

32. Ibid., 108.

33. Joel Beeke, "The Communion of Men with God," in *John Calvin: A Heart for Devotion, Doctrine and Doxology*, 231.

34. Calvin, *Institutes*, 3.20.2.

35. Ibid., 3.20.4-16.

36. Ibid., 3.20.4-5.

37. Ibid., 3.20.6.

38. "The Shorter Catechism," in *Constitution of the Presbyterian Church (USA)*, 185.

39. Calvin, *Institutes*, 3.20.10.

40. Ibid., 3.20.16.

41. Abraham Kuyper, "Sphere Sovereignty," in *Abraham Kuyper: A Centennial Reader* (Grand Rapids: Eerdmans, 1998), 488.

42. H. Richard Niebuhr, *Christ and Culture* (New York: Harper Torchbooks, 1956), 217.

43. Leith, *Introduction to the Reformed Tradition*, 67-85.

44. Calvin, *Institutes,* 1.5.7.

45. Ibid., 1.5.8; see also 1.6.2; 1.14.20; 3.9.2; and passim.

46. Ibid., 3.17.10; 3.23.12; 4.17.38.

47. "The Heidelberg Catechism," in *Constitution of the Presbyterian Church*, 29.

Chapter 7

1. For the most up-to-date information, consult the Anglican Communion's website, www.anglicancommunion.org, and particularly its "Press Section," where one can find the helpful "Anglican Communion Q & A."

2. See www.episcopalchurch.org.

3. Psalm 96:9, following the wording of the Psalter in *The Book of Common Prayer* (New York: Church Publishing Incorporated, 2015), 726. Hereafter cited as BCP 1979.

4. Many details about the evolution of the various rites, readings, and prayers can be found in Marion J. Hatchett's definitive work, *Commentary on the American Prayer Book* (New York: Seabury Press, 1980). See also Charles Hefling and Cynthia Shattuck, eds., *The Oxford Guide to the Book of Common Prayer: A Worldwide Survey* (Oxford, UK: Oxford University Press, 2006).

5. Matthew Towsend, "Changing Trains on Liturgical Revision," *The Living Church*, August 5, 2018, 7-8. I was privileged to serve in the House of Deputies at this seventy-ninth convention as part of the delegation from the Diocese of Kansas.

6. In his magisterial biography, Diarmaid MacCulloch argues that the BCP represents the archbishop's greatest achievement and enduring legacy. See *Thomas Cranmer: A Life* (New Haven, CT: Yale University Press, 1996), esp. 630-32.

7. See Brian Cummings, ed., *The Book of Common Prayer: The Texts of 1549, 1559, and 1662* (Oxford, UK: Oxford University Press, 2011), 4-6 (quotes from 4 and 5). I follow Cummings in not correcting Cranmer's original spelling.

8. Herbert's classical 1633 collection of poems, *The Temple*, may be found in John N. Wall Jr., ed., *George Herbert: The Country Parson, The Temple*, The Classics of Western Spirituality (New York: Paulist Press, 1981), 117-326.

9. Cummings, *Book of Common Prayer: The Texts*, 4-5. The Daily Office Lectionary of BCP 1979 (933-1001) settles, probably realistically, for getting through most of the Bible every two years.

10. Terrence Kardong, "*Lectio Divina*," in *The New Westminster Dictionary of Christian Spirituality*, ed. Philip Sheldrake (Louisville, KY: Westminster John Knox Press, 2005), 403-4.

11. Cummings, *Book of Common Prayer: The Texts*, 5.

12. In BCP 1979, morning and evening prayers are offered in two formats nearly identical in substance. Rite I (37-73) retains much traditional language, akin to the King James Version of the Bible, while terminology in Rite II (75-135) has been modernized and includes "An Order of Service for Noonday" (103-7) and "An Order for Compline" (127-35), as well as an alternative to evening prayer, "An Order of Worship for the Evening" (109-14). I recommend beginning with Rite II, so I shall refer to it exclusively below.

13. "The Invitatory and Psalter," Morning Prayer: Rite One, BCP 1979.

14. Dietrich Bonhoeffer, *Life Together: A Discussion of Christian Fellowship*, trans. John W. Doberstein (San Francisco: Harper and Row, 1954), 44-50.

15. From BCP 1979's baptismal rite, 308. I offer a more extended discussion of Holy Baptism in the next section.

16. From Suffrages A and B in Morning Prayer II (BCP 1979, 97-8). Suffrages A are also an option in Evening Prayer II (BCP 1979, 121-2).

17. From Morning Prayer II's "A Collect for the Renewal of Life" (BCP 1979, 99), "A Collect for Peace" (BCP 1979, 99), and "A Collect for Grace" (BCP 1979, 100).

18. Morning Prayer II (BCP 1979, 100-101; quote from the option on 101) and Evening Prayer II (BCP 1979, 124-25). The prayer for the care of all persons, the second option on 124, may also be employed in Compline (BCP 1979, 134) and comes from Augustine of Hippo (Hatchett, *Commentary on the American Prayer Book*, 143).

19. Morning Prayer II (BCP 1979, 102) and Evening Prayer II (BCP 1979, 126).

20. Morning Prayer II (BCP 1979, 101) and Evening Prayer II (BCP 1979, 125). See Hatchett, *Commentary on the American Prayer Book*, 130.

21. Morning Prayer II (BCP 1979, 102) and Evening Prayer II (BCP 1979, 126).

22. As summarized by Townsend's report on the most recent General Convention.

23. Paul Avis, "Anglicanism and Eucharistic Ecclesiology," in Avis's collection of essays, *The Identity of Anglicanism: Essentials of Anglican Ecclesiology* (London: T and T Clark, 2008), 81-108.

24. BCP 1979, 336 (in Eucharistic Prayer I) and 342 (Eucharistic Prayer II). (In Cranmer's original, Cummings, *Book of Common Prayer: The Texts*, 31). All of Holy Eucharist I may be found in BCP 1979, 322-49.

25. BCP 1979, 365-66, from Holy Eucharist II (354-82).

26. I first contributed to this lively discussion in "The Eucharist and World Hunger: An Episcopalian Reflection," *Anglican Theological Review* 73, no. 3 (Summer 1991), 267-79. I am currently working on the seminal Eucharistic theology of Bishop Charles Gore (1853-1932). I am grateful for ongoing discussions in a colloquy on Holy Communion at the Episcopal School for Ministry in St. Louis, convened by its former dean, Rev. Dr. Dan Handschy.

27. All contained in the section "Pastoral Offices" in BCP 1979, 411-507.

28. "Episcopal Services," BPC 1979, 509-79, which concludes with "The Dedication and Consecration of a Church," 566-79. In Episcopal polity all ordinations, licensing of canonically prescribed lay ministries, and consecrations must be performed by bishops. Since new ministries might also be celebrated by a parish, there

is a corresponding rite in the section "Pastoral Offices," "A Form of Commitment to Christian Service," 420-21.

29. "The Calendar of the Church Year," BCP 1979, 15-33. *The Revised Common Lectionary's* prescription of Bible texts for each Sunday in Years A, B, and C is found in BCP 1979, 887-922.

30. C.S. Lewis, "The Weight of Glory," in *The Weight of Glory and Other Addresses* (New York: Harper Collins, 1976), 25-46, esp. 46. The original edition appeared in 1949. Its contents are all the more remarkable for having been composed during the horrors of the Second World War.

31. BCP 1979, 339.

32. See, for instance, Clodovis Boff, "Methodology of the Theology of Liberation," in *Systematic Theology: Perspectives from Liberation Theology,* ed. Jon Sobrino and Ignacio Ellacuría (Maryknoll, NY: Orbis Books, 1993), 1-21 (and esp. 10-11).

33. Harmon L. Smith, "Contraception and Natural Law: A Half Century of Anglican Moral Reflection," in *The Anglican Moral Choice,* ed. Paul Elmen (Harrisburg, PA: Morehouse, 1983), 181-200.

34. In the case of the Episcopal Church, see *Constitution and Canons of the Episcopal Church, Together with the Rules of Order Adopted by the General Convention 1789–2015* (New York: General Convention of the Episcopal Church, 2016), Title I, canons 18 and 19 (58-59). See also the discussion of sexual ethics in influential Episcopal ethicist Timothy Sedgwick's *The Christian Moral Life: Practices of Piety* (Grand Rapids: Eerdmans, 1999), 53-76.

35. In the Episcopal Church all these matters are addressed in Title IV of the canons, tightened further at the General Convention of 2018.

36. George Conger, "Episcopal Church Adopts New Alcohol Policies in Wake of Heather Cook Affair," Anglican Link, July 4, 2015, http://anglican.ink/2015/07/04 /episcopal-church-adopts-new-alcohol-policies-in-wake-of-heather-cook-affair/. Heather Cook was an assistant bishop in the Diocese of Maryland who killed a cyclist while driving under the influence of alcohol. She was deprived of her ordained status and sentenced to prison.

37. R. C. D. Jasper and G. J. Cuming, eds. and trans., *Prayers of the Eucharist: Early and Reformed,* 3rd ed. (New York: Pueblo, 1987), 25-30.

38. Cummings, *Book of Common Prayer: The Texts,* 27.

39. Ibid. See also Colin Buchanan, *What Did Cranmer Think He Was Doing?,* Grove Liturgical Series 7 (Bramcote, UK: Grove Books, 1976), 11, 14, 28.

40. Henry Chadwick and Allison War, eds., *Not Angels, But Anglicans: A History of Christianity in the British Isles* (Norwich, UK: Canterbury Press, 2000) also covers overseas expansion of the church under the British Empire. Practicing economic dominance under the terms of the Monroe Doctrine, the US church also got into the colonial act, especially after the Spanish-American War. See Robert Prichard, *A History of the Episcopal Church,* rev. ed. (Harrisburg, PA: Morehouse, 1999), 193-97.

41. For one particularly powerful story of a clergy family, see Edward Ball, *Slaves in the Family* (New York: Farrar, Straus and Giroux, 1998).

42. Gardiner H. Shattuck Jr., *Episcopalians and Race: Civil War to Civil Rights* (Lexington, KY: University Press of Kentucky, 2000).

43. Seminarian Jonathan Myrick Daniels, an Episcopal martyr of the civil rights era, was greatly grieved by the strong resistance of the Episcopal Church in Alabama to admission of African Americans to Communion. See Rich Wallace and Sandra Neil Wallace, *Blood Brother: Jonathan Daniels and His Sacrifice for Civil Rights* (Honesdale, PA: Calkins Creek, 2016).

44. W. E. Tate, *The English Village Community and the Enclosure Movements* (London: Gollancz, 1967). Sanderson's six 1623 sermons may be found in *The Works of Robert Sanderson, D.D., Sometime Bishop of Lincoln*, ed. William Jacobson (Oxford, UK: Oxford University Press, 1854), vol. 2, "Ad Magistratum," 169-362.

45. Adam Hochschild, *Bury the Chains: Prophets and Rebels in the Fight to Free an Empire's Slaves* (New York: Houghton Mifflin, 2005).

46. This hymn originally appeared in Mrs. C. F. Alexander's *Hymns for Little Children* (London: J. Masters, 1848), no. 9, 27-28. Note that this lyric was part of the Christian formation of young people!

47. The theme of incarnation was never absent in Anglican thought, but it moved front and center in Charles Gore, ed., *Lux Mundi: A Series of Studies in the Religion of the Incarnation*. I own the US printing of the fifth edition (New York: John W. Lovell, n.d.). The original appeared in 1889 and rapidly went through numerous editions. I applied the Anglican approach to incarnation in *Listening to Popular Music* (Minneapolis: Fortress Press, 2013).

48. Bishop Charles Gore exemplifies the prophetic witness and describes the role of committed small groups in ecclesial transformation in *Christ and Society: The Halley Stewart Lectures, 1927* (New York: Charles Scribner's Sons, 1928). This book remains surprisingly relevant.

49. Cummings, *Book of Common Prayer: The Texts*, 46-57, quotes from 50. The overall emphasis, and interrogation, remained the same in the 1662 BCP, still the official book of the Church of England. See Cummings, 408-25 (interrogation for children, 411, and for those of "riper years," 422-23).

50. "Holy Baptism," BCP 1979, 302-3.

51. Ibid., 305.

52. Ibid.

53. Ibid.

54. Ibid., 307. Compare the rite in the alternative services book, *Common Worship: Services and Prayers for the Church of England* (London: Church House Publishing, 2000), 344-61. The final question is posed thus: "Will you acknowledge Christ's authority over human society, by prayer for the world and its leaders, by defending the weak, and by seeking peace and justice?" (359). Intercessions are included that pray for peace and justice and ask God to "deliver the oppressed, strengthen the weak, heal and restore your creation" (360).

55. As in Paul Avis, "Anglicanism and Baptismal Ecclesiology," in Avis, *The Identity of Anglicanism*, 109-17 (quote on 111).

56. Anglican Communion's website, http://www.anglicancommunion.org/. See section titled "Mission" as well as the material previously cited.

57. "General Convention Wrap-Up: Following the Way of Jesus," Episcopal News Service, July 16, 2019, https://www.episcopalnewsservice.org/2018/07/16 /general-convention-wrap-up-following-the-way-of-jesus/.

58. "Racial and Ethnic Composition among Members of the Episcopal Church," Pew Research Center, 2019, http://www.pewforum.org/religious-landscape-study /religious-denomination/episcopal-church/racial-and-ethnic-composition/.

59. The Church Pension Group's website includes an up to date directory of all clergy: https://www.ecdplus.org/.

Chapter 8

1. www.bbc.co.uk/religion/christianity/subdivisiones/baptists_1.shtml.

2. Yearbook of Churches, Association of Statisticians of American Religious Bodies, online data base 6-9-18, www.yearbookofchurches.org.

3. There is no definition or organizational expression of "progressive Baptists." There have been, however, across the years, Baptists who have combined historic Baptist distinctives such as the authority of Scripture and the priority of the born-again experience with liberal or progressive positions on issues such as civil rights, gender equality, and economic justice. Rauschenbusch, King, and Townes would be examples.

4. Asociación Bautista Argentina, Declaración de creencias y prácticas bautistas, Buenos Aires, http://www.bautistas.org.ar/prin_decia_doc.htm.

5. Dale Moody, *The Word of Truth: A Summary of Christian Doctrine Based on Biblical Revelation* (Grand Rapids: Eerdmans, 1981), 325.

6. James William McClendon Jr., *Doctrine*, vol. 2 of *Systematic Theology* (Nashville: Abingdon Press, 1994), 118. See also Augustus H. Strong, *The Doctrine of Salvation*, vol. 3 of *Systematic Theology* (Philadelphia: The Judson Press, 1909), 869; Stanley J. Grenz, *Created for Community: Connecting Christian Beliefs with Christian Living* (Grand Rapids: Baker Books, 1998), 198.

7. Moody, *Word of Truth*, 324.

8. Ibid.

9. John Calvin, *Institutes*, 4.1.17, cited in Moody, *Word of Truth*, 324. See Calvin, *Institutes of the Christian Religion*, vol. 2, 4.1.17, trans. Ford Lewis Battles, ed. John T. McNeill, The Library of Christian Classics, vol. 21, (Philadelphia: Westminster Press, 1960), 1031.

10. Carl F. H. Henry, *God Who Speaks and Shows: Fifteen Theses, Part Three*, vol. 4 of *God, Revelation and Authority* (Waco, TX: Word, 1979), 501.

11. Samuel Escobar, "Nuestra herencia evangélica," in *Ser Evangélico Hoy* (Barcelona, ESP: Editorial Andamio, 1988), 24.

12. Molly T. Marshall, *Joining the Dance: A Theology of the Spirit* (Valley Forge, PA: Judson Press, 2003), 98.

13. Molly T. Marshall, "Spiritual Formation: Humanity as Unfinished Presence," in *Freedom of Conscience: A Baptist/Humanist Dialogue*, ed. Paul D. Simmons (Amherst, NY: Prometheus Press, 2000), 196.

14. The books of R. J. Foster translated into Spanish that have enjoyed the greatest popularity are the following: *Alabanza a la disciplina* [Celebration of discipline] (Miami: Editorial Betania, 1986); *La oración, verdadero refugio del alma* [Prayer: True

refuge of the soul] (Miami: Editorial Betania, 1994); *Dinero, sexo y poder* [Money, sex, and power] (Miami: Editorial Betania, 1989); *Clásicos Devocionales* [Devotional classics)] (El Paso, TX: Editorial Mundo Hispano, 2004); *Rios de agua viva: El retorno a la Fuente de la renovación perdurable* [Rivers of living water: Essential practices from the six great traditions of Christian faith] (Miami: Editorial Peniel, 2010); *Santuario del alma: Descubre el gozo de la oración meditativa* [Sanctuary of the soul: Journey into meditative prayer] (El Paso, TX: Editorial Mundo Hispano, 2012); *Oración personal; Una guía para escuchar la voz de Dios y obedecer su Palabra* [Personal prayer: A guide to listening for the voice of God and obeying his word] (Buenos Aires: Certeza, 2013).

15. Grenz, *Created for Community*, 59.

16. Ibid., 78.

17. Jerry L. Ervin, "First Person: Pursuing Holiness," *The Baptist Messenger*, October 1, 2015, https://www.baptistmessenger.com/first-person-pursuing-holiness/.

18. Ibid.

19. Ibid.

20. "Neo-Calvinism," as per the teaching of nineteenth-century Dutch theologian Abraham Kuyper, emphasizes that in addition to the "special" or saving grace distributed among humans according to the will of a sovereign God, there is a "common" grace that restrains the destructive power of sin. This common grace enables even those not born again to recognize the good and the beautiful and to develop the "latent forces" of the universe for the common good. frcna.org/resources /student-society-speeches?download=3°.

21. Miguel Núñez, "Cómo reaccionar ante el pecado. Primera parte." *Integridad y Sabiduría* (blog), http://integridadysabiduria.org/como-reaccionar-ante-el-pecado -parte/.

22. See Martin Luther King Jr., "Letter from Birmingham Jail," April 16, 1963, African Studies Center, University of Pennsylvania, https://www.africa.upenn.edu /Articles_Gen/Letter_Birmingham.html.

23. Walter Rauschenbusch, *Christianizing the Social Order* (New York: Macmillan, 1912), 7, cited in Dennis L. Johnson, "Walter Rauschenbusch: A Baptist Model for Spiritual Formation in Baptist Congregations" (unpublished, 2017), 7.

24. Johnson, "Walter Rauschenbusch," 13.

25. Ibid., 11, citing Walter Rauschenbusch, *Selected Writings*, ed. Winthrop Hudson (New York: Paulist Press, 1984), 126-27.

26. David Shannon, Gayraud Wilmore, et. al. "Toward a Common Expression of Faith: A Black North American Perspective," *American Baptist Quarterly*, 4, no. 4 (December 1985): 392.

27. E. Y. Mullins, *The Axioms of Religion: A New Interpretation of the Baptist Faith* (Philadelphia: Griffith and Rowland Press, 1908), 40.

28. Ibid., 38.

29. Ibid., 41.

30. They influenced drafting the final 1974 Lausanne Covenant.

31. The Lausanne Covenant (1974), The Voice, http://www.crivoice.org/creed lausanne.html.

32. "Pacto de Lausanne," Movimiento de Lausanne, https://www.lausanne.org/es/contenido/pacto-de-lausanne/pacto (trans. author).

33. Ibid.

34. Mullins, *Axioms of Religion*, 155.

35. Marshall, "Spiritual Formation," 200.

36. Baptists certainly recognize that the Holy Spirit is the agent of the inspiration of Scripture (2 Tim. 3:16) and of the ongoing interpretation and application of Scripture. The listing of "teachers" among recipients of gifts of the Spirit in 1 Corinthians 12:28 implicitly makes this point.

37. Dale Moody, *Spirit of the Living God* (Philadelphia: Westminster Press, 1968), 120.

38. Ibid., 118-23.

39. Henry, *God Who Speaks and Shows*, 501. There is a strand of "Jesus only" piety among some Baptists. To correct that error it is important to state that the triune God, not just one member, is engaged in the ongoing transformation we call sanctification.

40. René Padilla, "El Espíritu Santo y la misión de la iglesia," in *El Trino Dios y la misión integral*, ed. Pedro Arana, Samuel Escobar, and René Padilla, (Buenos Aires: Editorial Kairós, 2003), 123.

41. Emilie M. Townes, *Womanist Ethics and the Cultural Production of Evil* (New York: Pelgrave Macmillan, 2006), 164.

42. Strong, *Doctrine of Salvation*, 869-70.

43. Grenz, *Created for Community*, 78.

Chapter 9

1. This is the final verse of the hymn "Love Divine, All Loves Excelling," written by Charles Wesley in 1747 (*Wesley Hymns* [Kansas City: Lillenas, 1982], no. 44). It is widely considered one of Charles Wesley's greatest hymns and one of the most important on the subject of holiness or sanctification.

2. For a detailed description of the contrast between John Calvin the systematic theologian and John Wesley's very practical and pastoral approach to theology, see Don Thorsen, *Calvin vs. Wesley: Bringing Belief in Line with Practice* (Nashville: Abingdon Press, 2013), xi-xxv.

3. John Wesley, "Preface," in *The Works of John Wesley*, 14 vols., 3rd ed. (Peabody, MA: Hendrickson, 1991), 5:2.

4. Ibid., 5:4.

5. See Randy L. Maddox, *Responsible Grace: John Wesley's Practical Theology* (Nashville: Kingswood Books, 1994), 83-84. And Albert C. Outler, "John Wesley: Folk Theologian," *Theology Today* 34 (July 1977): 150-60.

6. Wesley, "Sermon XI, The Witness of the Spirit," in *Works of John Wesley*, 5:124-25.

7. See C. S. Lewis, *The Lion, the Witch, and the Wardrobe* (London: Geoffrey Bles, 1950).

8. See in particular the work of Theodore Runyon in *The New Creation: John Wesley's Theology Today* (Nashville: Abingdon Press, 1988). In a less explicit Wesleyan way but within the Methodist-Anglican tradition and certainly in the Wesleyan

spirit, see N. T. Wright, *Surprised by Hope: Rethinking Heaven, the Resurrection, and the Mission of the Church* (New York: HarperOne, 2008).

9. Charles Wesley, "Christ, the Lord Is Risen Today," in *Wesley Hymns*, no. 157.

10. Wesley, "Sermon LXIII, The General Spread of the Gospel," in *Works of John Wesley*, 6:288 (emphasis mine).

11. Ibid.

12. Deism was a seventeenth- and eighteenth-century movement that, on the basis of reason, accepted the existence of a supreme being who does not intervene in the universe. God created the world according to natural laws by which the universe functions. God also established moral laws accessible by reason. Divine activity in the world is both impossible and unnecessary.

13. See Runyon, *New Creation*, 13.

14. Wesley, "Sermon XLV, The New Birth," in *Works of John Wesley*, 6:65-77.

15. Runyon, *New Creations*, 16.

16. Ibid., 18.

17. Wesley, "Sermon XLV, The New Birth," in *Works of John Wesley*, 6:66-67.

18. Timothy J. Crutcher, *John Wesley: His Life and Thought* (Kansas City: Beacon Hill Press of Kansas City, 2015), 120.

19. See Runyon, *New Creation*, 87.

20. Crutcher, *John Wesley*, 158.

21. Wesley, "Sermon XXIV, Upon Our Lord's Sermon on the Mount—Discourse IV," *Works of John Wesley*, 5:307 (author's paraphrase).

Chapter 10

1. For a very helpful discussion of the Holiness Movement as a forerunner to Pentecostalism, see Donald W. Dayton, *Theological Roots of Pentecostalism* (Grand Rapids: Baker Academic, 1987).

2. Various restorationist movements have sought to restore the church to greater conformity to primitive New Testament Christianity, as they have understood it.

3. This is not to overlook the importance of experience for Martin Luther and John Calvin. In Luther's "Preface to Romans" he speaks of God "pouring the Holy Spirit and His blessings upon us. . . . Both the gifts and the spirit must be received by us daily." Without a "corresponding experience" of "genuine faith . . . in the depth of the heart," faith is nothing more than a "human fabrication." It is "ineffective and not followed by a better life." *Martin Luther: Selections from His Writings*, ed. John Dillenberger (Garden City, NY: Anchor Books, 1961), 22-23.

John Calvin was no stranger to the importance of the inward testimony of the Holy Spirit. The truth of doctrine, Calvin insisted, "is not established until we have a perfect conviction that God is its author." Calvin particularly applied this to the authority of Scripture. "The highest proof of Scripture is uniformly taken from the character of him whose Word it is. . . . For as God alone can properly bear witness to his own words, so these words will not obtain full credit in the hearts of men, until they are sealed by the inward testimony of the Spirit. The same Spirit, therefore, who spoke by the mouth of the prophets, must penetrate our hearts." *Institutes of the Christian Religion*, trans. Ford Lewis Battles, 2 vols. (Philadelphia: Westminster, 1960), 1.7.4.

4. Todd M. Johnson, Gina A. Zurlo, et al., "Christianity 2018: More African Christians and Counting Martyrs," *International Bulletin of Mission Research* 42, no. 1 (January 2018), tables 2 and 3.

5. The term "classical Pentecostal" did not exist when I was young; we were just "Pentecostals." "Classical Pentecostal" is a term coined by my friend, the priest and Benedictine monk Dr. Kilian McDonnell, in a context of ecumenical dialogue. He used it to describe groups that grew out of, or that claim as a substantial part of their heritage, the Azusa Street revival, which took place in Los Angeles from 1906 to 1909, and to differentiate them from charismatics in the Catholic Church and mainline Protestant denominations.

6. The multiple, simultaneous origins theory links the beginning of the Pentecostal Movement to the many recorded incidents of glossolalia (speaking in tongues) in the late nineteenth century and the early twentieth century. But tongues by themselves are not enough to classify a person as a Pentecostal. Pentecostalism requires a theological linkage of speaking in tongues with the biblical concept of baptism in the Holy Spirit understood as empowering for witness. And while it is true that the Azusa Street revival was the launchpad from which Pentecostalism spread, in 1906 William Seymour himself acknowledged that Parham was "God's leader in the Apostolic Faith Movement." William Seymour, "Letter from Bro. Parham," *The Apostolic Faith* 1, no. 1 (September 1906): 1.

7. In general, the Wesleyan wing of Pentecostalism has spoken of three definite *experiences*, not three definite *works of grace*. Baptism in the Holy Spirit was viewed as an empowering, an addition to God's already completed saving activity. Seymour explained it this way, "Sanctification is the second work of grace and the last work of grace . . . . The Baptism with the Holy Ghost is a gift of power on the sanctified life." "The Apostolic Faith Movement," *The Apostolic Faith* 1, no. 1 (September 1906): 2.

The largest of the Wesleyan-Pentecostal denominations are the Church of God in Christ (COGIC), the Church of God (Cleveland), and the International Pentecostal Holiness Church (IPHC). Of these, the IPHC has the most purely Wesleyan roots, while the COGIC combines Wesleyan roots with Baptist roots, and the Church of God (Cleveland), while valuing its Wesleyan ancestry, no longer articulates a clearly Wesleyan approach to sanctification.

8. The largest of the Finished Work Pentecostal groups are the Assemblies of God and the International Church of the Foursquare Gospel.

9. Oneness Pentecostals prefer that the widely used descriptor "Jesus Only" Pentecostals not be used. See David K. Bernard, *A History of Christian Doctrine*, vol. 3, *The Twentieth Century* (Hazelwood, MO: World Aflame Press, 1999; Kindle edition), loc. 914. The largest of the Oneness Pentecostal groups are the United Pentecostal Church and the Pentecostal Assemblies of the World. In addition, there are many independent Oneness churches that use the words "apostolic faith" in their names.

10. The only Oneness group of which I am aware that takes a holiness Pentecostal approach to sanctification is the Apostolic and Overcoming Holy Church of God, founded in 1917 by William T. Phillips. See Bernard, *History of Christian Doctrine*, vol. 3, loc. 849.

11. I should also point out that this essay will focus almost entirely on the English-speaking world, especially the United States, since that is what I know and understand best.

12. The lists of gifts of the Spirit found in the New Testament do not appear to be comprehensive. Instead they are representative, and additional gifts might be included among both the oral gifts and the power gifts.

13. The formation of the Pentecostal Church of the Nazarene was a consolidation of several earlier holiness groups, a couple of which also had included the word "Pentecostal" in their previous names.

14. This fracture took place within the Finished Work wing of Pentecostalism. Although tensions began earlier, the split was formalized at the 1916 General Council of the Assemblies of God, which for the first time approved a statement of faith, the "Statement of Fundamental Truths." This statement devoted nearly half its length to excluding Oneness theology and practice.

15. While I believe this plea to make Jesus the Lord of one's life is appropriate, the expression's meaning in this context differs from the earliest Christian confession, "Jesus is Lord" (see Rom. 10:9; 1 Cor. 12:3; Phil. 2:11; Acts 10:36).

16. Important Higher Life conventions were organized by D. L. Moody at Northfield, Massachusetts, and by A. B. Simpson at Old Orchard, Maine, and elsewhere.

17. The first of the annual Keswick conventions took place in 1875. It had been preceded by an exploratory convention in Brighton earlier that same year.

18. Prominent names associated with the Keswick movement are Dwight L. Moody and his associate Reuben A. Torrey, Albert B. Simpson, and Robert Pearsall Smith and his wife, Hannah Whitall Smith. Hannah Whitall Smith's book *The Christian's Secret of a Happy Life*, published in 1875, became a holiness devotional classic. She also helped found the Women's Christian Temperance Union.

19. This was not the only distinctive characteristic of Keswick theology, but it is the one most pertinent to the topic at hand. Other emphases were premillennial eschatology and the importance of evangelism and missions.

20. Whereas Wesley's doctrine of entire sanctification was primarily Christological, the Keswick understanding of sanctification was more pneumatological.

21. Reuben A. Torrey was a very interesting figure associated with the Keswick Movement. Unlike many Keswick teachers, he emphasized baptism with the Holy Spirit as an empowering for witness and ministry rather than as another name for sanctification. In many ways he advanced the theology of three experiences that Pentecostals would later promote. However, his discomfort with tongues as a sign of Spirit baptism and his revulsion at Charles Parham, whom he considered the founder of Pentecostalism, led him to reject Pentecostalism when it arrived.

22. Donald W. Dayton discusses this common hermeneutic cogently in his 2004 article "John Fletcher as John Wesley's Vindicator and Designated Successor? A Response to Laurence W. Wood" *Pneuma* 26 no. 2 (Fall 2004): 359.

23. Ibid. While for many years the Reformed tradition dismissed Acts as "history" containing nothing of theological value, more recent developments in hermeneutical theory have vindicated the common holiness and Pentecostal reading of Acts as a theological document.

Pentecostals also understand the descent of the Spirit on those who are already believers in Acts 2:4 to set a model that is repeated in Acts 8:17, when the Spirit fills the recent converts in Samaria. This separation of conversion from a charismatic reception of the Spirit happens again in Acts 19:6 in Ephesus, when the Spirit comes on the "disciples" (as they are called in v. 1) after Paul lays his hands upon them. Pentecostals also read Acts 10:44-48, about the household of Cornelius, through the lens of Acts 2, although the focus in this passage is not on the separation of conversion from a subsequent reception of the Spirit but rather on speaking in tongues as evidence of the Holy Spirit's activity. The text itself notes the paradigmatic character of the Acts 2 account when in 10:47 Peter asks, "Can anyone forbid water for baptizing these people who have received the Holy Spirit *just as we have*?" (RSV, emphasis added).

24. The three-experience teaching of the earliest Pentecostals had already been anticipated in part by the holiness teachers William Arthur and especially the Canadian Ralph C. Horner. At least by 1891 Horner was teaching a baptism of the Spirit separate from, and subsequent to, sanctification. He differed from the Pentecostals that would emerge mainly in believing tongues was not a "permanent gift." See his books *Pentecost* (Toronto: William Briggs, 1891) and *The Feast of 1905: Seventeen Sermons and Addresses* (Ottawa: Holiness Movement Publishing House, 1905). Arthur taught an experience called the "tongue of fire," which was a third experience following sanctification, which he identified with baptism in the Spirit. In this way the experience of Pentecost was split in two. Arthur's *The Tongue of Fire* was published in multiple editions, beginning first in 1880.

25. The best treatment of Durham's biography is Edith L. Blumhofer, "William H. Durham: Years of Creativity, Years of Dissent," in *Portraits of a Generation: Early Pentecostal Leaders,* ed. James R. Goff Jr. and Grant Wacker (Fayetteville, AR: University of Arkansas Press, 2002), 123-42. The most extensive treatment of his theology is Thomas George Farkas, "William H. Durham and the Sanctification Controversy in Early American Pentecostalism, 1906-1916" (PhD diss., Southern Baptist Theological Seminary, 1993).

26. Durham did not coin "finished work of Calvary"; it had been used by teachers in the Keswick holiness tradition before him, and it is likely he encountered it in the World's Faith Missionary Association that had ordained him in 1902. It is possible that Durham also heard finished work terminology in the preaching of E. W. Kenyon. In 1912 Kenyon, who had conducted tent meetings in Chicago in 1908, claimed that Durham had adopted *his* view of "the finished work of Calvary." E. W. Kenyon, "Triumph for Truth," *Reality*, April 1912, 128. Cited in Blumhofer, "William H. Durham," in *Portraits of a Generation*, 136.

27. Although there seems to be no direct historical linkage, Durham's position was anticipated by Count Zinzendorf, the leader of the eighteenth-century movement known as the Moravians. He stated: "The moment someone is justified, he is sanctified wholly." See Nicholaus Ludwig Count von Zinzendorf, *Nine Public Lectures on Important Subjects in Religion*, trans. and ed. George W. Forell (Iowa City, IA: University of Iowa Press, 1973), xviii. Cited in Farkas, "William H. Durham," 200.

28. William H. Durham, *Articles Written by Pastor W. H. Durham Taken from Pentecostal Testimony and Printed in Booklet Form* (1912), 19.

29. The organizing General Council of the Assemblies of God occurred in Hot Springs, Arkansas, April 2-12, 1914. Pinson's address took place on April 5 and was based on Ephesians 4:24, arguing that "righteousness and true holiness" came with putting on "the new man" at conversion. This address was printed in 1964 in a Fiftieth Anniversary Special Jubilee Issue of the *Pentecostal Evangel*. See M. M. Pinson, "The Finished Work of Calvary," *Pentecostal Evangel*, April 5, 1964, 7, 26-27.

As observed earlier, the Assemblies of God first articulated a formal theological statement, its "Statement of Fundamental Truths," in 1916. Many have been puzzled by the seemingly Wesleyan title of its article "Entire Sanctification, the Goal for All Believers." Two observations should be kept in mind. First, in 1916 the fellowship was being split by controversy over the nature of the Godhead, and there was an urgent need to stem the exodus of, not only Pentecostals who had embraced the Oneness position, but also those troubled by the adoption of a formal statement of faith. This statement was the extension of an olive branch. Second, the statement does not affirm that entire sanctification may be achieved prior to death. It merely sets entire sanctification as the ultimate goal, which all present would have affirmed.

Edith Blumhofer (née Waldvogel) has provided a helpful investigation of sanctification in the Assemblies of God. See Edith Lydia Waldvogel, "The 'Overcoming Life': A Study in the Reformed Evangelical Origins of Pentecostalism" (PhD diss., Harvard University, 1977).

30. Farkas, "William H. Durham," 125.

31. I heard this story two or three times from Stanley Horton, Clara Fisher's grandson. A written account may be found in Stanley Horton, *Reflections of an Early American Pentecostal* (Baguio, Philippines: APTS Press, 2001), 14.

32. A friend of mine recently told me that when he was young and poorly instructed (in an Assemblies of God context), he believed he was likely to go to heaven because he was a "fast prayer." While he sinned many times each day, he followed his sins immediately with a quick prayer asking for God's forgiveness. He only felt he was in jeopardy during that short interval between his sin and the prayer that followed.

33. Declaration of Faith, Church of God (Cleveland, Tennessee), http://www.churchofgod.org/beliefs/declaration-of-faith.

34. Statement of Faith, Church of God in Christ, http://www.cogic.org/about-company/statement-of-faith/.

35. Church of God in Christ Official Manual (Memphis: Board of Publication of the Church of God in Christ, 1973; repr., 1991), 58.

36. Ibid.

37. International Pentecostal Holiness Church, Beliefs, arts. 9, 10.

38. The technical name for this dynamic is "inaugurated eschatology."

www.ingramcontent.com/pod-product-compliance
Lightning Source LLC
Chambersburg PA
CBHW070038100426
42740CB00013B/2722